The Courage of Hopelessness

For Jela, just like that, for no reason at all

SLAVOJ ŽIŽEK

The Courage of Hopelessness

Chronicles of a Year of Acting Dangerously

ALLEN LANE
an imprint of
PENGUIN BOOKS

ALLEN LANE

UK | USA | Canada | Ireland | Australia
India | New Zealand | South Africa

Allen Lane is part of the Penguin Random House group of companies
whose addresses can be found at global.penguinrandomhouse.com

First published 2017
001

Copyright © Slavoj Žižek, 2017

The moral right of the author has been asserted

Set in 9.75/13 pt Sabon LT Std
Typeset by Jouve (UK), Milton Keynes
Printed in Great Britain by Clays Ltd, St Ives plc

A CIP catalogue record for this book is available from the British Library

ISBN: 978–0–241–30557–7

Contents

Introduction:
V for Vendetta, Part 2

In a wonderful comment on Italo Svevo's novel *Zeno's Conscience*, Alenka Zupančič deploys a systematic matrix of the relations between repetition and ending.[1] The basic version is the false reference to the freedom of choice where (if we take the case of smoking) my awareness that I can stop smoking any time I want guarantees that I will never actually do it – the possibility of stopping smoking is what blocks the actual change; it allows me to accept our continuous smoking without bad conscience, so that the end of smoking is constantly present as the very source of its continuation. (As Zupančič perspicaciously notes, we should just imagine a situation in which the subject is under the sway of the following order: you can smoke or not, but once you start to smoke you have no choice, you are not allowed to end. Far fewer people would choose to smoke under this condition.) When I can no longer tolerate the hypocrisy of this endless excuse, the next step consists in an immanent reversal of this stance: I decide to smoke and I proclaim this to be the last cigarette in my life, so I enjoy smoking it with a special surplus provided by the awareness that this is my last cigarette . . . and I do this again and again, endlessly repeating the end, the last cigarette. The problem with this solution is that it only works (i.e., the surplus-enjoyment is only generated) if, each time that I proclaim this to be my last cigarette, I sincerely believe it is my last cigarette, so this strategy also breaks down. In Svevo's novel, the next step is that the subject's analyst (who, till now, has tried to convince Zeno that smoking is dangerous for his physical and mental health) changes his strategy and claims that Zeno should smoke as much as he wants since health is not really a problem – the only pathological feature is Zeno's obsession with smoking, his passion to stop doing it.

So what should be brought to an end is not smoking but the very attempt to smoke. Predictably (for anyone with analytic experience), the effect of this change is catastrophic: instead of finally feeling relieved and able to smoke (or not) without guilt, Zeno is totally perturbed and desperate. He smokes like crazy and nonetheless feels totally guilty, without getting any narcissistic satisfaction from this guilt. In despair, he breaks down. Whatever he does turns out to be wrong: neither prohibitions nor permissiveness work, there is no way out, no pleasurable compromise; and, since smoking has been the focus of his life, even smoking loses its sense, there is no point in it. So, in total despair – not as a great decision – he *stops smoking* . . . The way out thus emerges unexpectedly when Zeno accepts the total hopelessness of his predicament. And this same matrix should also be applied to the prospect of radical change. The predominant attitude among academic 'radical Leftists' is still the one that, back in 1937, George Orwell described apropos class difference:

> We all rail against class-distinctions, but very few people seriously want to abolish them. Here you come upon the important fact that every revolutionary opinion draws part of its strength from a secret conviction that nothing can be changed.[2]

Orwell's point is that radicals invoke the need for revolutionary change as a kind of superstitious token that should achieve the opposite, i.e. *prevent* the change from really occurring – like today's academic Leftist who criticizes capitalist cultural imperialism but is in reality horrified at the idea that his field of study might really become redundant. The stance is here the same as that of the smoker convinced that he can stop smoking if he chooses to do so: the possibility of change is evoked to guarantee that it will not be acted upon. Then we get an entire panoply of strategies that amount to the same thing, up to 'accelerationism' (capitalism will collapse through its overdevelopment, so let's engage in it to the end . . .). It is only when we despair and don't know any more what to do that change can be enacted – we have to go through this zero point of hopelessness. In short, we have to enact in politics a reversal similar to the one enacted in 'Der Leiermann', the song that concludes Schubert's

Winterreise. It appears to describe the utter despair of the abandoned lover who finally loses all hope, even the very ability to mourn and to despair, and conjures the man on the street playing his hurdy-gurdy. However, as many commentators have noticed, this last song can also be read as a sign of forthcoming redemption: while all the other songs in the cycle present the hero's inward brooding, here, for the first time, the hero turns outwards and establishes a minimal con tact, an emphatic identification, with another human being, although this identification is with another desperate loser who has lost even his ability to mourn and is reduced to performing blind mechanical gestures. Two years before his death, when it became clear that there would be no all-European revolution, and knowing that the idea of building socialism in one country was nonsense, Lenin reached this point when he wrote:

> What if the complete hopelessness of the situation, by stimulating the efforts of the workers and peasants tenfold, offered us the opportunity to create the fundamental requisites of civilization in a different way from that of the West European countries?[3]

The basic ideological operation of Stalin was precisely to turn around Lenin's reading of the situation: he presented the Soviet Union's isolation as a unique chance to build socialism in one country. In that historical situation, Stalin's formula was one of hope. However, the next decade made evident the price paid for the attempt to live up to this hope: purges, mass starvation, etc. The lesson of twentieth-century communism is that we have to gather the strength to fully assume the hopelessness. Giorgio Agamben said in an interview that 'thought is the courage of hopelessness' – an insight which is especially pertinent for our historical moment, when even the most pessimistic diagnosis as a rule finishes with an uplifting hint at some version of the proverbial light at the end of the tunnel. The true courage is not to imagine an alternative, but to accept the consequences of the fact that there is no clearly discernible alternative: the dream of an alternative is a sign of theoretical cowardice, functioning as a fetish that prevents us from thinking through to the end the deadlock of our predicament. In short, the true courage is to admit that the light at the end of the tunnel is probably the headlight of another train approaching us from the opposite direction.

This approaching train has lately assumed many forms. In the last few years, troubles in our global-capitalist paradise have exploded at four levels, with four figures of the enemy: the renewed fundamentalist-terrorist threat (the declaration of war against ISIS, Boko Haram . . .); geo-political tensions with and between non-European new powers (China and especially Russia); the rise of new radical emancipatory movements in Europe (Greece and Spain, for the time being); the flow of refugees crossing the Wall that separates 'Us' from 'Them', thereby 'posing a threat to our way of life'. It is crucial to see these threats in their interconnection – not in the sense that they are the four faces of the same enemy, but in the sense that they express aspects of the same immanent 'contradiction' of global capitalism. Although fundamentalism and the flow of refugees appear as the most threatening of the four (is ISIS not a brutal denial of our civilized values?), the tensions with Russia pose a much more serious danger to peace in Europe, while movements like Syriza prior to its capitulation undermine from within global capitalism in its neo-liberal version. But there should be no misunderstanding here: Western powers can easily co-exist with fundamentalist regimes; while in the case of Putin, the problem is how to contain Russia in geo-political terms (recall that his rise is the result of the catastrophic Yeltsin years marked by corruption, the years when Western economic advisors helped to humiliate Russia and to bring it to ruin). So although the US formally declared war on ISIS, and although there is constant talk about the threat of a war with Russia, the true danger are the moderate and 'gentle' new emancipatory movements from Syriza in Greece to the followers of Bernie Sanders in the US, and their putative radicalization. Because of this misperception of radical politics, we live in times of pseudo-conflicts: in the UK, Brexit 'yes' or 'no', in Turkey the military or Erdogan, in Eastern Europe, new Baltic-Polish-Ukrainian fundamentalists or Putin, in France, burkini or bared breasts, in Syria, Assad or Daesh . . . In all these cases, although one might slightly prefer one side to the other, the ultimate stance should be one of indifference, best rendered by Stalin who, when asked in the late 1920s which deviation is worse, the Right one or the Leftist one, snapped back: 'They are both worse!' Is there still the potential for true change beneath these pseudo-struggles? There is, since the function of these pseudo-struggles is precisely to block the explosion of the true ones.

Rage, rebellion and a new power offer a kind of dialectical triad of the revolutionary process. First, there is chaotic rage: people are dissatisfied and show it in a more or less violent way, but without any clear goal or organization. When this rage gets organized, we get a rebellion with minimal organization and a more-or-less clear awareness of who the enemy is and what is to be changed. Finally, if rebellion succeeds, the new power confronts the immense task of organizing the new society. (Remember the anecdote about the exchange between Lenin and Trotsky just prior to the October Revolution. Lenin said: 'What will happen with us if we fail?' Trotsky replied: 'And what will happen if we succeed?') The problem is that we almost never get this triad in its logical progression: chaotic rage gets diluted or turns into a Rightist populism; rebellion succeeds but loses steam and gets compromised in multiple ways. This is why rage occurs not only at the beginning but also at the end, the outcome of failed emancipatory projects. Recall, in the US, protests like those in Ferguson in August 2014, after the fatal shooting of Michael Brown by a police officer. Were they not today's exemplary cases of what Walter Benjamin called 'divine violence'? They are not part of a long-term strategy – as Benjamin put it, they are means without ends. Does not the same hold not only for other protests that followed Ferguson, like the Baltimore riots in April 2015, but also for the French suburban riots of autumn 2005, when we saw thousands of cars burning and a major outburst of public violence? In these protests, what strikes the eye is the total absence of any positive utopian prospect among the protesters: if May '68 was a revolt led primarily by students and workers with a utopian vision, the 2005 revolts in suburban Paris were outbursts among ghettoized immigrant communities with no pretence to a collective vision. If the oft-repeated commonplace that we live in a post-ideological era has any sense, it is here. The fact that there was *no* programme in the burning Paris suburbs is thus itself a fact to be interpreted. It tells us a great deal about our ideologico-political predicament. What kind of universe is it that we inhabit, which celebrates itself as a society of choice but in which the only option available to the enforced democratic consensus is a blind acting out?

Here is how Göran Therborn succinctly characterizes our predicament: 'Never before have the possibilities of a good world for the human species as a whole been greater. At the same time, the gap between human potential and the existing conditions of humankind in its totality has probably never been wider.'[4] Why this gap? In his *Idea of Socialism*,[5] Axel Honneth begins with the great paradox of today's situation: there is a growing dissatisfaction with global capitalism that often explodes in rage, but it is less and less possible to articulate this rage into a new Leftist political project. If the growing rage gets articulated into a programme, it is predominantly in the guise of a Rightist populism. When we wonder about the enigmatic rise of Muslim fundamentalism, should we not also wonder about the no less enigmatic rise of religious-nationalist fundamentalism in countries like Poland, Hungary and Croatia? In the last decades, Poland was one of the few definitive European success stories: after the fall of socialism, the per capita product more than doubled, and for the last couple of years, the moderate liberal-centrist government of Donald Tusk ruled – and then, almost out of nowhere, without any great corruption scandals as in Hungary, the extreme Right took over, and there is now a widespread movement to prohibit abortion even in the limit-cases of the mortal danger to the mother's health, rape, and deformity of the foetus. What is going on here?

The case of Poland is also important for another reason: it provides a strong empirical rebuttal to the predominant Left-liberal dismissal of authoritarian populism as a contradictory politics that is doomed to fail. While this is in principle true – in the long term, we are all dead, as J. M. Keynes put it – there can be many surprises in the (not so) short term:

> The conventional view of what awaits the US (and possibly France and the Netherlands) in 2017 is an erratic ruler who enacts contradictory policies that primarily benefit the rich. The poor will lose, because populists have no hope of restoring manufacturing jobs, despite their promises. And massive inflows of migrants and refugees

will continue, because populists have no plan to address the problem's root causes. In the end, populist governments, incapable of effective rule, will crumble and their leaders will either face impeachment or fail to win re-election. But the liberals were wrong. PiS (Law and Justice, the ruling Rightist-populist party) has transformed itself from an ideological nullity into a party that has managed to introduce shocking changes with record speed and efficiency [. . .] it has enacted the largest social transfers in Poland's contemporary history. Parents receive a 500 złoty ($120) monthly benefit for every child after their first, or for all children in poorer families (the average net monthly income is about 2,900 złoty, though more than two-thirds of Poles earn less). As a result, the poverty rate has declined by 20–40%, and by 70–90% among children. The list goes on: in 2016, the government introduced free medication for people over the age of 75. The minimum wage now exceeds what trade unions had sought. The retirement age has been reduced from 67 for both men and women to 60 for women and 65 for men. The government also plans tax relief for low-income taxpayers.[6]

PiS does what Marine le Pen also promises to do in France: a combination of anti-austerity measures – social transfers that no Leftist party dares to consider – plus the promise of order and security that asserts national identity and promises to deal with the immigrant threat. Who can beat this combination, which directly addresses the two big worries of ordinary people? We can discern at the horizon a weirdly perverted situation in which the official 'Left' is enforcing the austerity politics (while advocating multicultural rights and so on), while the populist Right is pursuing anti-austerity measures to help the poor (while pursuing the xenophobic nationalist agenda) – the latest figure of what Hegel described as *die verkehrte Welt*, 'the topsy-turvy world'.

And what if Trump moves in the same direction? What if his project of moderate protectionism and large public works, combined with anti-immigrant security measures and a new perverted peace with Russia, somehow works? The French language uses the so-called *ne explétif* after certain verbs and conjunctions; it is also called 'non-negative *ne*' because it has no negative value in itself – 'it is used in situations where the main clause has a negative (either negative-bad or negative-negated) meaning, such as expressions of fear, warning, doubt, and negation.'[7] For example: *Elle a peur qu'il ne soit malade* ('She's afraid that he is sick'). Lacan noted how this superfluous negation renders perfectly the gap that separates our true unconscious desire from our conscious wish: when a wife ids afraid that her husband is sick, she may well worry that he is not sick (desiring him to be sick). And could we not say exactly the same about the Left liberals horrified by Trump? *Ils ont peur qu'il ne soit une catastrophe.* What they really fear is that he will not be a catastrophe.

So let's jump to the other extreme, the construction of a new power. When, a day after winning the referendum against EU pressure and saying 'no' to austerity politics, the Syriza government fully surrendered to that pressure, this breathtaking reversal stands for the ultimate 'infinite judgement' (coincidence of the opposites) of contemporary Leftist politics in power: there was no gradual mediation between the two extremes, no slow sliding into a compromise, but a direct and brutal reversal – immediately after a resolute 'no' to the politics of austerity, Syriza became its faithful executor. We have to accept this paradox at its purest, not downplay it through references to particular circumstances (fear, or even outright corruption of the Syriza leadership, etc.). We are dealing with a properly Hegelian dialectical reversal, where the highest ethical stance becomes a no less principled subservience.

In the final scene of the film *V for Vendetta* (2006), thousands of unarmed Londoners wearing Guy Fawkes masks march towards Parliament; without orders, the military allows the crowd to pass into Parliament, and the people take over. As Finch asks Evey for V's identity, she replies: 'He was all of us.' OK, a nice ecstatic moment, but I am ready to sell my mother into slavery in order to see *V for Vendetta*, Part 2: what would have happened the day after the victory of the people; how would they (re)organize daily life?

Echoing the rise of big popular protests in the last years, with hundreds of thousands assembling in public places (from New York, Paris and Madrid to Athens, Istanbul and Cairo), 'assemblage' (not in the sense of the assemblage theory deployed by Latour and Delanda but in the sense of analysing the phenomenon of assembling in public spaces), its performative effects, its power to challenge the existing power relations, became a popular topic of theory. One should retain a sceptical distance towards this topic: whatever its merits, it leaves untouched the key problem of how to pass from assembling protest to the imposition of a new power, of how this new power will function in contrast to the old one. Jean-Claude Milner reports that Althusser once improvised a typology of revolutionary leaders worthy of Kierkegaard's classification of humans into officers, housemaids and chimney sweepers: those who quote proverbs, those who do not quote proverbs, those who invent (new) proverbs. The first are scoundrels (Althusser thought of Stalin), the second are great revolutionaries who are doomed to fail (Robespierre); only the third understand the true nature of a revolution and succeed (Lenin, Mao). If we leave aside Milner's reading of this triad (the successful authentic leaders imported the revolutionary idea from abroad, and to make it appear rooted in their country they have to dress it up in the popular form of proverbs[8]), its importance resides in the fact that it registers three different ways of relating to the big Other (the symbolic substance, the domain of unwritten customs and wisdoms best expressed in the stupidity of proverbs). Scoundrels simply re-inscribe the revolution into the ideological tradition of their nation (for Stalin, the Soviet Union was the last stage of the progressive development of Russia). Radical revolutionaries like Robespierre fail because they just enact a break with the past without succeeding in their effort to enforce a new set of customs (recall the utter failure of Robespierre's idea of replacing religion with a new cult of a Supreme Being). Leaders like Lenin and Mao succeeded (for some time, at least) because they invented new proverbs, which means that they imposed new customs that regulated daily life. One of the best Goldwynisms tells how, after being informed that critics sometimes complained that there were too many old clichés in his films, Sam Goldwyn wrote a memo to his scenario department: 'We need more new clichés!' He was right, and this is a revolution's most difficult task – to create 'new clichés' for ordinary daily life.

There is an idea circulating in the underground among many disappointed radical Leftists, a softer repetition of the decision for terror in the aftermath of the 1968 movement (Action Directe in

France, the Baader-Meinhof in Germany, for example): only a radical catastrophe (preferably an ecological one) can awaken the large crowds and thus give a new impetus to radical emancipation. The latest version of this idea relates to the refugees: an influx of a really large number of refugees could revitalize the European radical Left. I find this line of thought obscene: notwithstanding the fact that such a development would for sure give an immense boost to anti-immigrant brutality, the truly crazy aspect of this idea is that it attempts to fill the gap created by the absence of proletarians by importing them from abroad, so that we get the revolution by a surrogate revolutionary agent . . .

One can, of course, claim that the repeated defeats of the Left are just steps in a long educational process that may end in victory – say, Occupy Wall Street created the conditions for the Bernie Sanders movement, which in its turn may act as the first step in the rise of a large, organized Leftist movement. However, the least one can say is that, from 1968 onwards, the power edifice demonstrated an extraordinary ability to use movements of contestation as a source of its own renovation. But if the picture is so bleak, why then not call it a day and resign ourselves to modest reformism? The problem is, very simply, that global capitalism confronts us with a series of antagonisms that cannot be controlled or even contained within the frame of global capitalist democracy. None other than Elon Musk, the iconic Silicon Valley figure, the founder of SolarCity and Tesla, proposed the formula 'Robots will take your jobs, government will have to pay your wage':

> Computers, intelligent machines, and robots seem like the workforce of the future. And as more and more jobs are replaced by technology, people will have less work to do and ultimately will be sustained by payments from the government, predicts Elon Musk. According to Musk, there really won't be any other options: 'There is a pretty good chance we end up with a universal basic income, or something like that, due to automation.[9]

If this prospect is not the end of capitalism, then what is? One should also note that Musk's formula implies a strong government, not just some network of local cooperatives. So the only *true* question today is this: do we endorse the predominant acceptance of capitalism as a fact of (human) nature, or does today's global capitalism contain strong enough antagonisms to prevent its indefinite reproduction? There are four such antagonisms. They concern (1) *the commons of culture* in the broadest sense, of 'immaterial' capital: the immediately socialized forms of 'cognitive' capital, primarily language, our means of communication and education, not to mention the financial sphere with the absurd consequences of uncontrolled virtual money circulation; (2) *the commons of external nature*, threatened by human pollution: all particular dangers – global warming, dying of the oceans, etc. – are aspects of a derailment of the entire life reproduction system on earth; (3) *the commons of internal nature* (the biogenetic inheritance of humanity): with new biogenetic technology, the creation of a New Man in the literal sense of changing human nature becomes a realistic prospect; and, last but not least, (4) *the commons of humanity itself, of the shared social and political space*: the more capitalism gets global, the more new walls and apartheids are emerging, separating those who are IN from those who are OUT. This global division is accompanied by the rise of tensions between new geopolitical blocks (the 'clash of civilizations'). It is this reference to 'commons' that justifies the resuscitation of the notion of communism: it enables us to see the progressive 'enclosure' of the commons as a process of proletarianization of those who are thereby excluded from the very substance of their lives.

Only the fourth antagonism, the reference to the excluded, justifies the term communism: the first three effectively concern questions of humanity's economic, anthropological, even physical, survival, while the fourth one is ultimately a question of justice. But here we stumble upon the old boring question of the relationship between socialism and communism: why call the goal of a radical emancipatory movement communism? In the Marxist tradition, socialism was conceptualized as the (in)famous lower stage of communism, so that the 'progress' was supposed to run from socialism to communism. (No wonder that, with regard to the sad reality of life under 'really existing socialism', jokes abounded like the well-known one from the

Soviet Union where a group of people in Moscow are reading a big propaganda poster which says: 'In twenty years, we will live in full communism!' One of the people starts to laugh and jump with pleasure and joy, and when others ask him why, he replies: 'I have cancer, I will be dead for sure in twenty years!') But the reality was different; most socialist countries, rather, began with some version of primitive but radical communism (the Soviet Union in 1918–20, etc.), and then, in order to survive, they had to 'regress' and make compromises with the old society – so the line of development ran from communism to socialism (which combined the old and the new). The worst thing we can do today is to drop the name 'communism' and advocate a watered-down version of 'democratic socialism'. The task confronting us today is precisely the reinvention of communism, a radical change that moves well beyond some vague notion of social solidarity. Insofar as, in the course of the historical process of change, its goal itself should be redefined, we can say that 'communism' is to be reinvented as the name for what emerges as the goal after the failure of socialism.

The establishment reacts to today's 'radical' theory in the same way as the one described by Hegel in the Preface to the *Philosophy of Right*, where he mentions 'a letter of Joh. v. Müller who, speaking of the condition of Rome in the year 1803, when the city was under French rule, writes, "A professor, asked how the public academies were doing, answered, '*On les tolère comme les bordels!* ['They are tolerated, like brothels!']' " '[10] Is not most of what goes on today in 'radical' academia tolerated in the same way – it is considered that 'though not of much good, [they] can be of no great harm. Hence the recommendation, so it is thought, if useless, can do no injury.'[11] It is my contention that only a reinvented communism can return to theory its emancipatory force.

This approach to communism (expounded in many recent books of mine) has lately been submitted to a series of criticisms – basically, my critics identify five principal sins: my (openly admitted) eurocentrism, i.e., my insistence on the European roots of the project of universal emancipation; my rejection of the Greek Left Platform proposal to risk a more radical measure (Grexit, etc.) after the victory of the Syriza government at the referendum; my critique of the elevation of refugees and migrants into a new form of global proletariat and my insistence on the problems of cultural identity; my doubts about some ideological components of the LGBT+ movement; and, last but not least, my 'support' for the 'fascist' Donald Trump. As expected, all these reproaches are combined into the thesis that I am effectively a homophobic eurocentrist racist who opposes any authentic radical measure . . . The present book addresses systematically all these critical points.

The Courage of Hopelessness is indeed a dark book, but I prefer to be a pessimist: not expecting anything, I am here and there nicely surprised (since things are usually not as bad as they could be), while optimists see their hopes dashed and end up depressed all the time. The two parts of the book deploy the dark diagnosis at two levels: that of the economico-political mess we are in – 'The Ups and Downs of Global Capitalism' – and that of the ideological theatre where political and economic battles are fought – 'The Ideological Theatre of Shadows'. (This theatre is in no way just a secondary reflection of the 'true' economic struggle, but the very stage where 'true' battles are fought.) Part One first provides a quick overview of the impasses of global capitalism; it then describes the fate of Syriza as the attempt to break out of the global capitalist imbroglio; and it concludes with an overview of the return of religion as a political factor from China to Israel. Part Two begins with an analysis of the so-called 'terrorist threat' of religious fundamentalism; it then deals with the worldwide battle for sexuality raging between conservatives and the forces of political correctness; it concludes with the populist rage as the predominant reaction to these impasses. A short finale paints an even darker picture of how the ongoing geo-political tensions may lead to the Third World War.

PART ONE

The Ups and Downs of Global Capitalism

I

Global Capitalism and its Discontents

DISTURBANCES IN A CUPOLA

In Edgar G. Ulmer's classic horror movie *The Black Cat* (1934), the opposition between the Bela Lugosi character (Werdegast) and the Boris Karloff one (Poelzig) is the one between the two modes of the 'undead', both referring to the previous screen images of the actors – Lugosi is the spectral survivor obsessed with the traumatic past, while Karloff is a machine-like monster, i.e., we have the vampiric undead versus the Frankensteinian monster (this is clearly discernible from their acting: Lugosi's Dracula-like mannerisms versus Karloff's wooden gestures). The entire film thus points towards the final theatrically staged sadomasochistic torture scene, in which Lugosi starts to flay the skin off the living Karloff. Is this opposition not that of the class struggle reduced to its minimum, the opposition between the aristocratic vampire and the proletarian living dead? So what form does this flaying take in our times?

In the first half of 2015, Europe was preoccupied by radical emancipatory movements (Syriza, Podemos), while in the second half the attention shifted to the 'humanitarian' issue of the refugees – class struggle was literally repressed and replaced by liberal-cultural topics of tolerance and solidarity. With the Paris terror killings on Friday 13 November 2015, even the refugee crisis (which still refers to large socio-economic issues) was eclipsed by the simple opposition of all democratic forces caught in a merciless war with the forces of terror – and it is easy to believe what has followed: paranoiac searches for ISIS agents among the refugees, etc. (the media gleefully reported that two of the terrorists entered Europe through Greece as refugees[1]). The greatest victims of the Paris terror attacks will be refugees themselves, and the true winners behind the platitudes in the style of *Je suis Paris* will be simply the partisans of total war on both sides. This is how we should *really* condemn the Paris killings: not just by engaging in pathetic shows of anti-terrorist solidarity, but by insisting on the simple *cui bono* question. There should be no 'deeper understanding' of the ISIS terrorists (in the sense of 'their deplorable acts are nonetheless reactions to European brutal interventions'): they should be characterized as what they are, as the Islamo-fascist obverse of the European anti-immigrant racists – two sides of the same coin.

But there is another, more formal, aspect that should give us pause to think – the very form of the attacks: a momentary brutal disruption of normal life. (Significantly, the attacked objects do not stand for the military or political establishment but for everyday popular culture – restaurants, rock venues and so on.) Such a form of terrorism – a momentary disturbance – mainly characterizes attacks on developed Western countries, in clear contrast to many Third World countries in which violence is a permanent fact of life. Think about daily life in Congo, Afghanistan, Syria, Iraq, Lebanon – where are the outcries and declarations of international solidarity when hundreds die there? We should remember *now* that we live in a 'cupola' where terrorist violence is a threat that just explodes from time to time, in contrast to countries where (with the participation or complicity of the West) daily life consists of uninterrupted terror and brutality.

In his *In the World Interior of Capital* (2013), Peter Sloterdijk demonstrates how, in today's globalization, the world system completed its development and, as a capitalist system, came to determine all conditions of life. The first symbol of this development was the Crystal Palace in London, the site of the first world exhibition in 1851: the inevitable exclusivity of globalization as the construction and expansion of a world interior whose boundaries are invisible, yet virtually insurmountable from without, and which is now inhabited by the one and a half billion 'winners' of globalization. Three times this number are left standing outside the door. Consequently, 'the world interior of capital is not an *agora* or a trade fair beneath the open sky, but rather a hothouse that has drawn inwards everything that was once on the outside.' This interior, built on capitalist excesses, determines everything: 'The primary fact of the Modern Age was not that the earth goes around the sun, but that money goes around the earth.' After the process that transformed the world into the globe, 'social life could only take place in an expanded interior, a domestically and artificially climatized inner space.' As cultural capitalism rules, all world-forming upheavals are contained: 'No more historic events could take place under such conditions – at most, domestic accidents.'[2] What Sloterdijk correctly points out is that capitalist globalization does not stand only for openness and conquest, but also for a self-enclosed cupola separating the Inside from its Outside. The two aspects are inseparable: capitalism's global reach is grounded in the way it introduces a radical class division across the entire globe, separating those protected by the sphere from those outside its cover.

The latest Paris terrorist attacks, as well as the flow of refugees, are momentary reminders of the violent world outside our cupola, a world which, for us insiders, appears mostly on TV reports about distant violent countries – not as a part of our reality but encroaching on it. Our ethico-political duty is not just to become aware of the reality outside our cupola, but to fully assume our co-responsibility for the horrors outside it. James Mangold's *Cop Land* (1996) is set in Garrison (an imagined New Jersey city across the river from Manhattan), where Ray Donlan, a corrupt Lieutenant of the NY police (played by Harvey Keitel) has established a place in which New York policemen can live safely with their families. When Freddy Heflin, an honest local cop (Silvester Stallone), expresses his moral qualms about Donlan's mode of operation, Donlan replies:

Freddy, I invited men, cops, good men, to live in this town. And these men make a living, they cross that bridge every day to that city where everything is upside down, where the cop is the perp[etrator] and the perp is the victim. The only thing they did was to get their families out before it got to them. We made a place where things make sense, where you can walk the street without fear, and you come to me with the plan to set things right, everyone in the city holding hands, singing

5

'We are the world.' It's very nice. But, Freddy, your plan is a plan of a boy, it was made on the back of a matchbox without thinking, without looking at the cards. I look at the cards, I see this town destroyed. Now that's not what you want, is it?

It is easy to see in what way Donlan's quasi-ontological vision of social reality is false: the group of policemen create their safe haven by withdrawing from the corrupted Manhattan, but it is their full participation in the corrupted crime universe of Manhattan that enables them to keep crime at bay in their own hamlet and sustain their safe and friendly way of life. What this means is that it is their very concern for their safe haven that contributes to the regular reproduction of crime in Manhattan – and the same can be said for all the participants in the Manhattan crime, with the exception of the lowest-level street criminals. Are mafia bosses also not doing what they do to protect their safe family haven? One should note the circularity of this constellation: the effort to create a safe haven and protect it from the crazy world outside generates the very world it tries to protect us from. Do we not encounter exactly the same paradox in Song-do, a new city for quarter of a million inhabitants built out of nothing close to Seoul's Incheon airport in South Korea, a kind of supreme ideological manifesto in stone? in his report 'Song-do, the Global City Without Soul', Francesco Martone describes how Song-do is built

on 6.5 square kilometers reclaimed from the sea, by a human hand that alters boundaries and morphologies. It would eventually host 250,000 and is rapidly becoming a trendy location to the extent that various soap opera stars moved in to what they would like to see as the Beverly Hills of the East.

As it stands now, however, the city is composed of almost empty futuristic buildings, a few bikers rambling along its wide avenues, construction sites active around the clock. Canals filled with merchant vessels in the background. Walking among these high-rise buildings made of steel and crystal, semi-deserted roads waiting to be filled with cars, is like living in a Truman Show of liberalism with no limit [. . .] A sort of 'city-state' where investors enjoy all sort of exemptions, from tax breaks and beyond. A plastic and virtual performance of extreme liberalism, the reification of daily reality, of nature transformed into a consumption commodity, the impossible equation between a Green New Deal and growth, fake stones and trees plucked on flat sand, battered by gusts of wind, icy cold in winter, steaming hot in summertime [. . .]

Song-do is today considered and boasted [of] as the show-case of 'green economy', built at the cost of the displacement of a delicate ecosystem where as many as 11 species of migratory birds, among them the 'Platalea Minor', used to live, a site of major importance for the Ramsar convention. Supergreen zero-emission powerplants turn sea tides into energy, destroying fragile coastal habitats. Paradoxically, the world's biggest tidal wave powerplant, the Siwha Tidal Powerplant, has been registered by the Clean Development Mechanism, set up to reduce emissions and generate carbon credits. *'A Conflict of Greens: Green Development versus Habitat Preservation – the case of Incheon, South Korea'* is the eloquent title of an article that pointed to the contradiction between green capitalism and ecology. What sort of ecological conversion is possible in an artificial place, where rights are subject to the rule of market and finance? A place that pretends to be a laboratory of a Green New Deal, antiseptic and without soul?

It'll be those urban extraterritorial spaces, such as IFEX and many more, developed 'in vitro', suspended in space and time, black holes where exemption from labour legislation and tax breaks are the rule, that will represent the new frontier of wildcat liberalism, fuelled by the expoliation of resources elsewhere in the world. The fact of the matter is that Song-do is currently one of those 'extraterritorial' spaces, akin to the Export Processing Zones that together with tax havens draw a parallel geography of power, a cobweb of parallel governance, away from public scrutiny, that envisages no anomaly or alternative [. . .] So, Song-do, designed by planning firm Kohn Pedersen Fox, is a city that can be reproduced anywhere in the world, with its Central Park, its World Trade Center, its canals that evoke a futuristic Venice, a technopark and a biocomplex. Electronic closets in hotels offer various options to guests, from automatized enema to butt massages at varying temperatures. Supermarkets sell cosmetics produced with the genetic manipulation of stem cells, to whiten the skin and nurture the illusion of eternal youth.[3]

This new form of a city is, to put it blandly, neo-liberal ideology embodied, an impossible combination of market economy exempted from the state control with the usual 'progressive' ecological, educational and health concerns, the result being a 'green' environment built on a ravaged natural habitat. To get a full picture, one need only imagine a gigantic transparent cupola (similar to the one in the films *Zardoz* or *Elysium*) to keep the city safe from its polluted environs, plus transgender toilets to guarantee that all forms of segregation are left behind (in a city which is itself a segregated area).

CUPOLA, EAST AND WEST

In today's historical constellation, is the cupola limited to the Western affluent countries (and its copies all around the world), so that the proletarian struggle to break in to the cupola is to be identified with the struggle against the scarecrow of 'eurocentrism'? Along these lines, in his 'On the Twilight of the West', Pankaj Mishra advocates 'a return to the Ottoman-style confederal institutions that devolve power and guarantee minority rights':

> In the 21st century, that old spell of universal progress – whether through Western-style socialism, or capitalism and democracy – has been decisively broken. The optimistic assumptions dating from the 19th century that these universalist ideologies and techniques will deliver endless growth and political stability cannot be sustained [. . .] The global crisis, which is as much moral and intellectual as it is political and environmental, puts into question above all our long submission to Western ideas of politics and economy. Whether it is catastrophic wars in Iraq and Afghanistan or disastrous interventions in Libya, the financial crisis of 2008, soaring unemployment in Europe, which seems like a problem with no solution, and is likely to empower far-right parties across the continent, the unresolved crisis of the euro, hideous income disparities in both Europe and the United States, the widespread suspicion that big money has corrupted democratic processes, the absurdly dysfunctional American political system, Edward Snowden's revelations about the National Security

Agency, or the dramatic loss of a sense of possibility for young people everywhere – all of this separately and together has not only severely depleted the West's moral authority but also weakened its intellectual hegemony [. . .] This is why its message to the rest of the world's population can no longer be the smooth reassurance that the Western way of life is the best, which others should try to replicate diligently in their own part of the world through nation-building and industrial capitalism [. . .] Reflecting on the world's 'pervasive raggedness', the American anthropologist Clifford Geertz once spoke of how 'the shattering of larger coherences' into 'smaller ones, uncertainly connected one with another, has made relating local realities . . . with the world overall, extremely difficult. If the general is to be grasped at all,' Geertz continued, 'and new unities uncovered, it must, it seems, be grasped not directly, all at once, but via instances, differences, variations, particulars – piecemeal, case by case. In a splintered world, we must address the splinters' [. . .] The Western path to modernity can no longer be regarded as 'normal'; it cannot be the standard against which historical change in other parts of the world is measured. Europeans had created their own kind of modernity in the very particular historical circumstances of the 19th and 20th centuries, and other people have been trying since then, with varying degrees of success, to imitate it. But there are, and always were, other ways of conceiving of the state, society, economy, and the good life. They all have their own specific difficulties and challenges. Nevertheless, it will be possible to understand them only through an open and sustained engagement with non-Western societies, and their political and intellectual traditions. Such an effort, formidable in itself, would also go against every instinct of the self-regarding universalism the West has upheld for two centuries. But it will be needed if we wish to seriously confront the great problem confronting the vast majority of seven billion human beings: how to secure a dignified and sustainable life amid deepening inequality and animosity in an interdependent world.[4]

These long passages are worth quoting since they render in a concise way the post-colonial common sense: we should recognize the failure of Western civilization as a global model, and the failure of those decolonized nations that tried to emulate it. There is nonetheless a problem with this diagnosis: yes, the lesson of post-9/11 is the end of the Fukuyama dream of global liberal democracy; but at the level of economy, capitalism has triumphed worldwide – the Third World nations that are now growing at spectacular rates are those which endorsed it. The mask of cultural diversity is sustained by the actual universalism of global capital. And this new global capitalism functions even better if its political supplement relies on so-called 'Asian values'. Global capitalism has no problem in accommodating itself to a plurality of local religions, cultures, traditions. So the cruel irony of anti-eurocentrism is that, on behalf of anti-colonialism, one criticizes the West at the very historical moment when global capitalism no longer needs Western cultural values (egalitarianism, fundamental rights, the welfare state) in order to function smoothly, and is doing quite well with authoritarian 'alternative modernity'. In short, one tends to denounce Western cultural values at the very moment that, critically reinterpreted, many of them can serve as a weapon against capitalist globalization. And *vice versa*, as Saroj Giri pointedly noted, it is possible that

> the immigrants who secure rights thanks to the anti-racist anti-colonial struggle might be securing the right to free capitalist enterprise, refusing to see, refusing to 'open your eyes', as the angry black yelled at the post-colonial immigrant. This right to free enterprise is another way to capital accumulation powered by the post-colonial entrepreneur: it produces 'unfree labour' and racialized class relations in the name of challenging the colonial rule of difference [. . .] There is a closet Ayn Randian class position underpinning the anti-racism of hyperbolic anti-colonialists – it is then not difficult to see that the non-modern, radical alterity upon which the anti-colonial is premised now stands for the capitalist universal.[5]

Giri's last sentence should be taken in all its Hegelian stringency: the 'concrete universal' of today's global capitalism, the particular form which overdetermines and colours its totality, is that of the 'anti-colonial' non-European capitalist.

Giri's point is not simply to assert the primacy of economic 'class struggle' over other struggles (against racism, for sexual liberation, etc.) – if we simply decode racial tension as a reflection of class differences, such a direct displacement of race onto class is effectively a reductionist way of obfuscating the very dynamic of class relations. Giri refers here to Jared Sexton's writings in the aftermath of the 1992 Los Angeles uprising, where he

> critiques scholars like Sumi Cho who argue that 'the ability (of Korean Americans) to open stores (in black neighbourhoods) largely depends upon a class variable.' Hence, 'many of the tensions (between these groups) may be class-, rather than racially based, actually reflecting differences between the store-owning Korean immigrants and the African-American customers.' As Sexton shows, this class analysis does not have anything to do with class struggle as class is abstracted from any real unequal social relations. Secondly, 'the mention of class-based relation is done in order to mitigate the resentment and hostility supposedly born of "cultural differences and racial animosities".' Thus for Cho, 'the ability to open stores (Korean businesses) largely depends upon a class variable, *as opposed to* a racial one.' A watered-down politically sterile notion of class is invoked even as the question of anti-black racism is diluted. Sexton calls this approach 'subordinating the significance of race while pacifying the notion of class' [. . .] This is where we encounter the familiar story of the post-colonial immigrants making great entrepreneurs and keeping the American Dream alive even as other 'illegal' and undocumented migrants are pushed to the bottom and even as a vast majority of blacks are reduced to not just marginalization and deprivation but 'social death' [. . .] this backhanded emphasis on class is a way to reduce the overdetermined status of the black poor to what looks like the natural outcome of (free) market relations.[6]

Do we not encounter here an exemplary case of the very reference to class being a means of obfuscating the concrete functioning of class struggle? Class difference itself can be the fetish which obfuscates class struggle.

The Western legacy is effectively not just that of (post-)colonial imperialist domination, but also that of the self-critical examination of the violence and exploitation that the West brought to the Third

World. The French colonized Haiti, but the French Revolution also provided the ideological foundation for the rebellion that liberated the slaves and established independent Haiti; the process of decolonization was set in motion when the colonized nations demanded for themselves the same rights that the West took for itself. In short, one should never forget that the West provides the very standards by means of which it (as well as its critics) measures its criminal past. We are dealing here with the dialectic of form and content: when colonial countries demand independence and enact the 'return to roots', the very form of this return (that of an independent nation-state) is Western. In its very defeat (losing the colonies), the West thus wins, imposing its social form on to the other.

The three types of subjectivity that, according to Alain Badiou, are operative in global capitalism, do not cover the entire field. There is the hegemonic Western middle-class subjectivity that perceives itself as the beacon of civilization; there are those possessed by the desire for the West; and there are those who, out of the frustration of their desire for the West, turn towards (self-)destructive nihilism. But there is also the global-capitalist traditionalism: the stance of those who, while fully participating in global capitalist dynamics, try to contain its destabilizing excesses by relying on some traditional ethics or way of life (Confucianism, Hinduism, etc.).

The European emancipatory legacy cannot be reduced to 'European values' in the predominant ideological sense, i.e., to what our media refer to when they talk about how our values are threatened by Islam; on the contrary, the greatest threat to what is worth saving from the European legacy are today's (anti-immigrant populist) defenders of Europe themselves. Plato's thought is a European event; radical egalitarianism is European; the notion of modern subjectivity is European; communism is a European event if there ever was one. When Marxists celebrate the power of capitalism to disintegrate old communal ties, when they detect in this disintegration the opening of a space for radical emancipation, they speak on behalf of the emancipatory European legacy. That's why Walter Mignolo and other post-colonial anti-eurocentrists attack Badiou and other proponents of communism as all too European: they dismiss the (quite correct) idea of communism being European and, instead of communism, propose as the source of resistance to global capitalism some ancient Asian, Latin American or African traditions. There is a crucial choice to be made here: do we resist global capitalism on behalf of the local traditions it undermines, or do we endorse this power of disintegration and oppose global capitalism on behalf of a universal emancipatory project? The reason anti-eurocentrism is so popular today is precisely because global capitalism functions much better when its excesses are regulated by some ancient tradition: global capitalism and local traditions are no longer opposites, they are on the same side.[7]

Let us take an example, one that challenges the stance that local customs are sites of resistance. In the autumn of 2016, a 55-year-old former pastor in Santiago Quetzalapa, a remote indigenous community 450 kilometres south of Mexico City, raped an 8-year-old girl, and the local court condemned him to buy the victim's father two crates of beer. Santiago Quetzalapa is in Oaxaca state, where many indigenous communities are ruled by an idiosyncratic system popularly known as *usos y costumbres* ('traditions and customs'), supposed to enshrine the traditions of diverse indigenous populations. Officials in *usos y costumbres* communities have previously used the framework as a pretext to exclude women from local government; for example, Eufrosina Cruz Mendoza, an indigenous woman, won the mayoral election, but was denied office by local leaders because of her gender. Cases like these clearly demonstrate that local popular customs are in no way to be revered as a form of resistance to global imperialism. The task is rather to undermine them by supporting the mobilization against these customs of local indigenous people themselves, as in Mexico where indigenous women are organized in effective networks.

THE RIGGED CUPOLA I: WHY DOES A DOG LICK ITS BALLS?

The division between the inner space covered by the cupola and its outside is not just the outcome of some objective 'logic of capital' – the space of global capitalism is also quite deliberately 'rigged' to privilege those within the cupola, as was made clear by the disclosure of the so-called Panama Papers. The only truly surprising thing about the leaked financial information in the Panama Papers was that there was no surprise in them: didn't we learn *exactly* what we expected to learn about shadowy offshore finance? But it is one thing to know it in general, and another to get concrete data. It is a little bit like knowing that one's sexual partner is playing around – one can accept the abstract knowledge of it, but pain arises when one learns the steamy details, when one gets pictures of what they were doing . . . So, now, with the Panama Papers, we get some of the dirty pictures of financial pornography, and we can no longer pretend that we don't know.

A quick look at the papers reveals two prominent features, a positive one and a negative one. The positive one is the all-embracing solidarity of the participants: in the shadowy world of global capital, we are all brothers. The Western developed world is there, including the uncorrupted Scandinavians, and they shake hands with Putin and the Chinese President Xi; Iran and North Korea are also there; Muslims and Jews exchange friendly winks – it is a true kingdom of multiculturalism, where all are equal and all different. The negative feature: the blinding absence of the USA, which gives some credence to the Russian and Chinese claims that particular political interests were involved in the inquiry.

So what are we to do with all these data? There is a classic joke about a husband who returns home earlier than expected and finds his wife in bed with another man. The surprised wife asks him: 'What happened? You told me you'd be back three hours from now!' The husband explodes back: 'Be serious, what are you doing in bed with that guy?' The wife calmly replies: 'Don't change the subject, first answer my question!' Is something similar not happening with reactions to the Panama Papers? The first (and predominant) one is the explosion of moralistic rage: 'Horrible, how much greed and dishonesty there are in people; where are the basic values of our society?' What we should do is change the topic immediately from morality to our economic system: politicians, bankers and managers were always greedy, so what is it in our legal and economic system that enabled them to realize their greed in such a spectacular way?

The reality that emerges is one of class division, as simple as that. The revelations demonstrate how wealthy people live in a separate world in which different rules apply, in which legal processes and police authorities are heavily twisted not only to protect the rich, but even to systematically bend the rule of law to accommodate them. Does the same not hold for the Enron bankruptcy in January 2002, which can be interpreted as a kind of ironic commentary on the notion of a risk society? Thousands of employees who lost their jobs and savings were certainly exposed to a risk, but without any true choice – the risk appeared to them as blind fate. Those, on the contrary, who effectively did have an insight into the risks as well as a possibility of intervening in the situation (the top managers), minimized their risks by cashing in their stocks and options before the bankruptcy – so it is true that we live in a society of risky choices, but some (the Wall Street managers) do the choosing, while others (the common people paying mortgages) do the risking . . .

There are already many Rightist liberal reactions to the Panama Papers that put the blame on the excesses of our welfare states (or whatever remains of them): since wealth is so heavily taxed, no wonder owners try to move it to places with lower taxes, which is ultimately nothing illegal. Ridiculous as this excuse is (the papers expose transactions that do indeed break the law), this argument has a kernel of truth, and makes two points worth noting. First, the line that separates legal from illegal transactions is getting more and more blurred, and is often reduced to a matter of interpretation. Second, owners of wealth who move it to offshore accounts and tax havens are not greedy monsters but individuals who simply act like rational subjects trying to safeguard their wealth. In capitalism, you cannot throw out the dirty water of financial speculation and keep the healthy baby of the real economy: the dirty water effectively *is* the blood of the healthy baby. One should not be afraid to go to the end here: the global capitalist legal system itself is, in its most fundamental dimension, corruption legalized. The question of where crime begins (which financial dealings are illegal) is thus not a legal question but an eminently political question, a question of power.

So why did thousands of businessmen and politicians do what is documented in the Panama Papers? The answer is the same as

that of the old vulgar riddle-joke: Why do dogs lick their balls?
Because they can.

THE RIGGED CUPOLA II: 'FREE TRADE' AGREEMENTS

Our cupola is rigged not only through tolerated violation of the laws
but even more openly through systematic attempts to accommodate
these laws themselves to the interests of those covered by the cupola.
On 19 June 2014, the day after the second anniversary of Julian
Assange's confinement to the Ecuadorian embassy in London,
WikiLeaks rendered public the secret draft text for the Financial Services Annex of the Trade in Services Agreement (TISA), the largest
of three proposed multinational trade agreements. This draft, the
result of the last round of TISA talks which took place from 28 April
to 2 May in Geneva, covers fifty countries and most of the world's
trade in services. It sets rules which would assist the expansion of
financial multinationals into other nations by preventing regulatory
barriers. It prohibits more regulation of financial services, despite the
fact that the 2007–8 financial meltdown is generally perceived as
resulting from the lack of regulation. Furthermore, the US is particularly keen on boosting cross-border data flow, including personal
and financial data.

The draft document was classified to keep TISA secret not just
during negotiations but for five years after it enters into force. While
the TISA negotiations were not censored outright, they were barely
mentioned in our media – a marginalization and secrecy that are in
stark contrast with the world-historical importance of the TISA
agreement. If enforced, it will have global consequences, effectively
serving as a kind of legal backbone for the restructuring of the world
market. TISA would bind future governments, regardless of who
wins elections and what the courts say. It will impose a restrictive
framework on public services, from developing new ones to protecting the existing ones – the main reason for its secrecy, no doubt.
TISA is by no means a unique case with regard to secrecy: today
more than ever secret agreements and decisions play a key role in

economies and finance as well as in war (the decision to invade a country is often taken well before the broad public is prepared for it by reports on the threat this country represents). NAFTA was the last trade agreement widely debated in advance (although nobody read it in detail), and later agreements are kept secret precisely because the outcry about NAFTA taught those in power a lesson.

Is this discrepancy between politico-economic importance and secrecy really surprising? Is it not, rather, a sad but precise indication of where we, in Western liberal-democratic countries, stand with regard to democracy? A century and half ago, in *Capital*, Karl Marx characterized the market exchange between worker and capitalist as 'a very Eden of the innate rights of man. There alone rule Freedom, Equality, Property and Bentham.' For Marx, the ironic addition of Jeremy Bentham, the philosopher of egotist utilitarianism, provides the key to what freedom and equality effectively mean in capitalist society – to quote *The Communist Manifesto*: 'By freedom is meant, under the present bourgeois conditions of production, free trade, free selling and buying.' And by equality is meant the legal formal equality of buyer and seller, even if one of them is forced to sell his labour under any conditions (like today's precarious workers). Today, we can say that we have freedom, democracy and TISA. Freedom means the free flow of capital, as well as of the financial and personal data; both flows guaranteed by TISA. And what of democracy?

The main culprits of the 2008 financial meltdown, from big bank managers to high state administrators, now impose themselves as experts who can lead us on the painful path of financial recovery, whose advice should therefore overrule parliamentary politics; or, as Mario Monti put it: 'Those who govern must not allow themselves to be completely bound by parliamentarians.' Which, then, is the higher force whose authority can suspend the decisions of the democratically elected representatives of the people? Already back in 1998 the answer had been provided by Hans Tietmeyer, at that time the governor of the Deutsches Bundesbank, who praised national governments for preferring 'the permanent plebiscite of global markets' to the 'plebiscite of the ballot box'. Note the democratic rhetoric of this obscene statement: global markets are more democratic than parliamentary elections since the process of voting goes on in them permanently (and is permanently reflected in market fluctuations), not only every four years, and at a global level, not only within the limits of a nation-state. The underlying idea is that, freed from this higher control of markets (and experts), parliamentary-democratic decisions are 'irresponsible'.

Democracy is thus the democracy of the markets, the permanent plebiscite of market fluctuations. The space for democratically elected political agents to make decisions is severely limited, and the political process deals predominantly with issues towards which capitalism is indifferent (like cultural wars). This is why the release of the TISA draft marks a new stage in the WikiLeaks strategy: till now, their activity was focused on exposing the ways in which our lives are monitored and regulated by the intelligence agencies of the state – the standard liberal topic of individuals threatened by oppressive state apparatuses. Now, another controlling force appears – capital – which threatens our freedom in a much more twisted way, perverting our very sense of freedom.

Since, in our society, free choice is elevated into a supreme value, social control and domination can no longer appear as infringing on a subject's freedom – it has to appear as (and be sustained by) the very self-experience of individuals as free. There are a multitude of examples of un-freedom appearing in the guise of its opposite: when we are deprived of universal healthcare, we are told that we are given a new freedom of choice (to choose our healthcare provider); when we can no longer rely on long-term employment and are compelled to search for a new precarious position every couple of years, we are told that we are given the opportunity to re-invent ourselves and discover new unexpected creative potentials that lurked in our personality; when we have to pay for the education of our children, we are told that we become 'entrepreneurs of the self', acting like a capitalist who has to choose freely how he will invest the resources he possesses (or has borrowed) – in education, health, travel. Constantly bombarded by imposed 'free choices', forced to make decisions for which we are mostly not even properly qualified (or possess enough information about), we more and more experience our freedom as what it effectively is: a burden that deprives us of the true choice of change.

Let's imagine a single mother with two small children – let's call her Sophie. She wants the best for her children, but, lacking money, she has to make some hard choices: she can send only one of them to a good school, so which one will she choose? Should she organize a nice summer holiday for them, buy each of them a new PC, or should she rather provide better healthcare for them? Although her choice is not as tough and brutal as Sophie's choice from the well-known William Styron novel, where Sophie has to choose one of her children to be saved from the gas chamber, it runs along the same lines, and I would certainly prefer to live in a society that deprives her of this freedom of choice. No wonder parties that claim to represent people like Sophie effectively resent them.[8] One should re-read in view of these paradoxes Aaron Schuster's ironic observation that 'the great champion of free choice, the obsessional neurotic, is precisely the one who is unable to choose, who makes his home in an eternal "maybe".'[9]

Perhaps, this paradox also allows us to throw a new light on our obsession with the ongoing events in Ukraine, and even with the rise of ISIS in Iraq, both extensively covered by the media (in clear contrast to the predominant silence on TISA). What fascinates us in the West is not the fact that people in Kiev stood up for the mirage of the European way of life, but that they (as it seemed, at least) simply stood up and tried to take their fate into their own hands – ousting their president and demanding change to a corrupted political system. They acted as a political agent enforcing a radical change – something that, as the TISA negotiations demonstrate, we in the West no longer have the choice to do.

THE RIGGED CUPOLA III: A DESCENT INTO THE MAELSTROM

Sometimes, faces become symbols – not symbols of the strong individuality of their bearers, but symbols of anonymous forces behind them. Was the stupidly smiling face of Eurogroup president Jeroen Dijsselbloem not the symbol of the EU's brutal pressure on Greece? When the public spectre of TISA was supplemented by the new spectre of TTIP, yet another multinational trade agreement, a new face emerged: the cold one of Cecilia Malmström, the EU trade commissioner who, when asked by a journalist how she could continue her promotion of TTIP in the face of massive public opposition, responded without shame: 'I do not take my mandate from the European people.' (In an unsurpassable act of irony, her family name is a variation of the word 'maelstrom'.) To quote Lee Williams's acerbic comment:

> One of the main aims of TTIP is the introduction of Investor–State Dispute Settlements (ISDS), which allow companies to sue governments if those governments' policies cause a loss of profits. In effect it means unelected transnational corporations can dictate the policies of democratically elected governments [. . .] I would vote against TTIP, except . . . hang on a minute . . . I can't. Like you, I have no say whatsoever in whether TTIP goes through or not.[10]

The general picture of the social impact of TTIP is clear enough: it stands for nothing less than a brutal assault on democracy. Nowhere is this clearer than in the case of these so-called Investor–State Dispute Settlements (ISDS), which are already in place in some bilateral trade agreements, where we can see how they work. The Swedish energy company Vattenfall is suing the German government for billions of dollars over its decision to phase out nuclear power plants in the wake of the Fukushima disaster – a public-health policy put into place by a democratically elected government is threatened by an energy giant because of a potential loss of profit. But let us forget for a moment this overall picture and focus on a more specific question: what will TTIP mean for European cultural production?

In 'A Descent into the Maelström', Edgar Allen Poe's story from 1841, a survivor reports how he has avoided being sucked into a gigantic maelstrom, or whirlpool. He observed how the larger a body, the more rapid its descent, and that spherical objects were pulled in the fastest; so he abandoned his ship and held on to a cylindrical barrel until he was saved several hours later. Do proponents of so-called 'cultural exception' (treating the market for cultural products differently from that for general goods and services) not envisage something similar? Let our big economic companies get swallowed into the vortex of the global market, while we try to save cultural products . . . how? By simply exempting cultural products from free-market rules: allowing states to support their artistic industries (with state subsidies, lower taxes, etc.), even if this means 'unfair competition' with other countries. For example a country, France, say, may insist that this is the only way for its national cinema to survive the onslaught of Hollywood blockbusters.

Can this work? While such measures can play a limited positive role, I see two problems. First, in today's global capitalism, culture is no longer just an exception, a kind of fragile superstructure rising above the 'real' economic infrastructure, but is more and more a central ingredient of our mainstream 'real' economy. Over a decade ago, Jeremy Rifkin designated the latest stage of our economic development as 'cultural capitalism' (in a similar vein, Gerhard Schulze spoke of the 'society of experience'). The defining feature of 'postmodern' capitalism is the direct commodification of our experience itself: what we are buying on the market are less and less products (material objects) that we want to own, and more and more 'life-experiences' – experiences of sex, eating, communicating, cultural consumption, participating in a lifestyle – or, as Mark Slouka put it succinctly, 'we become the consumers of our own lives'. We no longer buy objects; we ultimately buy (the time of) our own life. Michel Foucault's notion of turning one's self itself into a work of art thus gets an unexpected confirmation: I buy my bodily fitness by visiting fitness clubs; I buy my spiritual enlightenment by enrolling in courses on transcendental meditation; I buy the satisfactory self-experience of myself as ecologically aware by purchasing only organic fruit, etc. Although these activities may have beneficial effects, their main importance is clearly ideological.

Second problem: even if Europe succeeded in imposing 'cultural exceptions' on to TTIP, what kind of Europe will survive the TTIP reign? The question is thus not whether European culture can survive TTIP, but what it will do to our economy. Will it not slowly become what ancient Greece was for imperial Rome, a preferred place for tourists (American and Chinese in the modern case), a destination for nostalgic cultural tourism with no effective relevance? More radical measures are thus needed: instead of *cultural* exceptions we need *economic* exceptions. Can we cover the costs? Our growing military expenses, as well as our support for superb scientific institutions like CERN, demonstrate that we can afford great investments without in any way crippling our economy.

In the post-Brexit atmosphere, opposition to TTIP exploded all around Europe, but the struggle is far from over. Even if TTIP or TISA are shelved, one should not forget that they are just expressions of a general tendency that works like a hydra – when its head is cut off, a new head grows up immediately. The (first) name of this new head is CETA, the Comprehensive Economic and Trade Agreement, a deal between the EU and Canada. George Monbiot writes:

> As far as transparency, parity and comprehensibility are concerned, it's the equivalent of the land treaties illiterate African chiefs were induced to sign in the nineteenth century. It is hard to see how parliamentarians could make a properly informed decision.
>
> Like TTIP, CETA threatens to lock in privatization, making renationalization (of Britain's railways, say) or attempts by cities to take control of failing public services (as Joseph Chamberlain did in Birmingham in the nineteenth century, laying the foundations for modern social provision) impossible. Like TTIP, it uses a broad definition of both investment and expropriation to allow corporations to sue governments when they believe their 'future anticipated profits' might be threatened by new laws. Like TTIP, it restricts the ways in which governments may protect their people. It appears to prohibit, for example, rules that would prevent banks from becoming too big to fail. It seems to threaten our planning laws and other commonsense protections [. . .] CETA claims to be a trade treaty, but many of its provisions have little to do with trade. They are attempts to circumscribe democracy on behalf of corporate power.

Monbiot's sad conclusion is that the struggle 'will continue throughout your life. We have to succeed every time; they have to succeed only once. Never drop your guard. Never let them win.'[11]

PROGRESS TOWARDS SLAVERY AND
THE PRECARIAT

But are we not simply exaggerating here, painting much too dark a picture? Advocates of capitalism often point out that, in spite of all the critical prophecies, capitalism is overall, from a global perspective, not in crisis but progressing more than ever – and one cannot but agree with them. Capitalism thrives all around the world (more or less), from China to Africa. It is definitely not in crisis – it is just the people caught in this explosive development that are in crisis. This tension between overall rapid growth and local crises and misery is part of capitalism's normal functioning: capitalism renews itself through such crises.

Let's take the case of slavery. While capitalism legitimizes itself as the economic system that implies and furthers personal freedom (as a condition of market exchange), it generated slavery on its own, as a part of its own dynamics: although slavery became almost extinct at the end of the Middle Ages, it re-emerged in colonies from early modernity till the American Civil War. And one can risk the hypothesis that today, with the new epoch of global capitalism, a new era of slavery is also arising. Although there is no longer a direct legal category of enslaved persons, slavery acquires a multitude of new forms: millions of migrant workers in the Saudi peninsula (UAE, Qatar, etc.), who are deprived of elementary civil rights and freedoms and subjected to restricted mobility; the total control over millions of workers in Asian sweatshops, often consciously organized as concentration camps; the massive use of forced labour in the exploitation of natural resources in many central African states (Congo, etc.). This new *de facto* apartheid, this systematic explosion of a number of different forms of contemporary slavery, is not a deplorable accident but a structural necessity of today's global capitalism.

Another blatant case of regress as part of the capitalist progress is the enormous rise of precarious work. Precarious work deprives workers of a whole series of rights that, till recently, were taken as self-evident in any country which perceived itself as a welfare state: precarious workers have to take care themselves of their health insurance and retirement options; there is no paid leave; the future becomes much more uncertain. Precarious work also generates an antagonism within the working class, between permanently employed and precarious workers (trade unions tend to privilege permanent workers; it is very difficult for precarious workers even to organize themselves into a union or to establish other forms of collective self-organization). One would have expected that this increasing exploitation would also strengthen workers' resistance, but it renders resistance even more difficult, and the main reason for this is ideological: precarious work is presented (and up to a point even effectively experienced) as a new form of freedom – I am no longer just a cog in a complex enterprise but an entrepreneur-of-the-self, I am a boss of myself who freely manages my employment, free to choose new options, to explore different aspects of my creative potential, to choose my priorities . . .

There is a clear homology between the precarious worker and today's typical consumer of TV and cultural programmes, where we are also ordained, as it were, to practise freedom of choice.[12] More and more, each of us is becoming the curator of our own TV and cultural life, subscribing to programmes that we prefer (HBO, History Channel), selecting movies on demand, etc., according to our own desire, exposed to a freedom of choice for which we are not really qualified since we are given no orientation, no criteria, and are thus left to the arbitrariness of our bad taste. The role of authorities, models, cannons even, is essential here: even when we aim at violating and overturning them, they provide the basic coordinates (orientation points) in the messy landscape of endless choices.

Faire Bouger les Choses

The key lesson of the combination of the precariat, which is expanding in the middle classes within the cupola, and the new slavery outside its boundaries is that a link between Leftist protests (Occupy, etc.) in the West and the Third World horrors is crucial to *faire bouger les choses*. Everyone agrees in principle this is the big task, but we have here a clear case of non-principled politics: one agrees in principle with a task, but one does nothing to actualize it; we can even say that the very principled position serves as an excuse to do nothing, a nothing that can assume many well-known forms. To quote Badiou:

> The 'Leftists' try in general to constitute 'autonomous' groups composed of students or dropouts of the Western world, and are interested in the third-level questions like that of 'zones to be defended' for ecological reasons or gatherings around the motif of 'let's change our life'. There are real initiatives which effectively concern the nomadic proletariat, but they require political conscience and considerable personal efforts.[13]

So, are immigrant refugees to be considered the 'nomadic proletariat'? There is an immense problem in transforming them into part of a radical emancipatory movement: their utopia is mostly to get integrated into (welfare) capitalism plus to retain their cultural identity. They are mostly not sustained by a vulgar 'desire for the West' but by a much more desperate combination of the need to survive and the desire to maintain some kind of cultural identity. On both counts, they will have to learn a hard and painful lesson. So, again, we can see the 'nomadic proletariat' as an agent caught in the terrible tension between an authentic proletarian position and the populist temptation. The reason one should focus on different ways of life is not that they have inherent value but that, if we do not confront these types of tension openly, the universal class struggle for emancipation (and the *only* true social universality today is that of class struggle) will be displaced on to the fake 'clash of civilizations'.

The basic gesture we in the West should make is not to engage in some kind of very dubious and patronizing 'respect' for the Other, but to fight within our own tradition for the emancipatory dimensions (the legacy of equality, social justice, etc.) that offer strong arguments against colonialism and racism. Furthermore, to establish the link between the Western Left and the Third World poor and displaced, it is crucial to overcome the tension between Western modernity and Third World anti-modernity (even if it is masked as 'anti-imperialism'). This link will only be built through a double self-critique: one side (the protesting Leftists in the West) should get rid of the obsession with middle-class cultural and sexual politics issues, while the other (Third World) side should endorse cultural and sexual modernization as the only way to break out of neo-colonialist exploitation, i.e., they should learn the hard lesson that anti-modernism ultimately serves new forms of imperialism. To quote Badiou again:

> the communist politics should wrest from Western capitalism the monopoly on modernity (concerning history of sexuality, customs, language, religion, and other aspects of symbolic identities). The first problem is here that this politics unites all those who consider global capitalism the principal enemy and a new communism the vector of this conflict. It is within this shared conviction that one should deal with the persisting contradictions, especially by showing, point by point, how abandoning to capital the monopoly on modernity (the death of gods, the symbolic of the sexes, internationalism, etc.) goes against the unity necessary to combat it. Only from this discussion will emerge a new modernity relieved of the commodity culture.[14]

Yes, the struggle for modernization should be led under the banner of anti-capitalism, but without the link to the struggle for modernization, the anti-capitalist struggle will remain a reactive movement destined to fail.

Furthermore, there are some other ambiguities at work here. Badiou proposes a semiotic square which encapsulates the basic coordinates of today's world; its two axes are a vertical one, the opposition between tradition and modernity, and a horizontal one, the opposition between capitalism and communism. The line between modernism and capitalism designates the space of the modern developed West, and the line between capitalism and tradition the space of fascism. On the opposite side, the line between tradition and communism designates the space of twentieth-century state socialism (Stalinism), while the line between modernism and communism opens up the space of a new political truth (newly reinvented communism). World wars take place in the triangle between the West, fascism and state socialism, while the Cold War takes place between the West and state socialism.

Although attractive in its explanatory power, this scheme raises many questions. How do capitalism and communism relate to modernity? Can capitalism reproduce itself without relying on a pre-modern core of traditional values and practices? Or is modernity (as Fredric Jameson sometimes suggests) another name for capitalism? I also find problematic the location of Stalinism on the line that connects communism and tradition: was Stalinism not primarily an extremely brutal modernization (forced collectivization, fast industrialization), and does the same not hold for Mao's Great Leap Forward? Was even fascism not a conservative modernization, a modernization legitimized as a return to pre-modern tradition (exemplarily in Japan), so that fascism should be rather located on the horizontal axis between tradition and modernity? Even ISIS is not simply traditional – as with every fascism, it combines pseudo-traditional content with ultra-modern form. On the other hand, if we are looking for elements that fit the communism–tradition axis, it is not so much the Stalinist 'really-existing socalism' that belongs here but many elements of the Third World new Left, which look for inspiration in some ancient tradition (Latin America is full of *indigenismo*). Furthermore, some forms of the most dynamic contemporary capitalism (India, China, etc.) refer to tradition in order to contain the disruptive effects of capitalist modernization.

DON'T MISUNDERESTIMATE THE FETISH OF DEMOCRACY!

The lesson of all these complications is that, to paraphrase President Bush, one should definitely not misunderestimate the destructive power of international capital. In such conditions, can a 'democratically elected' Leftist government effectively impose radical changes? The trap that lurks here is clearly perceptible in Thomas Piketty's *Capital in the Twenty-first Century*. For Piketty, capitalism has to be accepted as the only game in town, so the sole feasible alternative is to allow the capitalist machinery to do its work in its proper sphere, and to impose egalitarian justice politically, by a democratic power that regulates the economic system and enforces redistribution. Such a solution is *utopian* in the strictest sense of the term. Piketty is well aware that the model he proposes would only work if enforced globally, beyond the confines of nation-states (otherwise capital would flee to the states with lower taxes); such a global measure presupposes an already existing global power with the strength and authority to enforce it. However, such a global power is unimaginable within the confines of today's global capitalism and the political mechanisms it implies – in short, if such a power were to exist, *the basic problem would already have been resolved*. Plus, what further measures would the global imposition of high taxes proposed by Piketty necessitate? Of course, the only way out of this vicious cycle is simply to cut the Gordian knot and *act*. There are never perfect conditions for an act – every act by definition comes too early, but one has to begin somewhere; with a particular intervention, one just has to bear in mind the further complications that such an act will lead to. In other words, the true utopia is to imagine global capitalism as we know it today, still functioning the way it does, just with the high tax rates proposed by Piketty added to it. This same utopianism is at work in Joseph Stiglitz's comment 'Democracy in the Twenty-first Century' – the title obviously refers to Thomas Piketty's, but with an important twist, shifting the accent from capitalism to our liberal-democratic political system. Here is its concluding line of argument:

> What we have been observing – wage stagnation and rising inequality, even as wealth increases – does not reflect the workings of a normal market economy, but of what I call 'ersatz capitalism'. The problem may not be with how markets should or do work, but with our political system, which has failed to ensure that markets are competitive, and has designed rules that sustain distorted markets in which corporations and the rich can (and unfortunately do) exploit everyone else [. . .] Markets, of course, do not exist in a vacuum. There have to be rules of the game, and these are established through political processes [. . .] Thus, Piketty's forecast of still higher levels of inequality does not reflect the inexorable laws of economics. Simple changes – including higher capital-gains and inheritance taxes, greater spending to broaden access to education, rigorous

enforcement of anti-trust laws, corporate-governance reforms that circumscribe executive pay, and financial regulations that rein in banks' ability to exploit the rest of society – would reduce inequality and increase equality of opportunity markedly. If we get the rules of the game right, we might even be able to restore the rapid and shared economic growth that characterized the middle-class societies of the mid-twentieth century. The main question confronting us today is not really about capital in the twenty-first century. It is about democracy in the twenty-first century.[15]

In some formal sense this is, of course, true: the organization of a market economy is effectively possible only within legal coordinates that are ultimately decided by a political process. Stiglitz is also fully justified in pointing out that, in order to effectively change capitalism, we would also have to change the functioning of our democracy. Here, however, problems arise. In what precise sense is democracy a problem? It seems that, for Stiglitz, it is simply a question of enforcing new rules (laws regulating economic life) within the existing democratic framework – we need an elected government to pass some 'simple changes' like 'higher capital-gains and inheritance taxes, greater spending to broaden access to education, rigorous enforcement of anti-trust laws, corporate-governance reforms that circumscribe executive pay, and financial regulations that rein in banks' ability to exploit the rest of society'. But can we really imagine the transformation of society done like this? Here Marx's key insight remains valid, perhaps more than ever: for Marx, the question of freedom should not be located primarily in the political sphere proper (Does a country have free elections? Are its judges independent? Is its press free from hidden pressures? Does it respect human rights?). Rather, the key to actual freedom resides in the 'apolitical' network of social relations, from the market to the family. The change required is not political reform but a transformation of the social relations of production – which entails precisely revolutionary class struggle rather than democratic elections or any other 'political' measure in the narrow sense of the term. We do not vote on who owns what, or about relations in the factory, etc. – such matters remain outside the sphere of the political, and it is illusory to expect that one could effectively change things by 'extending' democracy into the economic sphere (by, say, reorganizing the banks to place them under popular control). Radical changes in this domain need to be made outside the sphere of legal 'rights'. In 'democratic' procedures (which, of course, can have a positive role to play), no matter how radical our anti-capitalism, solutions are sought solely through those democratic mechanisms that themselves form parts of the apparatus of the 'bourgeois' state that guarantees the undisturbed reproduction of capital. In this precise sense, Badiou was right in his apparently weird claim: 'Today, the enemy is not called Empire or Capital. It's called Democracy.'[16] When Badiou furthermore claimed that democracy is our fetish, this statement is to be taken literally, in the precise Freudian sense, not just in the vague sense that we elevate democracy into our untouchable Absolute: 'democracy' is the last thing we see before confronting the 'lack' that is constitutive of the social field, the fact that 'there is no class relationship' (if I may paraphrase Lacan's formula 'there is no sexual relationship'), the trauma of social antagonism. It is as if, when confronted with the reality of domination and exploitation, of brutal social struggles, we can always add: yes, but *we have democracy*, which gives us the hope of resolving or at least regulating struggles, preventing their destructive outcomes. It is the 'democratic illusion', the acceptance of democratic mechanisms as providing the only framework for any possible change, that prevents the radical transformation of society

The field of capitalist economy, of the organization of production, exchange and distribution, has its own inertia and immanent movement, and the democratic political frame is already accommodated to this capitalist structure. To really change this capitalist structure, one should also change this democratic political frame; one cannot do it by enforcing changes through democratic electoral procedures that remain the same as before. Here we encounter Stiglitz's second, Keynesian, limitation: does his designation of the present economic system as 'ersatz capitalism' not imply that there is another, proper, capitalism, in which markets are really and fairly competitive, not our 'distorted markets in which corporations and the rich can (and unfortunately do) exploit everyone else'? We can see Stiglitz's wager here: by democratically enforcing legal changes, we can replace ersatz-capitalism with a more just and efficient one, thus combining the best of capitalism with the best of democracy. But what if this entire idea is utopian in the strict sense of the term? What if what Stiglitz calls 'ersatz-capitalism' is simply capitalism as such, capitalism that follows its immanent development, and not some secondary perversion? That is to say, although capitalist markets 'do not exist in a vacuum', the political process of democracy also does not exist in a vacuum, but is always overdetermined by economic relations.

For this reason we should be suspicious of the critique of progressive movements or governments that is formulated, in pseudo-Leftist terms, as a libertarian critique of their 'authoritarian' features. Middle-class students and petit-bourgeois libertarians (who want more 'freedoms' and chances for themselves but abhor real change) complain about 'non-democratic' government decisions, etc. Such a critique is the most perfidious rejection of radical change, which, at first, has to appear 'authoritarian' in its resolute break with the established ways. Let's take the sad case of Venezuela. Although the Bolivarian revolution deserves a lot of criticism, we should nonetheless always bear in mind that it is lately the victim of a well-orchestrated counter-revolution, especially a long economic warfare. There is nothing new in such a procedure. Back in the early 1970s, in a note to the CIA advising them how to undermine the democratically elected Chilean government of Salvador Allende, Henry Kissinger wrote succinctly: 'Make the economy scream.' We can safely surmise that the economic difficulties faced by the Chavista government are not only the result of the ineptness of its own economic politics. Here we come to the key political point, difficult to swallow for some liberals: we are clearly not dealing with blind market processes and reactions (say, shop owners trying to make more profit by keeping some products off the shelves), but with an elaborate and fully planned strategy. In such conditions is a kind of terror (police raids on secret warehouses, detention of speculators and the coordinators of the shortages, etc.) not fully justified as a defensive counter-measure? When, on 9 March 2015, President Obama issued an executive order declaring Venezuela a 'national security threat', did he not thereby give a green light to a *coup d'état*? At a more 'civilized' level, the same is happening with Greece.

BEYOND CAPITALISM

So, how are we to make the idea of socialism operative again in such hopeless circumstances? Axel Honneth[17] outlines three main weaknesses of the classic model of socialism: (1) the focus on industrial productivity and on socializing the production process, which neglects political/public freedom (the democratic formation of public space) and freedom in the intimate sphere, as if it can be assumed that the socialization of the productive process will automatically entail actual freedom in the entire social body; (2) uncritical reliance on the notion of teleological historical necessity (socialism will arrive more or less automatically – it will replace capitalism following the logic of historical progress); (3) the presumption that there is a privileged subject of liberation (on account of its objective social situation, the working class is predestined to be the main agent of the transition from capitalism to socialism). According to Honneth, if the idea of socialism is to regain its power of mobilization, one has to leave behind all these three claims. Socialism should be (re)conceived as a process of expanding freedom that takes place in three spheres: cooperation and solidarity instead of competition in the sphere of productivity; the freedom of individuals in the public sphere, a freedom which renders possible the democratic formation of their collective will; and freedom from oppression in the intimate sphere. The agent and/or addressee of such an extended notion of freedom is no longer a privileged social subject (like a working class) but (potentially) all citizens.

Furthermore, the progressive enactment of such expanded freedom can no longer be conceived in deterministic terms, as a process regulated by a historical necessity; it can only be a process of complex social experimentation with no predetermined goal or procedure. For example, in economy, one should not adopt an *a priori* anti-market stance, but rather attempt to 'purify' the market of its capitalist distortions.

This vision of freedom extended to the three spheres implies the primacy (not of economy but) of the sphere of public communication: the socialization of economy as well as the freedoms gained in the private sphere can both be conceived as extensions of the logic of democratic freedom. But do we not stumble here upon a key weakness of Honneth's model? Are we not witnessing today precisely a complex situation in which (relative) political freedom and exploding freedom in the intimate sphere are counteracted by the growing non-transparency of the economic sphere? So, today, the key problem is precisely the problem of economy, of global capitalism and its antagonisms. This neglect of antagonisms is clearly discernible in Honneth's resort to the organic metaphor of 'Life', of a living organism as a model for the coexistence of three spheres. This model impels him to ignore radical antagonisms that are growing today, from ecology to biogenetics, from exploitation to new forms of social violence, antagonisms that resist being translated into communicational problems. So, when we talk about social totality, it would be appropriate to follow Hegel's assertion of the antagonistic totality, a totality oscillating from one extreme to another. Hegel's basic lesson is that the path to truth is not to be found by getting rid of 'unilateral' positions, thus creating a harmonious totality of Life, but by bringing each sphere to its extreme, thereby causing its reversal to the opposite. To put it another way, what is missing in Honneth's vision is an understanding of the paradoxical combination of growing freedom at one level with growing un-freedom at another level, a situation in which the new freedom is often the very mode of appearance for the un-freedom – just recall the desperate plight of precarious workers, a plight celebrated by some 'postmodern' sociologists as a new freedom to reinvent oneself every couple of years. If we want to reach some new freedom we have to get lost in this mad dance of freedom turning into un-freedom – there is no direct way to freedom.

Honneth ultimately remains an ethical socialist, i.e., he dismisses reference to a privileged social agent of change (the working class) as a hangover from nineteenth-century socialism, and instead grounds demands for change in ethical norms that concern all of us. But is it not reasonable to search for tendencies in today's reality itself that point beyond global capitalism, and to discern social groups that occupy a proletarian position? One can do this without any recourse to working-class essentialism and historical determinism. One of the great ironies of contemporary social theory is that Peter Sloterdijk, a resolutely anti-communist liberal conservative, whom some Habermasians even suspect of pursuing a Nazi eugenic agenda, takes a step further in outlining the antagonisms which make a move beyond global capitalism a matter of our survival.

In his new book, *What Happened in the Twentieth Century?*,[18] after rejecting the twentieth century's 'passion of the Real' as a harbinger of political extremism that leads to the extermination of enemies, Sloterdijk provides his own outline of what is to be done in the twenty-first century, best encapsulated in the title of the first two essays in the book, 'The Anthropocene' and 'From the Domestication of Man to the Civilizing of Cultures'. 'Anthropocene' designates a new epoch in the life of our planet in which we, humans, cannot any longer rely on the Earth as a reservoir ready to absorb the consequences of our productive activity: we cannot any longer afford to ignore the side effects (collateral damage) of our productivity. They cannot any longer be reduced to the background of the figure of humanity. We have to accept that we live on a 'Spaceship Earth', responsible and accountable for its conditions. Earth is no longer the impenetrable background/horizon of our productive activity: it emerges as a(nother) finite object that we can inadvertently destroy or transform to make it unliveable. This means that, at the very moment when we become powerful enough to affect the most basic conditions of our life, we have to accept that we are just another animal species on a small planet. A new way to relate to our environs is necessary once we realize this: no longer a heroic worker expressing his or her creative potentials and drawing from the inexhaustible resources of the environment, but a much more modest agent collaborating with the surroundings, permanently negotiating a tolerable level of safety and stability.

Is ignoring collateral damage not the very model of capitalism? What matters in capitalist reproduction is the self-enhancing circulation focused on profit, and the collateral damage done to the environment is in principle ignored – even the attempts to take it into account through taxation (or by directly putting a price tag on every natural resource one uses, including air) cannot but misfire.

So in order to establish this new mode of relating to our environment, a radical politico-economic change is necessary, what

Sloterdijk calls 'the domestication of the wild animal Culture'. Till now, each culture disciplined or educated its own members and guaranteed civic peace among them through state power; but the relationship between different cultures and states was permanently under the shadow of potential war, with each period of peace nothing more than a temporary armistice. As Hegel conceptualized it, the entire ethic of a state culminates in the highest act of heroism, the readiness to sacrifice one's life for one's nation-state, which means that the wild barbarian relations between states serve as the foundation of the ethical life within a state. Is today's North Korea, with its ruthless pursuit of nuclear weapons and rockets to carry them to distant targets, not the ultimate example of this logic of unconditional nation-state sovereignty? However, the moment we fully accept the fact that we live on a Spaceship Earth, the task that urgently imposes itself is that of civilizing civilizations themselves, of imposing universal solidarity and cooperation among all human communities, a task rendered all the more difficult by the ongoing rise of sectarian religious and ethnic 'heroic' violence and a readiness to sacrifice oneself (and the world) for one's specific cause.

Now, let us just take a step back and reflect upon what Sloterdijk is advocating. The measures he proposes as necessary for the survival of humanity – the overcoming of capitalist expansionism, wide international cooperation and solidarity that should lead to the creation of an executive power ready to violate state sovereignty, etc. – are these not all measures destined to protect our natural and cultural commons? If they do not point towards communism, if they do not imply a communist horizon, then the term 'communism' has no meaning at all. Although Sloterdijk critically rejects all twentieth-century extremism, the shift he advocates is extremely radical, much more 'extreme' than the standard communist vision (outlined originally by Marx) of a new society that continues to rely on unconstrained capitalist expansion. No wonder Sloterdijk remains vague about how to enact this immense transformation – a closer analysis would necessarily bring him to the old topic of the communist reorganization of society. The first step in this direction would have been the traditional Marxist move from external to internal antagonisms: the fact that relations between civilizations prosper under a permanent threat of war, i.e., remain barbarian, points towards a barbarian dimension that lurks within each civilization, the radical antagonism ('class struggle') on which each civilization is grounded. 'Civilizing civilizations' is thus not primarily a matter of external negotiations between civilizations but a matter of an immanent radical transformation of each civilization.

For Sloterdijk, the great political and ideological struggle that lies ahead of us and that will decide the fate of humanity is the struggle between the politics of sovereignty (where each agent is ready to risk everything for its ideologico-political cause, as is the case with Islamic and other fundamentalisms), and the politics of unity through negotiations (which strives to enact a moderate compromise as the only option for our survival). But, again, does the struggle against particular sovereignties not involve a radicality of its own, a clear break with the hitherto predominant mode of politics?

COOPERATIVE COMMONS

To resolve this deadlock, one should perhaps follow the good old Marxist path and shift the focus from politics to the signs of post-capitalism that are discernible within global capitalism itself, in particular the rise of what Jeremy Rifkin calls 'collaborative commons' (CC), a new mode of production and exchange that leaves behind private property and market relations. CC are to be opposed to the two other forms of social organization that were operative in modern history: market interaction (bottom-up spontaneous self-organization based on egotist competition and the search for profit) and centralized planning (the top-down regulation of society by a strong state, as in 'really-existing socialism'). The fourth form is the pre-state self-organization of 'primitive' societies, to which CC relates in an ambiguous way: the two are radically different, but at the same time they strangely resemble each other. How, then, does this square of four forms function? One possible path to understanding it was outlined by Kojin Karatani, whose basic premise is to use modes of exchange (instead of modes of production, as in Marxism) as a tool with which to analyse the history of humanity.[19] Karatani distinguishes four progressive modes of exchange: (A) gift exchange, which predominates in pre-state societies (clans or tribes exchanging gifts); (B) domination and protection, which predominates in slave and feudal societies (here, exploitation is based on direct domination, and the dominating class has to offer something in exchange, for example protecting its subjects from dangers); (C) commodity exchange of objects, which predominates in capitalism (free individuals exchange not only their products but also their own labour power); and (X) a further stage to come, a return to the gift-exchange at a higher level – this X is a Kantian regulative idea, a vision that has assumed different guises historically, from egalitarian religious communities relying on communal solidarity to anarchist cooperatives and communist projects. Karatani introduces here two further complications. (1) There is a crucial rupture, the so-called 'sedentary revolution', which takes place in pre-state early societies: the passage from nomadic hunter-groups to permanently settled groups organized in tribes or clans. At the level of exchange, we pass from 'pure' gift to the complex web of gift and counter-gift. This distinction is crucial insofar as the forthcoming passage to X will enact at a higher level the return to the nomadic mode of social existence. (2) In the passage from A to B, etc., the previous stage does not disappear, though it is 'repressed' and returns in a new form. With the passage from A to B, the community of gift-exchange survives as the spirit of religious reconciliation and solidarity; with the passage from B to C, A survives as nation, national community, and B (domination) survives as the state power. For this reason, capitalism is for Karatani not a 'pure' reign of B, but a triad (or, rather, a Borromean knot) of nation–state–capital: nation as the form of communal solidarity, state as the form of direct domination, and capital as the form of economic exchange; all three of them are necessary for the reproduction of the capitalist society.[20]

One could thus conceive of CC as the return, at a higher level, of the gift-exchange: in CC, individuals are giving their products free into circulation.[21] This emancipatory dimension of CC should, of course, be located in the context of the rise of the so-called 'internet of things' (IoT), combined with another outcome of today's development of productive forces, the explosive rise of 'zero marginal costs' (many products (and not only information) can be produced in greater numbers for no additional cost).

What lurks behind IoT is, of course, a properly metaphysical vision of the emergence of the so-called Singularity: our individual lives will be totally embedded in a divine-like digital Other that controls and regulates them. This extrapolation confronts us clearly with the utter ambiguity of the internet of things. Two mutually exclusive readings of IoT impose themselves: IoT as the domain of radical emancipation, a unique chance to combine freedom and collaboration in which, to paraphrase Juliet's definition of love from Shakespeare's *Romeo and Juliet*, 'The more I give to thee, the more I have, for both are infinite,' versus IoT as a complete submersion into the divine digital Other, where I am deprived of my freedom of agency. But are these two readings really mutually exclusive, in which case IoT is the ultimate field of the emancipatory struggle, or are they just two different views of the same reality?

The internet of things is the network of physical devices, vehicles, buildings and other items embedded with electronics, software, sensors, actuators and network connectivity that enable these objects to collect and exchange data; it allows objects to be sensed and controlled remotely across the existing network infrastructure, creating opportunities for more direct integration of the physical world into computer-based systems, and resulting in improved efficiency, accuracy and economic benefit. When IoT is augmented with sensors and actuators, the technology becomes an instance of the more general class of 'cyber-physical systems', which also encompasses technologies such as smart grids, smart homes, intelligent transportation and smart cities. Each thing is uniquely identifiable through its embedded computing system and is able to interact within the existing internet infrastructure. The interconnection of these embedded devices (including smart objects) is expected to usher in automation in nearly all fields, while also enabling advanced applications like a smart grid, and expanding to areas such as smart cities. 'Things' can also refer to a wide variety of devices – such as heart monitoring implants, biochip transponders on farm animals, electric dams in coastal waters, automobiles with built-in sensors, and DNA analysis devices for environmental/food/pathogen monitoring – that collect useful data with the help of various existing technologies and then autonomously flow the data between other devices. In this context, human individuals are also 'things', whose states and activities are continuously registered and transmitted without their knowledge. Data concerning their physical movements, their financial transactions, their health, their eating and drinking habits, what they buy and sell, what they read, listen to and watch, is all collected in digital networks that know them better than they know themselves.

The prospect of IoT seems to compel us to turn around Friedrich Hölderlin's famous line, from 'But where the danger is, also grows the saving power' to 'But where the saving power is, also grows the danger'. IoT's 'saving' aspect was described in detail by Jeremy Rifkin, who claims that, for the first time in human history, a path of overcoming capitalism is discernible as an actual tendency in social production and exchange (the growth of cooperative commons), and thus the end of capitalism is on the horizon. The crudest Marxist hypothesis seems re-vindicated: the development of new productive forces makes capitalist relations obsolete. The ultimate irony is that, while communists are today the best managers of capitalism (China, Vietnam), developed capitalist countries go furthest in the direction of collaborative or cooperative commons as the way to overcome capitalism:

> Markets are beginning to give way to networks, ownership is becoming less important than access, the pursuit of self-interest is being tempered by the pull of collaborative interests, and the traditional dream of rags to riches is being supplanted by a new dream of a sustainable quality of life [. . .] While the capitalist market is based on self-interest and driven by material gain, the social Commons is motivated by collaborative interests and driven by a deep desire to connect with others and share.[22]

> As capitalist markets and wage labor becomes less relevant, an economy built upon new principles and social values will progressively emerge: decentralized networks will take the place of markets; access to an abundance of shareable goods and services will reduce the significance of ownership and private property; open-source innovation,

transparency and collaborative co-creation will replace the pursuit of competitive self-interest and autonomy; a commitment to sustainable development and a reintegration with the Earth's biosphere will redress rampant materialism and overconsumption; and the re-discovery of our empathic nature will drive our pursuit for community engagement and social belonging in a rising Collaborative Commons.[23]

But this gives birth to new dangers, even if we discount false worries like the idea that IoT will boost unemployment. (Isn't this 'threat' a good reason to reorganize production so that workers work much less? In short, isn't this 'problem' its own solution?) At the concrete level of social organization, the threat is a clearly discernible tendency of the state and private sector to regain control over the collaborative commons:

> National governments are increasingly moving to enact their own legislations, citing sovereign rights, which threaten to undermine the open and accessible nature of the internet. The private sector is also moving away from the collective alliance, instead seeking to gain greater profits through more centralized control over how content is delivered. Similarly, large controlling companies on the web such as Google, Facebook and Twitter are increasingly 'selling the masses of transmitted Big Data that comes their way to commercial bidders and businesses that use it for targeted advertising and marketing campaigns' [Rifkin, *Zero Marginal Cost Society*, p. 199]. In essence, vertically scaled profit-seeking corporations of the capitalist era are exploiting a laterally scaled and distributed Collaborative Commons for their own private ends. In other words, 'companies are operating a social Commons as a commercial venture' [Ibid., p. 204].[24]

Personal contacts are thus privatized by Facebook, software by Microsoft, search by Google ... To grasp these new forms of privatization, one should critically transform Marx's conceptual apparatus: because of his neglect of the social dimension of 'general intellect', (the collective intelligence of a society), Marx didn't envisage the possibility of *the privatization of the 'general intellect' itself* – this is what is at the core of the struggle for 'intellectual property'. Antonio Negri is here right: within this frame, exploitation in the classic Marxist sense is no longer possible – which is why it has to be enforced more and more by direct legal measures, i.e., by a non-economic force. This is why, today, exploitation increasingly takes on the form of rent: as Carlo Vercellone put it, post-industrial capitalism is characterized by the 'becoming-rent of profit'.[25] And this is why direct authority is needed: it is needed to impose the (arbitrary) legal conditions for extracting rent, conditions that are no longer 'spontaneously' generated by the market. Perhaps, therein resides the fundamental contradiction of today's 'postmodern' capitalism: while its logic is de-regulatory, 'anti-statal', nomadic/de-territorializing, etc., its key tendency of the 'becoming-rent of profit' signals the strengthening role of the state, whose (not only) regulatory function is increasingly all-present. Dynamic de-territorialization co-exists with and relies on greater authoritarian interventions by the state and its legal and other apparatuses. What one can discern at the horizon of our historical becoming is thus a society in which personal libertarianism and hedonism co-exist with (and are sustained by) a complex web of regulatory state mechanisms. Far from disappearing, the state is strengthening today.

In other words, when, due to the crucial role of the 'general intellect' (knowledge and social cooperation) in the creation of wealth, forms of wealth are increasingly 'out of all proportion to the direct labour time spent on their production',[26] the result is not, as Marx seems to have expected, the self-dissolution of capitalism, but the gradual relative transformation of the profit generated by the exploitation of labour into rent appropriated by the privatization of the 'general intellect'. Let us take the case of Bill Gates: how did he become the richest man in the world? His wealth has nothing to do with the production costs of the products Microsoft is selling (one can even argue that Microsoft is paying its intellectual workers a relatively high salary), i.e., Gates's wealth is not the result of his success in producing good software for lower prices than his competitors, or in imposing greater 'exploitation' on his hired intellectual workers. If this were the case, Microsoft would have gone bankrupt long ago: people would have massively chosen programs like Linux, which are free and, according to specialists, of better quality than

Microsoft programs. Why, then, are millions still buying Microsoft? Because Microsoft has imposed itself as an almost universal standard, (almost) monopolizing the field, a kind of direct embodiment of the 'general intellect'. Gates became the richest man in a couple of decades through appropriating the rent generated by allowing millions of intellectual workers to participate in the new form of the 'general intellect' that he privatized and controls. Is it true, then, that today's intellectual workers are no longer separated from the objective conditions of their labour (they own their PC, etc.), which is Marx's description of capitalist 'alienation'? Yes, but more fundamentally *no*: they are cut off from the social field of their work, from a 'general intellect' that is not mediated by private capital.

The worst thing to do here is to simply oppose the 'good' and the 'bad' aspect, following the legendary US politician who, back in the Prohibition era, when asked what he thought about alcohol, answered: 'If you mean by alcohol the dreadful drink that ruins families and causes fight, then I am against it. But if you mean the wonderful drink that makes the evening relaxing and brings joy to a company, then I am for it.' Applied to digital commons, this stance amounts to: 'If you mean Google or another big corporation knowing us better than we know ourselves and regulating our lives, then I am against it; but if you mean free cooperation, then I am for it.' The predominant view is that such companies play an intermediate role in the passage from market to collaborative commons, and they will disappear by themselves through the expansion of CC:

> Companies such as Uber and Airbnb will attempt to bridge the gap between the two economies and take advantage of both. However, as truly decentralized peer-to-peer networks begin to take over at near zero marginal cost these hybrid companies will not last [. . .] Truly decentralized networks of exchange on the Commons will allow for direct peer-to-peer transactions without the need for third-party intermediary trust or involvement.[27]

Such a smooth solution avoids the real problem: is this encroaching of big corporations just a parasitism to be overcome, or is it that CC cannot stand alone and needs an external controlling and regulating agency? What if – while, of course, we should fight against corporations that privatize our commons – the direction of this fight should not be to dream about the moment when decentralized collaborative networks take over the entire field, but to find another organization and form of power external to the commons that will regulate its functioning? Even if we abstract from this re-privatization of the commons and imagine full collaborative commons with no external power regulating them, another problems arises. In the management of CC,

> the significance of reputation systems should be noted. Reputation rankings will play an important role in ensuring compliance with norms and regulating activities. These systems are designed to rank an individual's *social capital* in the Commons. With the growth of the Commons, 'expect social-capital ratings to become as important to millions of participants on the Collaborative Commons as credit ratings were to consumers in the capitalist marketplace' [Rifkin, *Zero Marginal Cost Society*, p. 258].[28]

OK, but how will reputations emerge, how will ratings be established? Envy enters here with a vengeance. In *An American Utopia*,[29] Jameson totally rejects the predominant optimistic view, according to which in communism envy will be left behind as a remainder of capitalist competition, to be replaced by solidary collaboration and pleasure in other's pleasures. Dismissing this myth, he emphasizes that, in communism, precisely insofar as it will be a more just society, envy and resentment will explode – why? Jean-Pierre Dupuy[30] proposes a convincing critique of John Rawls's theory of justice: in the Rawls model of a just society, social inequalities are tolerated only insofar as they also help those at the bottom of the social ladder, and insofar as they are not based on inherited hierarchies but on natural inequalities, which are considered contingent, not merits.[31] But what Rawls doesn't see is how such a society would create conditions for an uncontrolled explosion of *ressentiment*: in it, I would know that my lower status is fully 'justified', and I would thus be deprived of the ploy of excusing my failure as the result of social injustice. Rawls proposes a terrifying model of a society in which hierarchy is directly legitimized in natural properties, thereby missing Friedrich Hayek's[32] key lesson: it is much easier to accept inequalities if one can claim that they result from an impersonal blind force. The good thing about the 'irrationality' of the market and of success or failure in capitalism is that it allows me precisely to perceive my failure or success as 'undeserved', contingent. Remember the old motif of the market as the modern version of an imponderable Fate: the fact that capitalism is not 'just' is thus a key feature of what makes it acceptable.

There is another complication here. Marx always emphasized that the exchange between worker and capitalist is 'just' in the sense that workers (as a rule) get paid the full value of their labour-power as a commodity – there is no direct 'exploitation' here, that is, it is not that workers 'are not paid the full value of the commodity they are selling to the capitalists'. So while, in a market economy, I remain *de facto* dependent, this dependency is nonetheless 'civilized', enacted as a 'free' market exchange between me and other persons instead of as direct servitude or even physical coercion. It is easy to ridicule Ayn Rand, but there is a grain of truth in the famous 'hymn to money' from her *Atlas Shrugged*: 'Until and unless you discover that money is the root of all good, you ask for your own destruction. When money ceases to become the means by which men deal with one another, then men become the tools of other men. Blood, whips and guns or dollars. Take your choice – there is no other.'[33] Did Marx not say something similar in his well-known formula of how, in the universe of commodities, 'relations between people assume the guise of relations among things'? In the market economy, relations between people can appear as relations of mutually recognized freedom and equality: domination is no longer directly enacted and visible as such.

'Really-existing socialism' in the twentieth century proved that the overcoming of market-alienation abolishes 'alienated' freedom and with it freedom *tout court*, bringing us back to 'non-alienated' relations of direct domination. To what extent are collaborative commons exposed to the same danger? Can they survive without a regulating agency that controls the very medium of collaboration and thereby exerts direct domination?

2

Syriza, the Shadow of an Event

A SECOND RISE OF SYRIZA?

The attempt by the Syriza government to break out of the financial clutches of Brussels having ended in failure, the situation in Greece drags on in a depressing state. The time has come to reflect on what effectively happened.

Two texts appeared recently, both written by Greek theorists who were (and are) participants in the Syriza movement: Costas Douzinas and Stathis Kouvelakis. Their political paths split after Syriza succumbed to EU blackmail and agreed to implement the continuation of the austerity policy: Douzinas stayed with Syriza, while Kouvelakis, a prominent member of the Left Platform, formally split from the party. How do they justify their decisions? The titles of their texts are telltale: Kouvelakis's 'Syriza's Rise and Fall'[1] versus Douzinas's 'Syriza's Rise, Fall, and (Possible) Second Rise'.[2] So while they both agree that Syriza's surrender to EU pressure was a traumatic defeat, Kouvelakis rejects it as an unacceptable betrayal while Douzinas sees it as an enforced retreat that could be deftly exploited to lay the foundations of a new radical politics.

Here is, first, Kouvelakis's narrative. Things took a decisive turn back in the summer of 2012 when, after the elections, it became clear that, in some way, Syriza would take power. At this moment, the leadership of Alexis Tsipras made a series of decisions not only about the party line but also about the type of organization they needed: they advocated the transformation of Syriza from a coalition of disparate organizations and civil movements into a unified and centralized party. The great number of members of its Central

45

Committee made sure that *de facto* decisions were taken in advance in the narrow informal circle around Tsipras, the 'para-centre of power'. No wonder, then, that the surrender to Brussels decided by this 'para-centre' shocked Syriza's popular base, which mostly withdrew into despair and passivity, thereby depriving Syriza of the main source of its strength: the combination of electoral activity with popular mobilization.

However, when one talks about the loss of contact with a social movement's base, it is all too tempting to reproduce the old opposition of presence and representation, of basic social movements and their representation/alienation in party mechanisms and state apparatuses, from which ensues the mantra that the Left in power should at all costs keep alive its popular roots. But it is easy to show that this mantra covers up the true problem: how can we transform state mechanisms, make them function in a different way, instead of just supplementing them with popular pressure from outside? In short, it seems clear that, apart from two great models (social-democratic acceptance of parliamentary democracy, and the Stalinist state), the Left has no other practical model to offer – all the talk about active popular participation, about self-organization of the people (or 'multitude') in social movements, ultimately serves to obfuscate this lack. (Furthermore, one should also be attentive to the dark side of the reliance of a (Leftist) government on social movements: the case of Bolivia demonstrates that this reliance can also open the path to clientelism (different groups demanding privileges and financial gains in exchange for political support).)

Does this mean that Douzinas proposes a better interpretation? Surprisingly, although his text contains many precious insights and observations, it is ultimately a series of variations on one and the same motif: yes, there is a contradiction between Syriza's anti-austerity project and the politics it is forced to practise, but this contradiction is what characterizes the radical Left in power; there is no way to get rid of it:

> But is there a 'left' way of doing government? It is a difficult question not only because we don't have an answer, but also because we don't even have a fully worked out question. There is no precedent in

Western Europe. The government must experiment, take risks, use the imagination of party and movement, particularly that of young women and men who have consistently supported it. We have to learn to swim by jumping in the water.

The left in power in the current hostile international, European and domestic environment is a project marked by a series of paradoxes and contradictions. Its central expression is this, when a radical left party takes charge of the state, it encounters a hostile institution organized to frustrate its plans . . .

The denunciation of the imposed policies by Ministers manifests the contradictory and agonistic nature of left governmentality in a capitalist society . . . Nothing is more radical and scandalous than a government that proclaims its disagreement with the policies it has to implement, calls them the result of blackmail and develops a parallel programme to mitigate their consequences. Left governmentality means that critical distance, internal dissent and even active resistance form part of the government's negotiating strategy and the necessary correction to the seesaw between rupture and assimilation. Let me repeat: contradiction is the name of a left government that swims in a sea of neoliberal capitalism.[3]

Sounds nice, full of properly dialectical paradoxes, and Douzinas even wrote a text justifying Syriza's surrender in which he refers to critics of Syriza as examples of the Hegelian 'beautiful soul', who are not ready to dirty their hands and engage in hard political work full of necessary compromises. However, there is another of Hegel's insights that should be invoked here: Hegel always emphasized that what matters in an act is not the inner intent but its actual social outcome. Recall Marx's brilliant analysis of how, in the French revolution of 1848, deputies of the conservative-republican Party of Order perceived their republicanism as a mockery: in parliamentary debates, they generated royalist slips of the tongue and ridiculed the Republic to let it be known that their true aim was to restore the monarchy. What they were not aware of is that they themselves were duped as to the true social impact of their rule. They unknowingly established the conditions of bourgeois republican order that they despised so much (by, for instance, guaranteeing the safety of private property). So it is not that they were royalists who were just wearing a republican mask: although they experienced themselves as such, it was their 'inner' royalist conviction that was the deceptive front masking their true social role. In short, far from being the hidden truth of their public republicanism, their sincere royalism was the fantasmatic support of their actual republicanism – it was what provided the passion in their activity. Is it not, then, that the deputies of the Party of Order were also *feigning to feign* to be republicans, to be what they really were? And could something similar not be said about Syriza? It is possible that many of the Syriza members of government administration sincerely believe that they are doing some profoundly subversive work, superficially obeying EU orders but simultaneously using every opportunity to control the damage, to save what can be saved, to enforce progressive changes, and to organize forces for the inevitable future moment when the crisis strikes again. The Syriza government can, of course, do many things to de-clientelize and rationalize the ineffective state apparatus, to impose modern standards of human rights, etc., so it is difficult to pass a definitive judgement. However, what they are effectively doing is faithfully enforcing the EU demands, which amount to a *de facto* ceding of sovereignty (all government measures have to be approved by the EU troika); what if this is the truth of their activity, and the profound inner awareness of their resistance is an illusion enabling them to do what they are doing?

The question is here one of limits: how far does one go in compromises? At the extreme, there is the Vichy government in occupied France, which justified its collaboration with, 'We also hate the Germans, we secretly resist, and it's better for us to do what Germans want than to let the Germans themselves do it, because in this way we can minimize the damage.' (Many social-democratic governments play the same game: we hate austerity measures, but we have to be realists and . . .) Signs abound in Greece of symptomatic excessive compromises that belie the thesis of secret resistance. Among other things, Kouvelakis pointed out the discreet continuity in relations with Israel (masked by big public gestures like the recognition of the State of Palestine):

The Ministry of Foreign Affairs has issued a statement disagreeing with the EU policy of labelling products from the Occupied Territories. Tsipras visited Jerusalem and recognized it as the capital of Israel; even the Americans haven't done that. In September 2015 Greece took part in a military exercise on a scale unprecedented in the eastern Mediterranean, with Israel, Egypt, the US and Cyprus. It's a strategic orientation: they're panicking about the situation in the region and think that aligning themselves with the Americans and the Israelis provides some safety. This is what I mean by nihilism: Schäuble asked for pension cuts, for home repossessions by the banks; he didn't ask for subservience to Netanyahu.[4]

Instead of deciding who is right, Kouvelakis or Douzinas (and the answer is, of course, neither – the only chance of success was to try a third option along the lines proposed by the then minister of finance Varoufakis, i.e, remain in the euro and proclaim debt default), we should rather question their shared premise: that the radical Left in power, exerting state power, is a contradiction in terms, so that parliamentary state politics must be supplemented by and based on social movements. As long as the Left remains stuck within these coordinates, it is doomed. To justify this conclusion, let's take a look at the troubled rise of Syriza.

TROUBLES WITH LEFT GOVERNMENTABILITY

The difficulties the Syriza government found itself in gave rise to a series of extremely stupid criticisms. Apart from the expected standard reproaches (Syriza should return to its popular roots; Syriza should heroically risk Grexit), there were the complaints that the EU administration brutally ignored the plight of the Greek people in their blind obsession with humiliating and disciplining the Greek state, that even southern European countries like Italy or Spain didn't show any solidarity with Greece . . . but was there any surprise in all this? What did the critics expect? That the EU administration would magically understand the Syriza argument and act in compliance with it? The EU administration was simply doing what it was always doing. And there was the reproach that Greece was looking for help in Russia and China – as if Europe itself was not pushing Greece in that direction with its humiliating pressure.

Then there was the claim that phenomena like Syriza demonstrate how the traditional Left/Right dichotomy no longer exists. Syriza in Greece is called extreme Left, and Marine le Pen in France extreme Right, but these two parties have effectively a lot in common: they both fight for state sovereignty against multinational corporations. It is therefore quite logical that, in Greece itself, Syriza is in coalition with a small Rightist pro-sovereignty party. On 22 April 2015, François Hollande said on TV that Marine le Pen today sounds like George Marchais (a French communist leader) in the 1970s – the same patriotic advocacy of the plight of ordinary French people exploited by international capital – no wonder Marine le Pen supports Syriza. A weird claim that doesn't say a lot more than the old Liberal wisdom that fascism is also a kind of socialism. The moment we bring into the picture the topic of immigrant workers, this whole parallel falls apart. But the most depressing and demoralizing criticism of Syriza came from Joschka Fischer, the Green Party foreign minister in Gerhardt Schroeder's German government, who wrote a comment, 'Tsipras in Dreamland', where the title tells it all:

> The Tsipras government, with some justification, could have presented itself as Europe's best partner for implementing a far-reaching program of reform and modernization in Greece. Measures to compensate the poorest met with considerable sympathy in EU capitals [. . .] But Tsipras squandered Greece's opportunity, because he and other Syriza leaders were unable to see beyond the horizon of their party's origins in radical opposition activism. They did not understand – and did not want to understand – the difference between campaigning and governing. Realpolitik, in their view, was a sellout. Of course, it is precisely the acceptance of necessity that marks the difference between government and opposition. An opposition party may voice aspirations, make promises, and even dream a little; but a government party cannot remain in some imaginary world or theoretical system.[5]

These lines are not just disgustingly patronizing, they are simply wrong. When one compares Fischer's description with Varoufakis's programmatic declaration (which contains the ultimate strategic goal of the Syriza government), one cannot avoid the question: who is dreaming here? This is what Varoufakis wrote in his article 'How I Became an Erratic Marxist':

A Greek or a Portuguese or an Italian exit from the eurozone would soon lead to a fragmentation of European capitalism, yielding a seriously recessionary surplus region east of the Rhine and north of the Alps, while the rest of Europe would be in the grip of vicious stagflation. Who do you think would benefit from this development? A progressive left, that will rise Phoenix-like from the ashes of Europe's public institutions? Or the Golden Dawn Nazis, the assorted neo-fascists, the xenophobes and the spivs? I have absolutely no doubt as to which of the two will do best from a disintegration of the eurozone.

I, for one, am not prepared to blow fresh wind into the sails of this postmodern version of the 1930s. If this means that it is we, the suitably erratic Marxists, who must try to save European capitalism from itself, so be it. Not out of love for European capitalism, for the eurozone, for Brussels, or for the European Central Bank, but just because we want to minimise the unnecessary human toll from this crisis.[6]

And the financial politics of the Syriza government followed closely these guidelines: no deficit, tight discipline, more money raised through taxes. What is so shocking about the Syriza government is precisely the pragmatic modesty of its policy. Some German media recently characterized Varoufakis as a psychotic who lives in his own universe different from ours – but is he really so radical? What is so irritating about Varoufakis is not his radicality but his rational pragmatic modesty – if one looks closely at the proposals offered by Varoufakis, one cannot help noticing that they consist of measures which, forty years ago, were part of the standard moderate social-democratic agenda (in Sweden in the 1960s, the programme of the government was much more radical). It is a sad sign of our times that today you have to belong to a radical Left to advocate these same measures – a sign of dark times but also a chance for the Left to occupy the space that, decades ago, was that of the moderate Left centre.

But, perhaps, the endlessly repeated point about how modest Syriza's politics is ('just good old social democracy') somehow misses its target – as if, if we repeat it often enough, the eurocrats will finally realize we're not really dangerous and will help us ... But Syriza effectively *is* dangerous, it *does* pose a threat to the present orientation of the EU – today's global capitalism cannot afford a return to the old welfare state. So there is something hypocritical in the reassurances of the modesty of what Syriza wants: they effectively want something that is not possible within the coordinates of the existing global system. A serious strategic choice will have to be made here: what if the moment has come to drop the mask of modesty and openly advocate a much more radical change that is needed to secure even a small gain? Can such an act remain within the confines of parliamentary democracy?

YES, INDEBTED – BUT NOT GUILTY!

Critics of our institutional democracy often complain that elections as a rule do not offer a true choice: what we mostly get is the choice between a centre-Right and a centre-Left party whose programmes are almost indistinguishable. On Sunday 25 January 2015, this was definitely not the case – as on 17 June 2012, the Greek voters were facing a real choice: the establishment on one side, Syriza on the other. And, as is usually the case, such moments of real choice throw the establishment into panic: they paint a vista of social chaos, poverty and violence if the wrong side wins. The mere possibility of a Syriza victory had sent ripples of fear through markets all around the world, and, as is usual, ideological *prosopopoeia* has its heyday: markets started to talk again as living people, expressing their 'worry' at what will happen if the elections failed to produce a government with a mandate to continue the programme of fiscal austerity.

From this perspective, the Greek elections that brought Syriza to power cannot but appear as a nightmare – so how can this catastrophe be avoided? The obvious way would be to reflect the fright back on the voters – to scare them to death with the message: 'You think you suffer now, under austerity? You ain't seen nothing yet – wait for the Syriza victory and you will long for the bliss of the last years!' The alternative is either Greece stepping out (or being thrown out) of the European project, with unforeseeable consequences, or a 'messy compromise' where both sides moderate their demands – which raises another fear: not the fear of Syriza's 'irrational' behaviour after their victory, but, on the contrary, the fear that Syriza will accept a 'rational' messy compromise that would disappoint voters, so that discontent continues, but this time not regulated and moderated by Syriza . . . The only true solution is thus clear: since everyone knows Greece will never repay its debt, one will have to gather the courage and write the debt off. It can be done at a quite tolerable economic cost, just with political will. Such acts are our only hope of breaking out of the vicious cycle of cold Brussels neo-liberal technocracy and anti-immigrant passions. If we don't act, others, from Golden Dawn to UKIP, will do it.

The idea one gets from our media is that the Syriza government in Greece is a bunch of populist extremists who advocate 'irrational' and irresponsible populist measures. Nothing could be further from the truth. It is, on the contrary, the EU's policies that were and are obviously irrational. From 2008, Greece had to enact tough austerity measures in order to put its finances in order; in 2015 after the country had suffered a terrifying ordeal, the Greek finances were in an even greater disorder, since the country's debt rose from 120 to 180 billion euros – if this is not irrational, then the word has no meaning whatsoever. Varoufakis repeatedly pointed out that, in spite of all the fuss about austerity, the developed Western countries experience only a minimal amount of it (at the level of 1 or at worst 2 per cent) – it was Greece on which real full austerity was imposed, with reductions that changed the entire socio-economic landscape. One can easily venture the hypothesis that, as a punishment for electing the wrong government, Greece was sentenced to an extra measure of surplus-austerity. Recall the old Herbert Marcuse distinction (elaborated in his *Eros and Civilization*) between 'normal' repression (the renunciation of libidinal goals, necessary for the survival of the human race) and 'surplus' repression (necessary for the maintenance of the social relations of domination). The problem is that this distinction is theoretically false: in the same way that there is, in our libidinal economy, no 'normal' level of repression exceeded by some kind of 'surplus' repression, in capitalism there is also no 'normal' or 'surplus' level of austerity. 'Austerity' as such is a false notion; so why, then, is the EU doing this to Greece?

An ideal is gradually emerging from the European establishment's reaction to the Greek referendum, the ideal best rendered by the title of an article by Gideon Rachman in the *Financial Times*: 'Eurozone's Weakest Link is the Voters'.[7] In this ideal world, Europe gets rid of this 'weakest link' and experts gain the power to directly impose necessary economic measures – if elections take place at all, their function is just to confirm the consensus of experts. The problem is that this policy of experts is based on a fiction, the fiction of 'extend and pretend' (extending the payback period, and pretending that all debts will eventually be paid). Why is the fiction so stubborn? It is not only that this fiction makes debt extension more acceptable to German voters; it is also not only that a write-off of the Greek debt may trigger similar demands from Portugal, Ireland, Spain. It is that those in power *do not really want* the debt fully repaid. A decade or so ago, Argentina decided to repay its debt to the IMF ahead of time (with financial help from Venezuela), and the reaction was surprising – instead of being glad that it got its money back, the IMF (or, rather, its top representatives) expressed their worry that Argentina would use this new freedom and independence from international financial institutions to abandon tight financial policies and engage in careless spending. Debt is an instrument with which to control and regulate the debtor, and, as such, it strives for its own expanded reproduction.

The ongoing EU pressure on Greece to implement austerity measures fits perfectly what psychoanalysis calls 'superego'. Superego is not an ethical agency proper, but a sadistic agent that bombards the subject with impossible demands, obscenely enjoying the subject's failure to comply with them; the paradox of the superego is that, as Freud saw clearly, the more we obey its demands, the more we feel guilty. Imagine a vicious teacher who gives to his pupils impossible tasks, and then sadistically jeers when he sees their anxiety and panic. This is what is so terribly wrong with the EU demands/ commands: they don't even give Greece a chance. The Greek failure is part of the game.

The true goal of lending money is not to get the debt reimbursed with a profit, but the indefinite continuation of the debt so that the debtor is in permanent dependency and subordination . . . for most debtors, anyway, for there are debtors and there are debtors. Not only Greece but also the US and Japan will not be able even theoretically to repay their debts, as is now publicly recognized. So there are debtors who can blackmail their creditors because they cannot be allowed to fail (big banks), debtors who can control the conditions of their repayment (the US government), and, finally, debtors who can be pushed around and humiliated (Greece). Furthermore, one should be very careful in criticizing the 'extend and pretend' fiction: this fiction is not a local excess but an extreme expression of a tendency inscribed into the very core of capitalist economics, which thrives only through constantly borrowing from the future and endlessly postponing the final settlement of accounts.

From this perspective, the horror of Syriza was threefold: not only did it take democracy seriously, brought forward the voters' will and rejected the expertise of the 'experts'; not only did it refuse to play the 'extend and pretend' game; even worse, the debt providers and caretakers of debt basically accused the Syriza government of not feeling enough guilt. They are accused of feeling innocent. That's what was so disturbing for the EU establishment about the Syriza government: they admit debt, but without guilt. They got rid of the superego pressure. The very fact that they persist makes us all free: we all know that, as long as they are there, there is a chance for all of us.

As if they didn't suffer enough, Greeks are victims of a campaign that mobilizes the lowest egotist instincts. When they talk about writing off part of the debt, our media present this as a measure that will hurt ordinary taxpayers, so it's the lazy and corrupted Greeks against the hard-working ordinary people in other countries. In Slovenia, my own country, those who sympathize with Syriza were even accused of national treason. So when, back in the 2008 financial breakdown, big banks became insolvent, it was OK for the state to cover their losses by spending thousands of billions (of taxpayers' money, of course), but when a whole people finds itself in misery, the debt should be paid. (And among these banks were those that helped the Greek state to fake data in order to embellish its financial status.)

Varoufakis personified the resistance to this superego pressure in his dealings with Brussels and Berlin: he fully acknowledged the weight of the debt, and he argued quite rationally that, since the EU policy obviously didn't work, another option should be found. Paradoxically, the point Varoufakis and Tsipras made repeatedly was that the Syriza government is the only chance for the debt providers to get at least part of their money back. Varoufakis himself wonders about the enigma of why banks were pouring money into Greece and collaborating with a clientelist state while knowing very well how things stood; Greece would never have become so heavily indebted without the connivance of the Western establishment. His suspicion about the readiness of the EU and Western banks to extend credits to Greece sounds like a (fully justified) reversal of the old saying, 'Beware Greeks who bear gifts!' – today, it is rather Greeks themselves who should beware of receiving gifts in the form of easy credits. The Syriza government is well aware that the main threat does not come from Brussels – it resides in Greece itself, a clientelist corrupted state if there ever was one. What Europe (the EU bureaucracy) should be blamed for is that, while it criticized Greece for its corruption and inefficiency, it supported the very political force (New Democracy) that embodied this corruption and inefficiency.

What the Greek 'no' in the referendum and the ensuing compromise clearly demonstrated is that there is no illusion of democratic cooperation and solidarity in the EU: any serious analysis was blocked, Greece was brutally blackmailed into submission, and it was a heroic act on its own to state this publicly. The really catastrophic thing about the Greek crisis is that the moment the choice appeared as a choice between Grexit or capitulation to Brussels, the battle was already lost. Both terms of this choice move within the predominant eurocratic vision. The Syriza government was not fighting just for a greater debt relief and for more new money within the same overall coordinates, but for the awakening of Europe from its dogmatic slumber. The Europe that will win if Syriza is outmanoeuvred is a 'Europe with Asian values' (which, of course, has nothing to do with Asia, but with the clear and present tendency of contemporary capitalism to suspend democracy). So it is not only that Greece's fate is in the hands of Europe. We from Western Europe like to look upon Greece as if we are detached observers who follow with compassion and sympathy the plight of an impoverished nation. Such a comfortable standpoint relies on a fateful illusion. What went on in Greece concerns all of us – it is the future of Europe that is at stake. So when we read about Greece these days, we should always bear in mind that, as the old saying goes, *de te fabula narratur* ('this story is about you').

Leftists all around Europe complain how today no one dares to really disturb the neo-liberal dogma. The problem is real, of course – the moment one violates this dogma, or, rather, the moment one is just perceived as a possible agent of such disturbance, tremendous forces are unleashed. Although these forces appear as objective economic factors, they are effectively forces of illusion, of ideology – but their material power is nonetheless utterly destructive. We are today under the enormous pressure of what we should call enemy propaganda. Let me quote Alain Badiou: 'The goal of all enemy propaganda is not to annihilate an existing force (this function is generally left to police forces), but rather to annihilate an *unnoticed possibility of the situation*.'[8] In other words, they are trying to *kill hope*: the message of this propaganda is a resigned conviction that the world we live in, even if not the best of all possible worlds, is the least bad one, so that any radical change can only make it worse.

Somebody has to make the first move and cut the Gordian knot of neo-liberal dogma. (Let us not forget that those who preach this dogma – from the US to Germany – violate it freely when it suits them.) Gandhi's motto 'Be yourself the change you want to see in the world' fully holds for Syriza. They not only contributed to universal solidarity, they *were* universal solidarity at work. We often hear today that the Left doesn't have any alternatives to propose. Syriza *was* the alternative, its struggle reaching far beyond a simple struggle for welfare. It is the struggle for an entire way of life, the resistance of a *world* threatened by rapid globalization. 'World' stands here for a specific horizon of meaning, for an entire civilization or, rather, *culture*, with its daily rituals and manners that are threatened by post-historical commodification. Can this resistance actually be seen as conservative? Today's mainstream self-declared political and cultural conservatives are not really conservatives: fully endorsing capitalist continuous self-revolutionizing, they just want to make it more efficient by supplementing it with some traditional institutions (religion, etc.) to contain its destructive consequences for social life and social cohesion. A true conservative today is the one who fully admits the antagonisms and deadlocks of global capitalisms, the one who rejects simple progressivism, and is attentive to the dark obverse of progress. So, in this sense, only a radical Leftist can be today a true conservative.

FROM SYNTAGMA TO PARADIGMA

In what, then, did the authentic greatness of Syriza reside? Insofar as the icons of the popular unrest in Greece were the protests on Syntagma (Constitution) Square, Syriza engaged in a Herculean labour of enacting the shift from *syntagm* to *paradigm*, in the long and patient work of translating the energy of rebellion into concrete measures that would change the everyday life of the people. We have to be very precise here: the 'no' of the Greek referendum was not a 'no' to 'austerity' in the sense of necessary sacrifices and hard work, but a 'no' to the EU dream of just going on with business as usual. Varoufakis repeatedly made this point clear: no more borrowing but a genuine overhaul was needed to give the Greek economy a chance to rebound. The first step in this direction should be an increase in the democratic transparency of our power mechanisms. Our democratically elected state apparatuses are more and more redoubled by a thick network of 'agreements' (TISA, TTIP, etc.) and non-elected 'expert' bodies that wield the real economic (and military) power. Here is Varoufakis's report on an extraordinary moment in his dealings with Jeroen Dijsselbloem:

> There was a moment when the President of the Eurogroup decided to move against us and effectively shut us out, and made it known that Greece was essentially on its way out of the eurozone [. . .] There is a convention that communiqués must be unanimous, and the President

can't just convene a meeting of the eurozone and exclude a member state. And he said, 'Oh I'm sure I can do that.' So I asked for a legal opinion. It created a bit of a kerfuffle. For about 5–10 minutes the meeting stopped; clerks, officials were talking to one another, on their phone, and eventually some official, some legal expert addressed me, and said the following words: 'Well, the Eurogroup does not exist in law, there is no treaty which has convened this group.' So what we have is a non-existent group that has the greatest power to determine the lives of Europeans. It's not answerable to anyone, given it doesn't exist in law; no minutes are kept; and it's confidential. So no citizen ever knows what is said within [. . .] These are decisions of almost life and death, and no member has to answer to anybody.[9]

Sounds familiar? Yes, to anyone who knows how Chinese power functions today, after Deng Xiaoping set in action a unique dual system: the state apparatus and legal system are redoubled by the Party institutions, which are literally illegal – or, as He Weifang, a law professor from Beijing, put it succinctly: 'As an organization, the Party sits outside, and above, the law. It should have a legal identity, in other words, a person to sue, but it is not even registered as an organization. The Party exists outside the legal system altogether.'[10] It is as if, in Walter Benjamin's words, the state-founding violence remains present, embodied in an organization with an unclear legal status. The journalist Richard McGregor says:

it would seem difficult to hide an organization as large as the Chinese Communist Party, but it cultivates its backstage role with care. The big party departments controlling personnel and the media keep a purposely low public profile. The party committees (known as 'leading small groups') which guide and dictate policy to ministries, which in turn have the job of executing them, work out of sight. The make-up of all these committees, and in many cases even their existence, is rarely referred to in the state-controlled media, let alone any discussion of how they arrive at decisions.[11]

No wonder that exactly the same thing that happened to Varoufakis happened to a Chinese dissident who, some years ago, tried

THE COURAGE OF HOPELESSNESS

formally to bring to court the Chinese Communist Party, accusing it of being responsible for the Tiananmen Square massacre. After a couple of months he got a reply from the ministry of justice: they cannot pursue his charge since there is no organization called the 'Chinese Communist Party' officially registered in China. And it is crucial to note how the obverse of this non-transparency of power is false humanitarianism. After the Greek defeat, there is, of course, time for humanitarian concerns: Jean-Claude Juncker, president of the European Commission, immediately stated in an interview that he was so glad about the bailout deal because it would immediately ease the suffering of the Greek people, which worried him very much. It was a classic scenario: after a political crack-down, humanitarian concerns and aid . . . postponing debt payments, etc.

What should one do in such a hopeless situation? One should especially resist the temptation of Grexit, seeing it as a great heroic act of rejecting further humiliations and stepping outside – into what? What new positive order are we stepping into? The Grexit option appears as the 'real-impossible', as something that would lead to an immediate social disintegration. Paul Krugman has written:

> Tsipras apparently allowed himself to be convinced, some time ago, that euro exit was completely impossible. It appears that Syriza didn't even do any contingency planning for a parallel currency (I hope to find out that this is wrong). This left him in a hopeless bargaining position.[12]

Krugman's point is that Grexit is an impossible-real that can happen with unpredictable consequences and which, as such, can be risked:

> all the wise heads saying that Grexit is impossible, that it would lead to a complete implosion, don't know what they are talking about. When I say that, I don't mean that they're necessarily wrong – I believe they are, but anyone who is confident about anything here is deluding himself. What I mean instead is that nobody has any experience with what we're looking at.[13]

While in principle this is true, there are nonetheless too many indications that a sudden Grexit now would lead to utter economic and social catastrophe. Syriza economic strategists (including Varoufakis) were well aware that such a gesture would cause an immediate further fall in the standard of living by (a minimum of) 30 per cent, bringing misery to a new unbearable level, with the threat of popular unrest and even military dictatorship. The prospect of such heroic acts is thus a temptation to be resisted.

It is nonetheless not enough to say that, yes, Syriza put up a heroic fight, testing what is possible, but it's now over. The fight goes on, it has just begun. Instead of dwelling on the 'contradictions' of Syriza policy (after a triumphant 'no' they accept the very programme that was rejected by the people), and of getting caught in mutual recriminations about who is guilty (did the Syriza majority commit an opportunistic 'treason', or was the Left irresponsible in its preference for Grexit?), one should rather focus on what the enemy is doing: the 'contradictions' of Syriza are a mirror image of the 'contradictions' of an EU establishment that is gradually undermining the very foundations of a united Europe. In the guise of Syriza 'contradictions', the EU establishment is merely hearing its own message echoed in its true form. And this indicates what Syriza should be doing now. With a ruthless pragmatism and cold calculation, it should exploit the tiniest cracks in the opponent's armour. It should use all those who resist the predominant EU politics. It should shamelessly flirt with Russia and China, playing with the idea of giving an island to Russia as its Mediterranean military base, just to scare the shit out of NATO strategists. To paraphrase Dostoyevsky, now that the EU God has failed, everything is permitted.

The heroism of Syriza was that, after winning the democratic political battle, they risked a step further into disturbing the smooth flow of the reproduction of capital. The lesson of the Greek crisis is that capital, though ultimately a symbolic fiction, is our Real. That is to say, today's protests and revolts are sustained by the combination (overlapping) of different levels, and this combination accounts for their strength: they fight for ('normal' parliamentary) democracy against authoritarian regimes; against racism and sexism, especially the hatred directed at immigrants and refugees; for welfare states against neo-liberalism; against corruption in politics and in the economy (companies polluting the environment, etc.); for new forms of democracy that reach beyond multi-party rituals (participation, etc.); and, finally, they question the global capitalist system as such, trying to keep alive the idea of a non-capitalist society. Two traps are to be avoided here: false radicalism ('what really matters is the abolition of liberal-parliamentary capitalism; all other fights are secondary'), as well as false gradualism ('now we fight against military dictatorship and for simple democracy; forget your socialist dreams, that comes later – maybe. . .'). When we have to deal with a specific struggle, the key question is: how will our engagement in it or disengagement from it affect other struggles? The general rule is that, when a revolt begins against an oppressive half-democratic regime, as was the case in the Middle East in 2011, it is easy to mobilize large crowds with slogans that one cannot but characterize as crowdpleasers – for democracy, against corruption, etc. But then we gradually approach more difficult choices: when our revolt succeeds in its direct goal, we come to realize that what really bothered us (our un-freedom, humiliation, social corruption, lack of prospect of a decent life) goes on in a new guise. In Egypt, protesters succeeded in getting rid of the oppressive Mubarak regime, but corruption remained, and the prospect of a decent life moved even further away. After the overthrow of an authoritarian regime, the last vestiges of patriarchal care for the poor can fall away, so that the newly gained freedom is *de facto* reduced to the freedom to choose the preferred form of one's misery – the majority not only remains poor, but, to add insult to injury, it is being told that, since they are now free, poverty is their own responsibility. In such a predicament, we have to admit to there having been a flaw in our goal itself, that this goal – say, standard political democracy – was not specific enough. Standard political democracy can also serve as the very form of un-freedom: political freedom can easily provide the legal framework for economic slavery, with the underprivileged 'freely' selling themselves into servitude. We are thus brought to demand more than just political democracy – we need the democratization also of social and economic life. In short, we have to admit that what we first took as the failure to fully realize a noble principle (of democratic freedom) is a failure inherent to this principle itself – understanding this is *the* big step of political pedagogy.

REFERENDUM

The double U-turn that took the Greek crisis in July 2015 cannot but appear as a step not just from tragedy to comedy but, as Stathis Kouvelakis noted, from tragedy full of comic reversals directly into a theatre of the absurd – is there any other way to characterize the extraordinary turn from one extreme into its opposite that would bedazzle even the most speculative Hegelian philosopher? Tired of the endless negotiations with the EU executives in which one humiliation followed another, the Syriza referendum on Sunday 5 July asked the Greek people if they supported or rejected the EU proposal of new austerity measures. Even though the government clearly stated that it supported 'no', the result was a surprise for the government itself: an overwhelming majority of over 61 per cent voted 'no' to European blackmail. Rumours began to circulate that the result – victory for the government – was a bad shock for Tsipras himself, who secretly hoped that the government would lose, so that a defeat would allow him to save face in surrendering to the EU demands ('we have to respect the voters' voice'). However, literally the morning after, Tsipras announced that Greece was ready to resume the negotiations, and days later Greece negotiated an EU proposal that was basically the same as what the voters rejected (in some details even harsher) – in short, he acted as if the government had lost, not won, the referendum. Kouvelakis writes:

> How is it possible for a devastating 'no' to memorandum austerity policies to be interpreted as a green light for a new memorandum? [. . .] The sense of the absurd is not just a product of this unexpected reversal. It stems above all from the fact that all of this is unfolding before our eyes as if nothing has happened, as if the referendum were something like a collective hallucination that suddenly ends, leaving us to continue freely what we were doing before. But because we have not all become lotus-eaters, let us at least give a brief résumé of

what has taken place over the past few days [. . .] From Monday morning, before the victory cries in the country's public squares had even fully died away, the theatre of the absurd began [. . .] The public, still in the joyful haze of Sunday, watches as the representative of the 62 per cent subordinated to the 38 per cent in the immediate aftermath of a resounding victory for democracy and popular sovereignty [. . .] But the referendum happened. It wasn't a hallucination from which everyone has now recovered. On the contrary, the hallucination is the attempt to downgrade it to a temporary 'letting off of steam', prior to resuming the downhill course towards a third memorandum.[14]

And things went on in this direction. On the night of 10 July, the Greek parliament gave Tsipras the authority to negotiate a new bailout by 250 votes to 32, but 17 government MPs didn't back the plan, which means he got more support from the opposition parties than from his own. Days later, the Syriza Political Secretariat, dominated by the left wing of the party, concluded that the EU's latest proposals were 'absurd' and 'exceed the limits of Greek society's endurance' – Leftist extremism? The IMF itself (in this case a voice of minimally rational capitalism) made exactly the same point: an IMF study published a day earlier showed that Greece needs far more debt relief than European governments have been willing to contemplate – European countries would have to give Greece a thirty-year grace period on servicing all its European debt, including new loans, and a dramatic maturity extension. No wonder that Tsipras himself publicly aired his doubts about the bailout plan: 'We don't believe in the measures that were imposed upon us,' he said during a TV interview, making it clear that he supported it out of pure despair, to avoid a total economic and financial collapse. The eurocrats use such confessions with breathtaking perfidy: now that the Greek government has accepted their tough conditions, they doubt the sincerity and seriousness of their commitment. How can Tsipras really fight for a programme he doesn't believe in? How can the Greek government be really committed to the agreement when it opposes the referendum result?

However, statements like those from the IMF demonstrate that the true problem lies elsewhere. Does the EU really believe in their own bailout plan? Does it really believe that the brutally imposed measures will set in motion economic growth and thus enable the payment of debts? Or is it that the ultimate motivation for the brutal extortionist pressure on Greece is not purely economic (since it is obviously irrational in economic terms) but politico-ideological – or, as Krugman puts it, 'substantive surrender isn't enough for Germany, which wants regime change and total humiliation – and there's a substantial faction that just wants to push Greece out, and would more or less welcome a failed state as a caution for the rest.'[15] One should always bear in mind what a horror Syriza is for the European establishment – a conservative Polish member of the European parliament even directly appealed to the Greek army to stage a *coup d'état* in order to save the country . . .

Why this horror? Greeks are now asked to pay the high price, but not for a realistic prospect of growth. The price they are asked to pay is for the continuation of the 'extend and pretend' fantasy. They are asked to accept their actual suffering in order to sustain another's (the eurocrats') dream. Gilles Deleuze said decades ago: '*Si vous êtes pris dans le rêve de l'autre, vous êtes foutus*' ('If you are caught in another's dream, you are fucked'), and this is the situation in which Greece finds itself now. The one who now needs awakening is not Greece but Europe. Everyone who is not caught in this dream knows what awaits us if the bailout plan is enacted: another 90 or so billion euros will be thrown into the Greek basket, raising the Greek debt to 400 or so billion (and most of that will quickly return back to Western Europe – the true bailout is the bailout of German and French banks, not of Greece), and we can expect the Greek crisis to explode in a couple of years.

But is such an outcome really a failure? At an immediate level, if one compares the plan with its actual outcome, obviously yes. At a deeper level, however, it may be that, as we suggested earlier, the true goal is not to give Greece a chance but to change it into an economically colonized semi-state kept in permanent poverty and dependency, as a warning to others. But at an even deeper level, there is another failure – not of Greece, but of Europe itself, of the emancipatory core of the European legacy.

One should never forget that the unexpectedly strong 'no' in the Greek referendum was a historical vote cast in a desperate situation. In my work I often used the well-known joke from the last decade of the Soviet Union about Rabinovitch, a Jew who wants to emigrate. I am told that a new version of this joke is now circulating in Athens. A young Greek man visits the Australian consulate in Athens and asks for a work visa. 'Why do you want to leave Greece?' asks the official. 'For two reasons,' replies the Greek. 'First, I am worried that Greece will leave the EU, which will lead to new poverty and chaos in the country. . .' 'But,' interrupts the official, 'this is pure nonsense. Greece will remain in the EU and submit to financial discipline!' 'Well,' responds the Greek calmly, 'that is my second reason. . .' Quoting Stalin again: there is no worse choice, both choices are worse.

But are both choices worse? The moment has come to move beyond the irrelevant debates about the possible mistakes and misjudgements of the Greek government. The stakes are now much too high.

The fact that a compromise formula eluded Greece and the EU administrators is in itself deeply symptomatic, since it doesn't really concern actual financial issues – at this level, the difference is minimal. The EU usually accuse Greeks of talking only in general terms, making vague promises without specific details, while Greeks accuse the EU of trying to control even the tiniest details and imposing on Greece conditions that are more harsh than those imposed on the previous government. But what lurks behind these reproaches is another, more significant, conflict. Tsipras recently remarked that if he were to meet alone with Angela Merkel for dinner, they would have found a formula in two hours. His point was that he and Merkel, the two politicians, would treat the disagreement as a political one, in contrast to technocratic administrators like the Eurogroup head, Jeroen Dijsselbloem. If there is an emblematic bad guy in this whole story, it is Dijsselbloem, whose motto is: 'If I get into the ideological side of things, I won't achieve anything.'

This brings us to the crux of the matter: Tsipras and Varoufakis talk as if they are part of an open political process where decisions that are ultimately 'ideological' (based on normative preferences) are to be made, while the EU technocrats talk as if it is all a matter of detailed regulatory measures. And when the Greeks reject the EU approach and raise more fundamental political issues, they are accused of lying, of avoiding concrete solutions, etc. And it is clear that the truth is here on the Greek side: the denial of 'the ideological side' by Dijsselbloem is ideology at its purest: it masks (falsely presents) as purely expert regulatory measures decisions that are effectively grounded in politico-ideological premises (advocacy of deregulations, etc.).

On account of this asymmetry, the 'dialogue' between Tsipras or Varoufakis and their EU partners often appears as a dialogue between a young student who wants a serious debate on basic issues, and an arrogant professor who, in his answers, humiliatingly ignores the issue and scolds the student with technical points ('You didn't formulate that correctly! You didn't take into account that regulation!'), or even as a dialogue between a rape victim who desperately reports what has happened to her and a policeman who continually interrupts her with requests for administrative details. This passage from politics proper to 'neutral expert administration' characterizes our entire political process: strategic decisions based on power are increasingly masked as administrative regulations based on neutral 'expert' knowledge, and they are more and more negotiated in secrecy and enforced without democratic consultation – recall TTIP.

This is why the Syriza government was fighting a battle for all of us. It was a battle in which the very meaning of democracy was to be decided. Many critics of the Greek referendum claimed that it was a case of pure demagogic posturing, mockingly pointing out that it's not clear what this referendum was about – at that moment, there was no EU proposal on the table to be accepted or rejected, so what should the Greeks vote about? The claim was that the referendum was really about the euro versus the drachma, about Greece in the EU or outside it – but this is patently untrue. The Greek government repeatedly emphasized its desire to remain in the EU and in the eurozone. Again, the critics automatically translate the key political question raised by the referendum into an administrative decision about particular economic measures. In his interview on Bloomberg on 2 July, Varoufakis made clear the true stakes of the referendum.[16] The choice was between the continuation of the EU's politics of the previous years, which brought Greece to the edge of ruin – the already-mentioned fiction of 'extend and pretend' – and a new realist beginning that would no longer rely on such fictions, i.e. that would provide a concrete plan to start the actual recovery of the Greek economy. Without such a plan, the crisis would just reproduce itself again and again. On the same day, even the IMF conceded that Greece needed large-scale debt relief to create 'a breathing space' and get the economy moving (they proposed a twenty-year moratorium on debt payments), thereby confirming Varoufakis's point that a new approach is needed to really resolve the crisis.

The referendum was thus much more than a simple choice between two different approaches to economic crisis. The Greek people have heroically resisted the despicable campaign of fear that mobilized the lowest instincts of self-preservation. They have seen through the brutal manipulation of their opponents, who falsely presented the referendum as a choice between the euro and the drachma, between Greece in Europe and Grexit. Their 'no' was a 'no' to the eurocrats who prove daily that they are unable to drag Europe out of its inertia. It was a 'no' to the continuation of business as usual (a foreshadowing of what was to come with Trump supporters – though in a different guise), a desperate cry telling us all that things cannot go on in the same way.

It was a decision for an authentic political vision against the strange combination of cold technocracy and hot racist clichés about the lazy free-spending Greeks which coloured the EU pressure on Greece. It was a rare victory of principles against egotist and ultimately self-destructive opportunism. The 'no' was a 'yes' to a full awareness of the crisis Europe is in, a 'yes' to the need to enact a new beginning. After the referendum, it is up to the EU to act: will it be able to awaken from its self-satisfied inertia and understand the sign of hope delivered by the Greek people? Or will it unleash its wrath on Greece in order to be able to continue its dogmatic dream?

THE APOCALYPSE

When a short essay of mine on Greece after the referendum was republished by *In These Times*, its title was changed to 'How Alexis Tsipras and Syriza Outmanoeuvred Angela Merkel and the Eurocrats'. Although I effectively think that accepting the EU terms was not a simple defeat, I am far from such an optimistic view. The reversal of the 'no' of the referendum to the 'yes' to Brussels was a genuinely devastating shock, a shattering, painful catastrophe. More precisely, it was an apocalypse in both senses of the term, the usual one (catastrophe) and the original, literal one (disclosure, revelation): the basic antagonism, the deadlock, of the situation was clearly disclosed.

But we are not at the end. The Greek retreat is not the last word, for the simple reason that the crisis will hit again, in a couple of years if not earlier, and not only in Greece. The task of the Syriza government is to get ready for that moment, to patiently occupy positions and plan options. Keeping political power in these impossible conditions may provide a minimal space for preparing the ground for future action and for political education. Therein resides the paradox of the situation: although the bailout plan will not work, one should not lose nerve and withdraw but follow it till the next explosion – why? Because of the obvious non-preparedness of Greece for Grexit – there was no plan for how to do this very difficult and complex operation. Till now, the Syriza government operated without really controlling the state apparatus, with its 2 million employees – the police and judiciary mostly belong to the political Right, the administration is part and parcel of the corrupted clientelist machine, etc. – and it is precisely this vast state machinery that would have to be relied on to undertake the immense work of Grexit. (We should also bear in mind that Grexit was the enemy's plan – there are even rumours that Schauble offered 50 billion euros to Greece if it left the eurozone.) What makes the Syriza government so troubling is precisely the fact that it is the government of a country inside the eurozone: 'the vehemence with which it has been opposed is due precisely to Greece's existence within the eurozone. Who would really care, now that there is no Cold War, if a government of the Left had come to power in a little country with the drachma as its currency?'[17]

What space for manoeuvre does the Syriza government have when it is reduced to enacting the politics of its enemy? Should it step down and call new elections rather than enact the policy that is directly opposed to its programme? Syriza needs most of all to gain time, and the EU powers are doing everything they can to deprive Syriza of that time. They try to push Syriza into a corner, enforcing a fast decision: either total capitulation or Grexit. Time for what? Not only for preparing itself for the next crisis. We should always bear in mind that the basic task of the Syriza government concerns neither the euro nor the settling of accounts with the EU but, above all, the radical reorganization of Greece's long-term corrupt social and political institutions: 'Syriza's extraordinary problem – which would not be faced by any other political party in government – was to alter *internal* institutional frameworks under conditions of *external* institutional assault'[18] (like Germany itself did in the early 1800s under French occupation).

The problem Greece is confronting now is the one of 'Left governmentability':[19] the hard reality of what it means for the radical Left to govern in the world of global capital. What options has the government? The obvious candidates – simple social-democratization, state socialism, withdrawal from the state and reliance on social movements – are obviously not enough. The true novelty of the Syriza government is that it is a *governmental event* – the first time that a Western radical Left (not the old-style communist one) has taken state power. The entire rhetoric, so beloved by the New Left, of acting at a distance from the state, has to be abandoned: one has to heroically assume full responsibility for the welfare of the entire people and leave behind the basic Leftist 'critical' attitude of finding a perverse satisfaction in providing sophisticated explanations of why things had to take a wrong turn.

The 'no' that won the referendum should not be mystified into some principled readiness to break out of global capitalism even if it would still bring immense suffering. For the large majority of voters, 'no' meant they had had enough of suffering and misery and wanted a better life, *with no clear strategic idea of what this means.* This is also why I think it is too simplistic to say that 'the government was not at the level of its people': the game was decided in advance, there was no real chance. The talk about subjective 'betrayal' obfuscates the objective deadlock: in whatever way we redefine what is (im)possible, there was no authentic revolutionary opening in the situation. The accusations of betrayal by the Syriza government are made to avoid the true big question: how can we confront capital in its modern shape? How can we govern, how can we run a state, 'with people'? It is too easy to say that Syriza is not just a government party but has its roots in popular mobilization and social movements:

> [Syriza] is a loose, self-contradictory, and internally antagonistic coalition of leftist thought and practice, very much dependent on the capacity of social movements of all kinds, thoroughly decentralized and driven by the activism of solidarity networks in a broad sphere of action across class lines of conflict, gender and sexuality activism, immigration issues, anti-globalization movements, civil and human rights advocacy, etc.[20]

One can thus easily understand the calls for Syriza to return to its roots. Syriza should not become just another governing parliamentary party: true change can only come from the grass-roots, from the people themselves, from their self-organization, not from the state apparatuses . . . However, such calls are ultimately just another case of empty posturing, since they avoid the crucial problem, which is how to deal with the international pressure concerning debt, or, more generally, how to exert power and run a state. Grass-roots self-organization cannot replace the state, and the question is how to reorganize the state apparatus to make it function differently.

The big question remains: how does or should this reliance on popular self-organization affect running a government? Can we even imagine today an authentic communist power? What we seem to get is disaster (Venezuela), capitulation (Greece) or a full return to capitalism (China, Vietnam). The Bolivarian Revolution 'has transformed social relations in Venezuela and had a huge impact on the continent as a whole. But the tragedy is that it was never properly institutionalized and thus proved to be unsustainable.'[21] It is all too easy to say that authentic emancipatory politics should remain at a distance from the state: the big problem that lurks behind is what to do with the state. Can we indeed imagine a society without a state? We should deal with these problems here and now: we can't wait for some future situation and in the meantime keep a safe distance from the state.

The choice that the Syriza government faced was a genuinely difficult choice that should be dealt with in brutally pragmatic terms; it is *not* a big principled choice between the true act and opportunistic betrayal. In his 'Greece Has Been Betrayed', Tariq Ali wrote:

> At the beginning of the month they were celebrating the 'No' vote. They were prepared to make more sacrifices, to risk life outside the eurozone. Syriza turned its back on them. The date 12 July 2015, when Tsipras agreed to the EU's terms, will become as infamous as 21 April 1967. The tanks have been replaced by banks, as Varoufakis put it after he was made finance minister.[22]

I consider this parallel between 2015 and 1967 convincing but simultaneously profoundly deceiving. Yes, tanks does rhyme with banks, which means: Greece is now *de facto* under financial occupation, with strongly reduced sovereignty and all government proposals having to be approved by the troika before they are submitted to parliament. Not only financial decisions but even data are under foreign control (Varoufakis didn't have access to the data of his own ministry – he was accused of treason for trying to obtain it), and, to add insult to injury, insofar as the democratically elected government obeys these rules, it voluntarily provides a democratic mask to this financial dictatorship. We are dealing here with obscenity at its purest: while billions disappeared in the last decades, and the state manufactured fabricated financial reports, the only person charged was the journalist who rendered public the names of the owners of illegal foreign bank accounts.

Should, then, Grexit be risked? We are confronting here *la tentation événementielle*, the 'evental temptation' – the temptation, in a difficult situation, to accomplish the crazy act, to do the impossible, to take the risk whatever the costs, with the underlying logic that 'things cannot be worse than they are now'. The catch is that they certainly *can* get much worse, up to developing into a full-scale social and humanitarian crisis. The key question is: was there really an objective possibility of a proper emancipatory act, drawing all the politico-economic consequences from the 'no' vote?

When Badiou talks about an emancipatory Event, he always emphasizes that an occurrence is not an Event in itself – it only becomes one retroactively, through its consequences, through the hard and patient 'work of love' of those who fight for it, who practise fidelity to it. One should thus abandon ('deconstruct', even) the topic of the opposition between the 'normal' run of things and the 'state of exception' characterized by the fidelity to an Event that disrupts the 'normal' run of things. In a 'normal' run of things life just goes on, following its inertia, and we are immersed in our daily cares and rituals. Then something happens, an evental Awakening, a secular version of a miracle (social emancipatory tumult, a traumatic love encounter. . .). If we opt for fidelity to this Event, our entire life changes: we are engaged in the 'work of love' and endeavour to inscribe the Event into our reality. Then at some point the evental sequence is exhausted and we return to the normal flow of things . . . But what if the true power of an Event should be measured precisely by its disappearance, when the Event is erased in its result, in the change in 'normal' life? Let's take a socio-political Event: what remains of it in its aftermath, when its ecstatic energy is exhausted and things return to normality – how is this normality different from the pre-evental one?

So, back to Greece. It is easy to count on the heroic gesture of promising blood, sweat and tears, to repeat the mantra that authentic politics means one should not remain within the confines of the possible but rather risk the impossible – but what would this imply in the case of Grexit? First, let's not forget that, as we have seen, the referendum result was a demand for a better life, not a readiness for more suffering and sacrifice. Second, in the case of Grexit, would the Greek state not be compelled to enforce a series of measures (nationalization of banks, higher taxes, etc.) that would constitute simply a revival of the old national-sovereignty/state-socialist economic policies? There may be nothing against such politics, but would it work in the specific conditions of today's Greece, with its inefficient state apparatus, and as part of the global economy? Here are the three main points of the Left Platform anti-austerity plan, listing a series of 'absolutely manageable' measures:

(1) The radical reorganization of the banking system, its nationalization under social control, and its reorientation towards growth.

(2) The complete rejection of fiscal austerity (primary surpluses and balanced budgets) in order to effectively address the humanitarian crisis, cover social needs, reconstruct the social state, and take the economy out of the vicious circle of recession.

(3) The implementation of the beginning procedures leading to exit from the euro and to the cancellation of the major part of the debt. There are absolutely manageable choices that can lead to a new economic model oriented towards production, growth, and the change in the social balance of forces to the benefit of the working class and the people.

Plus two additional specifications:

The elaboration of a development plan based on public investment, which will however also allow in parallel private investment. Greece needs a new and productive relationship between the public and private sectors to enter a path to sustainable development. The realization of this project will become possible once liquidity is reestablished, combined with national saving.

Regaining control of the domestic market from imported products will revitalize and enhance the role of small and medium-sized enterprises, which remain the backbone of the Greek economy. At the same time exports will be stimulated by the introduction of a national currency.[23]

This plan advocated by the Left Platform (debt default, nationalization of banks, capital controls, alternative currency; and then printing new money for investments, etc.) does not do what is required – if enacted, it would merely amount to a new version of state socialism. The weak point of the Left Platform was its advocacy of Grexit: they presented Grexit as a heroic step into the unknown, an act of defying the EU technocracy, and therefore found it difficult to explain why Grexit was directly suggested by Schauble when he promised Varoufakis financial help if Greece temporarily left the eurozone. (It's like today in the UK, where a weird coalition of Left and Right advocated Brexit.) Varoufakis sensed correctly that Grexit ultimately amounts to the same as surrendering to Brussels demands: the eurozone remains intact, totally subordinated to Brussels rules. What was so subversive about the Syriza government was that it wanted to stay *in* the eurozone and disturb its rules. (In a homologous way, the moment Syriza split into those who accepted the EU blackmail and the Left Platform, its moment was over; the explosive combination fell apart into its two traditional components, Social Democracy and the radical Left.)

Measures advocated by the Left Platform, if properly calibrated, might work – but would they work for Greece, with an enormous foreign debt of private individuals and companies (which cannot be cancelled) and an economy fully integrated into and dependent on Western Europe, reliant on food, industrial and medical imports? In other words, where, in what 'outside', would Greece find itself? In an outside of Belarus and Cuba? As Paul Krugman recently wrote (see above, p. 60), one has to admit that nobody really knows what the consequences of Grexit would be – it's uncharted territory. But one thing is nonetheless clear· 'Grexit is a name for none other than a politics of national independence,'[24] so no wonder that some partisans of the Left Platform even resort to the extremely problematic and (for me) totally unacceptable self-characterization 'national populism'.[25]

So the choice was not simply 'Grexit or capitulation': the Syriza government found itself in a unique situation, obliged to do what it was opposed to. To persist in such a difficult situation and not to leave the field is true courage. The enemy of the Syriza government is now not primarily the Left Platform but those who take 'sincerely' the defeat and really want to play the EU card. This danger becomes clear when one takes into account the effect of the capitulation on Syriza itself. The capitulation, Varoufakis says,

> de-radicalized those left in the ministries, the result being that they are either incapable of or unwilling to (lest they upset the troika) plan for the next rupture. Moreover the troika is keeping them like guinea

pigs on a treadmill, making them run faster and faster to implement its toxic measures. Within days they have become co-opted and incapable of planning anything of the sort that you mention.

[. . .] crucially, the troika is cleverly forcing upon the government legislation that spreads and entrenches further its own fiefdoms within the state. So, the tax fighting units are now absorbed by the General Secretariat of Public Revenues (whose ownership by the troika I exposed), so that the government has no instruments left at its disposal to fight tax evasion by the oligarchs. Similarly with privatizations. The troika is setting up new 'organs' that it controls fully.[26]

The true miracle of the situation was that, in spite of the capitulation to Brussels, around 70 per cent of Greek voters still supported the Syriza government – the majority perceives the Syriza government as doing the right thing in an impossible situation.

There is a risk that the Syriza capitulation will turn out to be just that and nothing more, enabling the full reintegration of Greece into the EU as a humble, bankrupt member, in the same way that there was a risk of Grexit turning into a large-scale catastrophe. There is no clear *a priori* answer here: any decision can only be retroactively justified by its consequences. And, lately, signs are multiplying that the Syriza government is not doing properly even the job of efficient state administration – there are factional struggles for power and influence that occasionally involve physical violence. It looks like the old Greek politics of mismanagement and corruption is coming back at full speed. What one should fear is not only the prospect of the further suffering of the Greek people, but also the prospect of another fiasco that will discredit the Left for years to come, while the surviving Leftists argue how their defeat proves yet again the perfidiousness of the capitalist system . . .

A PLEA FOR BUREAUCRATIC SOCIALISM

Is, then, today's radical Left really 'condemned to fight tooth and nail for social democracy, to prove it cannot work'?[27] In order to break out of this perverted cycle, one has to change the entire perspective. When one hears anarchists deploying their idea of local communities working in a transparent way, with no 'alienated' representative mechanisms, with all members actively engaged in organizing their lives, the first thing that comes to mind is Thomas Metzinger's definition of transparency: 'For any phenomenal state, the degree of phenomenal transparency is inversely proportional to the introspective degree of attentional availability of earlier processing stages.'[28] Transparency is thus paradoxically 'a special form of darkness':[29] we are not able to see something because it is transparent; rather, we see through it. Metzinger's basic thesis is that such transparency is formative of our consciousness at two levels – first, generally, we

> do not experience the reality surrounding us as the content of a representational process nor do we represent its components as internal placeholders [. . .] of another, external level of reality. We simply experience it as *the world in which we live our lives*.[30]

Then, the same holds for our conscious self, for the immediacy of our self-awareness, which is a representation in our mind and thus also relies on such an illusion, on an epistemically illegitimate short-circuit of perceiving what effectively is a mere representation, a model our organism formed of itself, as 'the thing itself':

> We do not experience the contents of our self-consciousness as the contents of a representational process, and we do not experience them as some sort of causally active internal placeholder *of* the system *in* the system's all-inclusive model of reality, but simply as *ourselves, living in the world right now*.[31]

The basic mechanism of 'transparency' is well-known from the Hegelian-Marxian tradition of the critique of fetishist illusion: the agent's own 'reflexive determination' (their wish or desire) is misperceived as a property of the (perceived) object itself; the ruler is misperceived as an embodiment of some quality – love, fear. What Metzinger does is to bring the logic of this illusion to its extreme, *applying it to the perceiving agent itself*: the logic of (mis)perceiving our phenomenal experience as directly referring to 'objects out there' is applied to the *subject itself*. I myself do not 'really exist' but only appear as the result of a fetishist illusion. There never can be a subject (self) fully 'opaque' to itself (you can never fully 'know' yourself) in the sense of perceiving one's own generative mechanism – every such understanding is limited, embedded in a global context: 'cognitive self-reference always takes place against the background of transparent, pre-conceptual self-modelling.'[32] A sense of self is ultimately a part of naive, everyday experience.

Are not communities imagined by anarchists 'transparent' in a similar way? Their survival relies on a thick texture of 'alienated' institutional mechanisms: where do electricity and water come from? Who guarantees the rule of law? To whom do we turn for healthcare? The more a community is self-ruling, the more this network has to function smoothly and invisibly. Maybe, we should change the goal of emancipatory struggles from overcoming alienation to enforcing the right kind of alienation, achieving a smooth functioning of 'alienated' (invisible) social mechanisms which sustain the space of 'non-alienated' communities?

We have an old name for these alienated mechanisms: bureaucracy, which is why what the Left needs today is to reinvent bureaucratic socialism. The standard characterization of Stalinist regimes as 'bureaucratic socialism' is totally misleading and (self-)mystifying: it is the way the Stalinist regime itself perceived its problem, the cause of its failures and troubles. If there are not enough products in the stores, if the authorities do not respond to people's demands, etc., what is easier than to blame the 'bureaucratic' attitude of indifference, petty arrogance, and so on. No wonder that, from the late 1920s onwards, Stalin was writing attacks on bureaucracy, on bureaucratic attitudes. 'Bureaucratism' was nothing but an effect of the functioning of Stalinist regimes, and the paradox is that it is the ultimate misnomer: what Stalinist regimes really lacked was precisely an efficient 'bureaucracy' (an 'alienated', depoliticized and competent administrative apparatus).

Although it ended in a failure, the Great Proletarian Cultural Revolution was unique in attacking the key point: not just the takeover of state power, but the new economic organization and reorganiz-ation of daily life. Its failure was precisely the failure to create a new form of everyday life: it remained a carnivalesque excess, with the state apparatus (under Zhou Enlai's control) guaranteeing the con-tinuation of daily life, of production. The lesson of this failure is that the focus should be shifted from the utopian goal of the full reign of productive expressivity that no longer needs representation (state order, capital, etc.) to: what kind of representation should replace the existing liberal-democratic representative state? Is Negri's proposal of a 'citizen's income' not an indication in this sense? It is a measure enacted by the state, not by some kind of people's self-organization; it is not linked to an individual's productivity, but it is the repre-sentative *condition and frame* for opening up the possible space of expressive productivity. Trotsky advocates the same duality when he makes a plea for the interplay between class self-organization and the political leadership of the revolutionary vanguard party. (Espe-cially interesting is one of Trotsky's arguments for the need for a vanguard party: the self-organizing councils cannot also take on the role of the party, for a politico-psychological reason – people 'cannot live for years in an uninterrupted state of high tension and intense activity'.[33]) Lenin was fully aware of this problem, and his solution was an almost Kantian one: freely debate at public meetings during weekends, but obey and labour hard while at work. He wrote of the common man:

> Before the October Revolution he did *not* see a single instance of the propertied, exploiting classes making any real sacrifice for him, giv-ing up anything for his benefit. He did *not* see them giving him the land and liberty that had been repeatedly promised him, giving him peace, sacrificing 'Great Power' interests and the interests of Great Power secret treaties, sacrificing capital and profits. He saw this only *after* October 25, 1917, when he took it himself by force, and had to defend by force what he had taken [. . .] Naturally, for a certain time, all his attention, all his thoughts, all his spiritual strength, were con-centrated on taking a breath, on unbending his back, on straightening his shoulders, on taking the blessings of life that were there for the taking, and that had always been denied him by the now overthrown

exploiters. Of course, a certain amount of time is required to enable the ordinary working man not only to see for himself, not only to become convinced, but also to feel that he cannot simply 'take', snatch, grab things, that this leads to increased disruption, to ruin, to the return of the Kornilovs. The corresponding change in the conditions of life (and consequently in the psychology) of the ordinary working men is only just beginning. And our whole task, the task of the Communist Party (Bolsheviks), which is the class-conscious spokesman for the strivings of the exploited for emancipation, is to appreciate this change, to understand that it is necessary, to stand at the head of the exhausted people who are wearily seeking a way out and lead them along the true path, along the path of labour discipline, along the path of co-ordinating the task of arguing at mass meetings *about* the conditions of work with the task of unquestioningly obeying the will of the Soviet leader, of the dictator, *during* the work [. . .] We must learn to combine the 'public meeting' democracy of the working people – turbulent, surging, overflowing its banks like a spring flood – with *iron* discipline while at work, with *unquestioning obedience* to the will of a single person, the Soviet leader, while at work.[34]

It is easy to make fun of Lenin here (or to be horrified by what he is saying), easy to accuse Lenin of being caught in the industrialist paradigm, etc., but the problem remains. The main form of direct democracy for the 'expressive' multitude in the twentieth century were so-called councils ('soviets') – (almost) everybody in the West loved them, up to liberals like Hannah Arendt, who perceived in them the echo of the old Greek life of *polis*. Throughout the age of 'really-existing socialism', the secret hope of 'democratic socialists' was the direct democracy of the soviets, local councils as the form of self-organization; and it is deeply symptomatic how, with the decline of 'really-existing socialism', this emancipatory shadow, which haunted it all the time, has also disappeared. Is this not the ultimate confirmation of the fact that the council version of 'democratic socialism' was just a spectral double of the 'bureaucratic' 'really-existing socialism', its inherent transgression with no substantial positive content of its own and unable, therefore, to serve as the permanent basic organizing principle of a society? What both 'really-existing socialism' and council democracy shared is a belief in the possibility of a self-transparent organization of society that would preclude political alienation (state apparatuses, institutionalized rules of political life, legal order, police, etc.); and is the basic experience of the end of 'really-existing socialism' not precisely the rejection of this *shared* feature, the resigned 'postmodern' acceptance of the fact that society is a complex network of 'sub-systems', which is why a certain level of alienation is constitutive of social life, so that a totally self-transparent society is a utopia with totalitarian potentials.[35] No wonder, then, that the same holds for contemporary examples of 'direct democracy', from *favelas* to the 'post-industrial' digital culture (do the descriptions of the new 'tribal' communities of computer-hackers not often evoke the logic of council democracy?): they all have to rely on a state apparatus, i.e., for structural reasons they cannot take over the entire field.

Apart from the obvious associations with 'really-existing socialism', there is another more serious reproach to our plea for bureaucratic socialism: is bureaucracy – as we learned from Kafka, at least – not (in principle, not for contingent reasons of bad organization) inefficient, caught in its own circular *jouissance*? As the saying goes, the true aim of bureaucratic machinery is not to pursue its goal, to solve the problems it is dealing with, but to repeatedly re-create or even magnify these problems and in this way reproduce the reason for its own existence. Bureaucracy thus confronts us again with surplus-enjoyment: the enjoyment generated not by fulfilling its official goal (solving a problem) but by the self-reproducing cycle of its own movement.

Kafka's genius was to eroticize bureaucracy, *the* non-erotic entity if ever there was one. In Chile, Isabel Allende tells us, when a citizen wants to identify himself to the authorities,

> the clerk on duty demands that the poor petitioner produce proof that he was born, that he isn't a criminal, that he paid his taxes, that he registered to vote, and that he's still alive, because even if he throws a tantrum to prove that he hasn't died, he is obliged to present a 'certificate of survival'. The problem has reached such proportions that the government

itself has created an office to combat bureaucracy. Citizens may now complain of being shabbily treated and may file charges against incompetent officials . . . on a form requiring a seal and three copies, of course.[36]

This is state bureaucracy at its most crazy. Yet are we aware that this is our only true contact with the divine in our secular times? What can be more 'divine' than the traumatic encounter with the bureaucracy at its craziest – when, say, a bureaucrat tells us that, legally, we don't exist? It is in such encounters that we get a glimpse of another order beyond the mere terrestrial everyday reality. Like God, bureaucracy is simultaneously all-powerful and impenetrable, capricious, omnipresent and invisible. Kafka was well aware of this deep link between bureaucracy and the divine: it is as if, in his work, Hegel's thesis on the state as the terrestrial existence of God is 'buggered', given a properly obscene twist. It is *only* in this sense that Kafka's works engage in a search for the divine in our barren secular world – more precisely, they not only search for the divine, they *find* it in state bureaucracy.

There are two memorable scenes in Terry Gillian's *Brazil* (1985) that perfectly express the crazy excesses of bureaucratic *jouissance* perpetuating itself in its auto-circulation. After the hero's plumbing breaks down and he leaves a message with the official repair service asking for urgent help, Robert de Niro arrives, a mythical-mysterious criminal whose subversive activity is that he listens in to emergency calls and then immediately goes to the customer, repairing his plumbing for free, by-passing the inefficient state repair service's paperwork. Indeed, in a bureaucracy caught in a vicious cycle of *jouissance*, the ultimate crime is to simply and directly do the job one is supposed to do – if a state repair service actually does its job, this is (at the level of its unconscious libidinal economy) considered an unfortunate by-product, since the bulk of its energy goes into inventing complicated administrative procedures that enable it to invent ever-new obstacles and thus postpone the work indefinitely. In a second scene, we meet – in the corridors of a vast government agency – a group of people permanently running around, a leader (a big-shot bureaucrat) followed by a bunch of lower administrators who shout at him all the time, asking him for a specific opinion or decision, and he nervously spurts out fast, 'efficient' replies ('This is to be done tomorrow latest!' 'Check that report!' 'No, cancel that appointment!'). The appearance of nervous hyperactivity is, of course, a façade that masks a self-indulgent nonsensical spectacle of imitating, of playing 'efficient administration'. Why do they walk around all the time? The leader, whom they follow, is obviously not on the way from one meeting to another – the meaningless fast walk around the corridors is all he does. The hero from time to time stumbles on this group, and the Kafkaesque explanation is, of course, that this entire performance is here to attract his gaze, staged for his eyes only. They pretend to be busy, but all their activity is here to provoke the hero while he addresses a demand to the group's leader, who then snaps back, 'Can't you see how busy I am!', or, occasionally, does the reverse – greets the hero as if he has been waiting for him for a long time, mysteriously expecting his presence.

Is the idea of an efficient bureaucracy not therefore self-defeating, the worst of utopias? The art of good social management is to turn around the entire perspective: not diminishing the surplus-enjoyment and making bureaucracy as efficient as possible, but accepting the bureaucratic surplus-enjoyment as a fact and limiting oneself to restructuring it in such a way that, as a kind of secondary by-product, it also solves some real problems. One should also value the anonymous coldness of the bureaucratic treatment of individuals: yes, we are all mistreated by bureaucracy, but this also means that we are all treated in the same way. While one cannot even imagine a bureaucracy that treats us in a warm, human way (except a robotic voice programmed to do so), we can imagine a bureaucracy that reduces personal favour and ignores us all equally.

So, to recapitulate. At the time of the Greek referendum, there were two 'possibles': follow the Brussels dictates and accept the imposed austerity politics (the line adopted by the Tsipras government), or step out of it, perform Grexit and endeavour to get the national economy in motion through autonomous fiscal politics (the Left Platform proposal). There is no risking the 'impossible' in this second option: it remains entirely within the global capitalist system, which without any problem can allow local states to disengage – no wonder that, as we have already mentioned, when Varoufakis threatened Schauble with Grexit, Schauble accepted this immediately and even offered Greece financial help to facilitate it. Schauble's position was: you don't want to follow our proposal of continuing austerity politics, so, OK, no problem, get out. In spite of all his problematic and naive ideas, especially about 'democratizing Europe', the *only* political agent who touched on an 'impossible' and caused panic in the European establishment was Varoufakis – and he had to step down as the finance minister before the referendum. The proof that his plan touched the impossible was that, after the referendum, the liberal-conservative party New Democracy (ND) proposed to the parliament the establishment of a special committee of inquiry assigned to probe 'Plan X', the imposition of capital controls in June 2015 – in short, they wanted to criminalize what Varoufakis had been doing. The ND proposal was rejected, but, interestingly, the social-democratic party PASOK voted for it, while both the 'hard-line' communist KKE and the fascist Golden Dawn voted 'present' and not against (i.e. they abstained). What Varoufakis proposed was that Greece should remain in the eurozone but act independently within it – this would have been an authentic act, an act of disturbing the lines of separation that define the possibilities of a situation and intervening in the European system *from within*, enforcing a change in its rules.

It is difficult to do the impossible; it means much more than just saying 'no' and heroically resisting pressure. Castro said 'no' to the US, but no really new social form was invented in Cuba. One gets tired of the conflicting stories: the economic failure and human rights abuses pointed to by Cuba's opponenets, and the successes in education and healthcare constantly evoked by the friends of the revolution. One gets tired even of the really great story of how a small country resisted the biggest superpower (with the help of the other super-power, it's true). All these stories do not change the sad fact that the Cuban revolution did not produce a social model relevant for the eventual communist future. The even sadder thing about today's Cuba is a feature clearly portrayed in Leonardo Padura's Mario Conde police procedurals, set in contemporary Havana: the atmos-phere is one not so much of poverty and oppression as of missed chances, of living in a part of the world to a large extent bypassed by the tremendous economic and social changes of the last decades.

Recently, a Cuban guide made a bitter comment to a group of European tourists: 'I know why you are here. You know we are doomed, a weird eccentricity, and you just want to catch the last moment to see this Cuba before it will disappear.' Is being the object of a gaze looking at us as if we are already dead not the most tragic comment imaginable on twentieth-century communism?

The gradual opening of the Cuban economy is a compromise that does not resolve the deadlock but just allows the predominant inertia to drag on. After the fall of Chavismo in Venezuela, Cuba had three choices: (1) continue to vegetate in a mixture of communist party regime and pragmatic concessions to the market; (2) embrace fully the Chinese model (wild capitalism with party rule); (3) simply abandon socialism and, in this way, admit the full defeat of the revolution. Whatever happens, the distressing prospect is that, under the banner of democratization, all the small but important achievements of the revolution, from healthcare to education, will be undone, and the Cubans who escaped to the US will enforce a violent re-privatization. There is a small hope that this extreme fallback will be prevented and a reasonable compromise negotiated.

So what is the overall result of the Cuban revolution? What comes to my mind is Arthur Miller's experience on Havana's Malecon, where two men were sitting at a bench near him, obviously poor and in need of a shave, engaged in a vociferous discussion. A taxi then pulled up to the curb in front of them and a lovely young woman stepped out with two brown paper bags full of groceries. She was juggling the bags to get her purse open, while a tulip in one of the bags was waving dangerously close to snapping its stem. One of the men got up and took hold of one of the bags to steady it, while the other joined him to steady the other bag, and Miller wondered if they were about to grab the bags and run. Nothing like this happened – instead, one of them gently held the tulip stem between forefinger and thumb until she could get the bags secured in her arms; she thanked them with a certain formal dignity and walked off. Miller's comment:

I'm not quite sure why, but I thought this transaction remarkable. It was not only the gallantry of these impoverished men that was impressive, but that the woman seemed to regard it as her due and not at all extraordinary. Needless to say, she offered no tip, nor did they seem to expect any, her comparative wealth notwithstanding.

Having protested for years the government's jailing and silencing of writers and dissidents, I wondered whether despite everything, including the system's economic failure, a heartening species of human solidarity had been created, possibly out of the relative symmetry of poverty and the uniform futility inherent in the system from which few could raise their heads short of sailing away.[37]

It is at this most elementary level that our future will be decided – what global capitalism cannot generate is precisely such 'heartening species of human solidarity'. So, in the spirit of *de mortuis nihil nisi bonum*, this scene on Malecon is perhaps the nicest thing I can remember about Castro. And one cannot say even this for the Khmer Rouge, who also said 'no' to the US and their own collaborators, but whose very murderous radicality again bears witness to the fact that no new social form was created. Were the Khmer Rouge really 'extreme'? In a way, yes, their reign set new standards of brutality; but was it not that they precisely *failed* in their 'extremism'? They utterly failed to effectively change human nature: instead of creating a New Man, their brief reign just collapsed in a destructive rage, and the old 'human nature' swiftly returned. One can argue that the explosive mixture of biogenetics and the digitalization of our lives is far more efficient in pursuing this goal – a New Man is effectively emerging here.

This is why if one wants to produce something truly new in politics, it is not enough to have a government directly relying on a strong popular presence: the unique enthusiasm of such a situation gets soon diluted into inertia or even despair if a political organization does not propose a concrete plan of what to do (and, once again, in Greece only Varoufakis had something at least resembling it). Furthermore, there is nothing arrogant about mentioning ordinary people's material concerns: the poor have the right to do it, and to talk about a readiness for great sacrifices, or suffering 'whatever the price', is as a rule the ideology of the privileged, who are quite content to let the people suffer for them. So do I display distrust in the people? Yes, there is nothing non-communist in it. 'People' are an inconsistent multiplicity capable of breathtaking acts of solidarity that surprise cynical intellectuals, but they can also get lost in the lowest fascist passions.

It may appear that, while the basic theoretical problems have been properly dealt with for a long time, what is missing is actual politics, since the spirit of capitulation predominates in the last decades. Actual politics is not failing because the spirit of capitulation has been winning for the last thirty years; on the contrary, the spirit of capitulation is spreading around because actual politics lacks a vision that can only be provided by theory. The big problem of the Left is that, after the breakdown of 'really-existing socialism' and of the welfare-state social democracy, it lacks any serious vision of how to reorganize society. The true event is not the enthusiastic mobilization of the people but a change in everyday life, felt when things 'return to the normal'. This does not justify capitulation: one should look around for any place, any particular struggle, where there is a chance to *faire bouger les choses*, for moments which may trigger what you call the return of history, and which may open up the way for a true political event.

3

Religion and its Contents

CHINA'S ALTERNATIVE MODERNITY

The Three-Body Problem, writer Liu Cixin's sci-fi masterpiece[1] and the first part of the trilogy *Remembrance of Earth's Past*, begins in Mao's China during the Cultural Revolution, in which Ye Wenjie, a young woman, has just seen her father killed for continuing to teach (and proclaim his belief in) Einstein's theory of relativity. Disgusted by humanity, she hijacks a government programme meant to make contact with aliens and attempts to encourage extraterrestrials to invade Earth. The story then moves to the near future, where the now old Wenjie is contacted by Wang Miao, a researcher developing a new nanotechnology who has started having strange experiences. Scientists he knows are killing themselves because they say the laws of physics are no longer working as expected. When he takes photos with his fancy new camera, there's a number on each negative when it is developed. When he tries to explore possible linkages between these phenomena, he finds himself drawn into a virtual-reality game, 'Three Body', in which players find themselves on an alien planet called Trisolaris, whose three suns rise and set at strange and unpredictable intervals and positions: sometimes too far away, making the planet horribly cold, sometimes far too close and destructively hot, and sometimes not at all for long periods of time. The players can somehow dehydrate themselves and the rest of the population to weather the worst seasons, but life is a constant struggle against apparently unpredictable elements. Despite that, players slowly find ways to build civilizations and attempt to predict the strange cycles of heat and cold. After contact between the two civilizations is established in reality, outside the game, our Earth appears to the desperate Trisolarians as an ideal world of order, and they decide to invade it to ensure the survival of their race. The outcome of this encounter will probably be that both civilizations have to 'de-idealize' the other, realizing that the other also has its faults – something akin to what Lacan called 'separation'. There is another Lacanian motif in the novel: the virtual game that turns out to simulate the real life on Trisolaris reminds us of Lacan's motto that truth has the structure of a fiction.

However, the most interesting feature of the novel is how the opposition between Earth and Trisolaris echoes the opposition between the traditional Confucian view of heaven as the principle of cosmic order and Mao's praise for heaven in disorder: is the chaotic life on Trisolaris, where the very rhythm of seasons is perturbed, not a naturalized version of the chaos of the Cultural Revolution? Is the terrifying insight that 'there is no physics', no stable natural laws (the insight that, in the novel, pushes many scientists to suicide), not the recognition of how, as Lacan put it, there is no big Other? This tension between the order of heaven and disorder in heaven also provides the basic coordinates of the ideological turmoil that pervades contemporary China, as is clear from *The China Wave*,[2] a bestseller in China and abroad in which Zhang Weiwei presents, in a popular way, a justification of the Chinese authoritarian political system.

Zhang's starting point is that China is a unique 'civilizational state', a state that overlaps with an entire civilization defined by the Confucian tradition. Its values (not in the Western sense of values opposed to facts, but rather values as principles that sustain and are embedded in a life-form) are, among others: practical humanism, i.e., the rejection of otherworldly spiritualism and a focus on the good and harmonious life on this earth; an organic approach that avoids extremes of individualism and totalitarian centralized order, of fossilized tradition and rushed modernization, and combines openness to other cultures with fidelity to one's own roots; a pragmatic approach versus hanging on to unrealistic principles (for example, instead of clinging to the formal rules of democracy, one should focus on the true goal of democracy: people should be ruled by competent and virtuous men who work for their welfare, dignity and freedom); human rights should be conceived holistically, not just as a set of political and personal freedoms (of speech, etc.) but also as the right to a safe and satisfied life, with all material and spiritual needs met (what's the use of a free press and a multi-party system if the result is social chaos and pointless struggles)? Zhang's point is that it was fidelity to this Confucian tradition that enabled China to enact the economic miracle of the last decades: combining rapid social and economic development (which lifted hundreds of millions out of poverty and created a gigantic middle class) with social stability. In short, China succeeded in realizing an alternative modernity: engaging in the process of capitalist modernization at record-breaking speed while avoiding the explosion of social antagonisms.

So how did this work? Zhang quotes Martti Ahtisaari, ex-president of Finland, who said on 18 January 2009:

> the Politbureau of the Communist Party of China was like the board of directors of a corporation, the general secretary of the Party was like the chairman of the board, the premier was like the CEO of the corporation and the governance of China was more or less like managing a company.[3]

Zhang replies:

> Indeed, we have reflected on this question. Why do no companies in the world elect its CEO through one-person-one-vote? If it is done this way, the company may risk bankruptcy. Likewise, in terms of political system, we should consider how a country can be best governed. To my mind, the essence of democracy is the will of the people and good governance of a country, rather than democracy for the sake of democracy or election for the sake of election.[4]

One is almost tempted to add to this a variation of Heidegger's thesis that the essence of technique is nothing technical: the essence of democracy is nothing democratic (since, as Zhang implies, a strong authoritarian regime can be more 'essentially democratic' than a simple democracy).

One should be nonetheless careful here not to dismiss Zhang's arguments as hypocritical demagoguery fabricated to legitimize China's autocratic regime. The paradox is that, precisely because it lacks democratic legitimacy, an authoritarian regime can sometimes be more responsible towards its subjects than a democratically elected government: since it lacks democratic legitimacy, it has to legitimize itself by providing services to the citizens, with the underlying reasoning being, 'True, we are not democratically elected, but, as such, since we do not have to play the game of striving for cheap popularity, we can focus on citizens' real needs.' A democratically elected government, on the contrary, can fully exert its power for the narrow private interests of its members; they already have the legitimacy provided by elections, so they don't need any further legitimization and can feel safe doing what they want – they can say to those who complain, 'You elected us, now it's too late . . .'

However, things take a weird turn when Zhang recommends avoiding 'the European-style excessive welfare state'[5] – a recommendation that is already followed by most European countries through austerity politics, thus belying Zhang's point that, in the West, 'the welfare package can only go up, not down. Therefore it is impossible to launch such reforms as what China did to its banking sector and state-owned enterprises.'[6] To blame the 'excesses' of the welfare state on too much democracy is an insight that would be met with enthusiasm by every neo-conservative . . . In many cases, the principle evoked by Zhang may appear fair and reasonable, but one particular example used to illustrate it provides a specific twist, i.e., it points towards the true political aim underlying the principle. Zhang claims that

> individual rights could also be pursued at the expense of collective rights, as in the case of the freedom of expression exercised by one individual Danish cartoonist that has affected the collective right of a billion Muslims to religious freedom.[7]

There is a strange non-sequitur in this argument: maybe millions of Muslims did feel hurt and humiliated, but how does this affect their religious freedom? Religious freedom is affected much more by bans on burkas on public transport, for example. And in another of Zhang's problematic claims he states that 'the banning of Muslim headscarves in schools in France and other European countries is inconceivable in China.'[8] Really? In August 2014, in Xinjiang, home to the Muslim Uighur minority, 'five types of people' were banned from public transport: people wearing headscarves, veils, burkas or clothes adorned with the crescent moon and star symbol, and 'youths with long beards'. 'Passengers who do not co-operate, particularly the "five types of people", will be reported to the police,' said the authorities, who added that all commuters would be subject to bag checks: 'The security measures will ensure social stability and protect the lives, property and safety of citizens of all races.'[9] (Other prohibitions followed – for example, authorities also banned Ramadan fasting and ordered food stores to remain open during Ramadan.)

A similar problem arises when Zhangs' mentions the situation in Haiti:

> In many poverty-stricken countries, giving priority to democratization leads to a situation of failed states like Haiti, where poverty causes chaos and anarchy, and eventually the country can only rely on the UN peacekeeping forces to restore peace and stability.[10]

It is, to put it mildly, very strange to blame too much democracy for the continuing misery of Haiti, a country marked by a long history of dictatorship and military rule ... But the basic problem resides elsewhere, in Zhang's reliance on the Confucian notion of organic social harmony:

> In Chinese culture, you are born into a social role as a son, a daughter, a father, a mother, a colleague of others, and rights and obligations are always linked. I genuinely feel that China's humanistic culture can enrich the Western individual-based concept of human rights.[11]

This opposition is deceptive: the opposite of a 'harmonious' hierarchic society in which everyone plays his or her role is not (just) unconstrained individualism but (also) an egalitarian society, a society whose first great model is the Christian Holy Ghost. That's why Christ's words, 'If any man come to me, and hate not his father, and mother, and wife, and children, and brethren, and sisters, yea, and his own life also, he cannot be my disciple' (*Luke* 14:26), do not designate a society of extreme individualism, where everyone just cares for him- or herself and hates or exploits others, but a society kept together by a universal bond of love.

It is difficult not to read Zhang's reference to 'the traditional concept of *tian* or the heaven, which means the core interest and conscience of Chinese society'[12] in contrast to Mao Zedong's old motto: 'Everything under heaven is in utter chaos; the situation is excellent.' The basic insight of the radical Left is that, although crises are painful and dangerous, they are inevitable, and they are the terrain on which battles have to be waged and won. Zhang refers to the Chinese Communist Party (CCP) as the embodiment of *tian* (heaven), as a 'disinterested' organization elevated above social conflicts and basically caring only for the harmonious development of all its parts. But what guarantees this neutrality? Is there not a struggle also in heaven, is heaven not also divided (and, incidentally, is 'the divided heaven' not one of the best characterizations of class struggle)?

Beneath Confucian wisdom versus individualist Western democracy there is another battle going on: Confucianism versus legalism. For the Confucians, the land was in chaos because old traditions were not obeyed, and states like Qin, with their centralized military organization dismissive of the old customs, were perceived as the embodiment of what can go wrong. In contrast to this approach, which perceived nations like Qin as a threat to peace, the great legalist Han Fei 'proposed the unthinkable, that maybe the way of the Qin government was not an anomaly to be addressed, but a practice to be emulated'.[13] The solution resided in what appeared as the problem: the true cause of the troubles was not the abandonment of old traditions, but *these traditions themselves*, which daily demonstrated their inability to serve as guiding principles of social life. As Hegel put it in the Foreword to his *Phenomenology of Spirit*, the standard by which we measure a situation and establish that the situation is problematic is part of the problem and should be abandoned. Exactly the same reversal is at work in democracy. As Claude Lefort has demonstrated,[14] the achievement of democracy is to turn what is in traditional authoritarian power the moment of its greatest crisis – the time of transition from one master to another, when, briefly, 'the throne is empty', which causes panic – into the very source of its strength: democratic elections are the moment of passing through the zero-point when the complex network of social links is dissolved into a purely quantitative multiplicity of individuals, whose votes are mechanically counted. The moment of terror, of the dissolution of all hierarchic links, is thus re-enacted and transformed into the foundation of a new and stable positive political order.

Zhang's arguments against Western democracy as a political order that brings instability and conflicts should thus be transposed back into the Chinese context. He rehabilitates Confucian organicist corporatism in opposition to the Maoist egalitarian orientation that culminated in the 'terror' of the Cultural Revolution. It is wrong and meaningless to interpret the 'excesses' of the Cultural Revolution as the result of Western influence on China: such millenarian explosions of social negativity are a feature of all societies; they are the shadow that accompanies every hierarchic social order. And if anything can be said about Western democracy, it is precisely that (where it functions well) it enables a society to operate in a more stable way than any traditional hierarchic society, because it integrates conflicts and outpourings of negativity into the normal functioning of society, thereby rendering violent explosions superfluous (power can be changed democratically, so there is no need for a violent overthrow when people are not satisfied with it). So although democracy has its own limitations, the destabilization of society is certainly not one of them – on the contrary, it provides the scaffolding for arguably the most stable societies. Authoritarian societies are today much more unstable, since they perceive every demand for social and political change as a threat.

Democracy is effectively an egalitarian social link based on terror: 'terror' stands here for the negative act of sweeping away all social hierarchies. If the democratic axiom is that the place of power is empty, that there is no one who is directly qualified for this post either by tradition, charisma or, say, expertise and leadership qualities, then, before democracy can enter the stage, terror has to do its work so that the summit of state power is kept apart from the experts. Interestingly, Hegel's solution to this same problem is to keep apart the monarch and the state bureaucracy. While bureaucracy rules by expertise, i.e., while bureaucrats are chosen on account of their abilities and qualifications, the king is a king by his birth, i.e., ultimately, by lottery, on account of natural contingency. The danger Hegel is thereby trying to avoid emerged a century later in Stalinist bureaucracy, which is precisely the rule of (communist) experts: Stalin is *not* a figure of a master, but the one who 'really knows', who is an expert in all imaginable fields, from economics to linguistics, biology to philosophy.

For this reason, fully 'rational' elections would not be elections at all, but a transparent, objectivized process. Traditional (pre-modern) societies resolved this problem by invoking a transcendent source that 'verified' the result, conferring authority on it (God, king . . .). Therein resides the problem of modernity: modern societies perceive themselves as autonomous, self-regulated, i.e., they can no longer rely on an external (transcendent) source of authority. But, nonetheless, the moment of hazard has to remain operative in the electoral process, which is why commentators like to dwell on the 'irrationality' of votes (one never knows where votes will swing in the last days before elections). In other words, democracy would not work if it were to be reduced to permanent opinion polling – fully mechanized and quantified, deprived of its 'performative' character; as Lefort has pointed out, voting has to remain a (sacrificial) ritual, a ritualistic self-destruction and rebirth of society.[15] The reason is that this hazard itself should not be transparent, it should be minimally externalized/reified: 'people's will' is our equivalent of what the Ancients perceived as the imponderable God's will or the hand of Fate. What people cannot accept as their direct arbitrary choice, the result of a pure hazard, they can accept if it refers to at least a minimum of the 'real'. Hegel knew this long ago; it is the entire point of his defence of monarchy. And, last but not least, the same goes for love: there should be an element of the 'answer of the real' in it ('we were for ever meant for each other'); I cannot really accept that my falling in love hinges on a pure contingency.

And, perhaps, this brings us to the ultimate difference between the modern secular West and traditional societies. The latter still fully trust the authority of the big Other (the symbolic authority that sustains a way of life, like heaven in Chinese ideology), while the secular West increasingly assumes the void, inconsistency, impotence, etc., of the big Other, not only in ethics but also in politics. Back to Lefort's theorization of democracy as a political order in which the place of power is originally empty, and is only temporarily filled by the elected representatives: democracy admits the gap between the symbolic (the empty place of power) and the real (the agent who occupies this place), postulating that no empirical agent 'naturally' fits the empty place of power. Other systems are incomplete: they have to engage in compromises, in occasional shake-ups or revolutions, to function. Democracy elevates incompleteness into a principle: it institutionalizes the regular shake-up in the guise of elections. Democracy here goes further than the 'realistic' stance, according to which, in order to actualize a certain political vision, one should allow for concrete unpredictable circumstances and be ready to make compromises, to leave the space open for people's vices and imperfections; democracy instead turns imperfection itself into a positive asset. Far from being a limitation, the fact that elections do not pretend to select the most qualified person is what protects them from the totalitarian temptation – which is why, as was clear to the Ancient Greeks, the most democratic form of selecting who will rule us is a lottery.

Such a reversal of a negative feature into a positive one is the core mechanism of what we can call the dialectic of historical progress: what initially appeared as an obstacle or threat turns into the grounds for a new order. A similar reversal takes place when a traditional ideology finds a new lease of life functioning as an unexpected support of modernization, as in Japan when, after the Meiji restoration, the reassertion of strong state authority and the divinization of the Emperor provided the institutional framework for rapid industrialization. Is it not the same with Confucianism in China? It has returned trans-functionalized, like Zen Buddhism for corporate managers, to sustain capitalist rhythm. The re-discovered Confucianism is a profoundly reactive phenomenon: it is a defence mechanism destined to keep in check the exponential growth of capitalism and the forces of disintegration it unleashes.

This obsession on the part of the Chinese authorities with stability and harmony during the capitalist transformation of their economy, when economic inequalities are growing rapidly, means primarily one thing: no class struggle, no free trade unions. One has to bear in mind that the process of change in the last decades in China has been extremely violent in its social impact: communities were ruined, families were torn apart, elementary forms of solidarity are disappearing – see the films of Jia Zhangke, but also reports of how, when a woman or man is beaten or molested, passers-by just look the other way. In April 2016, a man approached a woman in a Beijing hotel as she entered her room and then tried to drag her violently into the corridor:

> In an online account published on Tuesday, the victim, who uses the online alias Wanwan, said bystanders and hotel staff did nothing as she was beaten and dragged by the man. 'I kept asking the cleaner for help and said, "I don't know him, he can't even say my name," but the cleaner didn't pull him away.' [. . .] The attack has sparked an impassioned debate about violence against women and triggered a renewed bout of soul-searching as to why witnesses to violent incidents or accidents so often failed to intervene in China.[16]

So when Zhang writes that 'top-level decision-makers or members of the Standing Committee of the Political Bureau of the Communist Party of China are selected by criteria that usually include two terms as provincial governors or ministers,'[17] we should highlight the passive verb form: 'are selected'. So who selects them, and how? At a Party congress every eight years or so, a new centre of power – the nine (now seven) members of the Standing Committee of the Politburo – is presented as a mysterious revelation, with no prior public debate; the selection procedure involves complex and totally opaque behind-the-scenes negotiations, so that the assembled delegates, who unanimously approve the list, learn about it only when they vote. We are not dealing here with some kind of secondary 'democratic deficit': this impenetrability is structurally necessary (within the authoritarian system, the only alternatives are a *de facto* monarchy, as in North Korea, or the traditional Stalinist model of a leader who simply stops ruling when he dies).

One can argue that the CCP works like the British aristocracy in the early growth of capitalism: as Marx put it, the bourgeoisie wisely left party politics to the old aristocracy, thereby avoiding the transposition of its internal conflicts into the political sphere. The aristocracy, the non-bourgeois class, appeared as the best representative of the class interests of the bourgeoisie in its entirety, rather than of just certain factions within it. Similarly, one could claim that the CCP, a non-bourgeois organization, is the best representative of the entire new capitalist class, protecting China from struggles between different factions of the bourgeoisie, and thus the new bourgeoisie has been wise to leave political power in the hands of the CCP.

The true opposition that underlies Zhang's edifice is thus the one between the Confucian 'harmonious' hierarchic state, where everything is in its proper place and antagonisms are absent (or kept in check, at least), and the Maoist populist-egalitarian orientation (whose historical model is legalism). One should note that, with all the talk about 'unity in diversity', about finding a proper position between the opposite extremes, Zhang privileges the Confucian model in a 'one-sided' way, i.e., he does not (as one would have expected) advocate a 'holistic' balance between the two extremes in the guise of a historical rhythm of exchange between order and chaos, between hierarchic stability and egalitarian explosions.

A closer look at how the Chinese state actually functions makes it clear that it is not a new version of the old Confucian state: the big difference is that state power is redoubled, something absent in the Confucian state. With Deng Xiaoping's 'reforms', at the level of economy (and, up to a point at least, of culture) what is usually perceived as 'communism' was abandoned, and the gates were opened wide for what, in the West, is called 'liberalization' (private property, profit-making, the lifestyle of hedonist individualism, etc.), while the Party maintained its ideologico-political hegemony – not in the sense of doctrinal orthodoxy (in the official discourse, Confucian references to a 'harmonious society' practically replaced references to communism), but in the sense of maintaining the unconditional political hegemony of the Communist Party as the only guarantee of China's stability and prosperity. In this way, the Chinese communists can have their cake and eat it: the radical change in social politics (economic 'liberalization') is combined with the continuation of the same Party rule as before.

But how does this combination work in (institutional) practice? How do you combine the political hegemony of the Party with the modern state apparatus needed to regulate a rapidly expanding market economy? What institutional reality sustains the official slogan that good stock-market performance (high returns on investments) is the way to fight for socialism? That is to say, what we have in China is not simply a private capitalist economy and communist political power: one should bear in mind that, through a series of transparent and non-transparent channels, state and Party own the majority of (especially large) companies. It is the Party itself that demands that these corporations perform well on the market. An anecdote from the times of Deng Xiaoping illustrates this weird situation. When Deng was still alive, although already retired from the post of General Secretary of the CCP, one of the top *nomenklatura* was purged, and the official reason given to the press was that, in an interview with a foreign journalist, he divulged a state secret, namely, that Deng was still the supreme authority, making effective decisions. The irony is that this fact was common knowledge: everybody knew that Deng was still pulling the strings – it was in all the media all the time. The difference was just with regard to the big Other – this fact was never officially stated. A secret is thus not simply a secret: it lets itself be known as a secret, i.e., people are not supposed simply not to know of the hidden Party structure redoubling the state agencies; they are supposed to be fully aware of it as a hidden network. The front stage is occupied by 'the government and other state organs, which ostensibly behave much like they do in many countries':[18] the Ministry of Finance proposes the budget, courts deliver verdicts, universities teach and deliver degrees, even priests lead rituals. So, on the one hand, we have the legal system, the government, the elected national assembly, the judiciary, the rule of law, etc. But – as the officially used term 'party and state leadership' indicates, with its precise hierarchy of who comes first and who second – this state power structure is redoubled by the Party, which is all-present while remaining in the background. Is this redoubling not yet another case of diffraction, of the gap between the 'two vacuums': the 'false' summit of state power, and the 'true' summit of the Party? There are, of course, many states, some even formally democratic, in which a half-secret exclusive club or sect *de facto* controls the government; in apartheid South Africa, it was the exclusive Boer Brotherhood, for example. However, what makes the Chinese case unique is that this redoubling of power into public and hidden is itself institutionalized, done openly.

All decisions on nominating people to key posts (in the Party and state organs, but also in large companies) are first made by a Party body, the Central Organization Department, whose large headquarters in Beijing has no listed phone number and no sign indicating the tenant inside. Once the decision is made, legal organs (state assemblies, manager boards) are informed and go through the ritual of confirming it by a vote. The same double procedure – first in the Party, then in the state – is reproduced at all levels, up to basic economic policy decisions, which are first debated in the Party organs and, once the decision is reached, formally enacted by government bodies.

This gap that separates the pure voluntarist power above the law from the legal bodies is most palpable in the anti-corruption struggle: when there is a suspicion that some high functionary is involved in corruption, the Central Commission for Discipline Inspection, a Party organ, enters the scene and investigates the charges unbound by any legal niceties – they basically kidnap the suspected functionary and can hold him for up to six months, subjecting him to harsh interrogations. Significantly, the only limitation imposed on the interrogators is the extent to which the suspected functionary is protected by some top-ranking Party cadre, like a Politburo member. Once the verdict is reached (and this verdict doesn't just depend on any facts discovered but is also the result of complex behind-the-scenes negotiations between different Party cliques), and if the functionary is found guilty, he is finally delivered to the organs of law; at this level, things are already decided and the trial is a formality – the only thing (sometimes) negotiable is the length of the sentence.

One of the consequences of such a power structure is that, while certain things are clearly prohibited in China, some of these prohibitions cannot be publicly stated but are themselves prohibited: it is not merely prohibited to raise the question of workers' self-organization against capitalist exploitation as the central tenet of Marxism, it is also prohibited to publicly claim that it is prohibited to raise this question.[19]

While I was doing my military service in the Yugoslav People's Army in 1975–6, I remember noticing a clear case of an unwritten rule that it was prohibited to pronounce openly. According to the Yugoslav constitution, all languages spoken among the nations and nationalities of Yugoslavia were equal, which is why in the National Assembly all speeches and debates were translated from the language in which they were spoken (Serbocroat, Slovene, Macedonian, Albanian) into the other three. The constitution also specified that all these four languages were equal in the army, with the exception of issuing commands, where orders were given in Serbocroat, the language spoken by most people (a quite understandable exception since, in the midst of a battle, one cannot shout orders in four languages). However, de facto, in everyday life, not only in education but also in conversations, only Serbocroat was used, and this clear violation of the constitution was imposed without debate. I remember once an Albanian soldier in my unit raised the obvious question: he asked the officer at a class of political education, 'Why are we not allowed to use our own language, although the constitution claims it is equal to others in the army?' Before he could finish the question he was interrupted by the officer with a threat: if he asks questions like that, he will be arrested for spreading separatist propaganda ... Another clear case of a prohibition whose open proclamation was itself prohibited.[20]

In this way, we violate what Kant called the 'transcendental formula of public law': 'All actions relating to the right of other men are unjust if their maxim is not consistent with publicity.' A secret law, a law unknown to its subjects, would legitimize the arbitrary despotism of those who exercise it. Compare with this formula the title of a recent report on China: 'Even What's Secret is a Secret in China'.[21] Troublesome intellectuals who report on political oppression, ecological catastrophes, rural poverty, etc., can get years in prison for betraying a state secret. The catch is that many of the laws and regulations that make up the state-secret regime are themselves classified, making it difficult for individuals to know how and when they're in violation – and what Edward Snowden's revelations made palpable is the extent to which the agencies that monitor terrorists' secret plans function in the Chinese way.

The problem is, of course, that the Party itself, with its complex network outside public control, is the ultimate source of corruption. The inner circle of *nomenklatura*, the top party and state functionaries as well as managers, are connected through an exclusive phone network, the 'Red Machine'; possessing one of its unlisted numbers is the clearest indicator of one's status. However, what do people talk about when they use the Red Machine?

> One vice-minister told me that more than half of the calls he received on his 'red machine' were requests for favours from senior party officials, along the lines of: 'Can you give my son, daughter, niece, nephew, cousin or good friend and so on, a job?'[22]

One can easily concoct here a scene reminiscent of Kafka's *The Castle*, where the hero (K.) accidentally gets connected to the exclusive phone line of the castle; overhearing a conversation between two high officials, he hears only muffled, eroticized, obscene whispers. In the same way, one can imagine an ordinary Chinese accidentally being connected to a Red Machine conversation: expecting to hear top party political or military debates and decisions, he finds himself overwhelmed by dirty private exchanges concerning personal favours, corruption, sexuality . . .

So we should render more complex the formula of party–state as the defining feature of twentieth-century communism: there is always a gap between the two, corresponding to the gap between ego-ideal (symbolic law) and superego, i.e., the Party remains a half-hidden obscene shadow redoubling the state structure. There is no need to demand a new politics of distance towards the state: the Party *is* this distance. Its organization gives body to a kind of fundamental distrust of the state, its organs and mechanisms, as if they need to be controlled, kept in check, all the time. A true twentieth-century communist never fully accepts the state: there always has to be a vigilant agency outside the control of the (state) law, with the power to intervene in the state – such as the army or the secret police controlled by the Party.

The deadlock in which the CCP finds itself can be best illustrated by Rick Yancey's novel *The 5th Wave*, in which the human race stands on the brink of extinction as a series of alien attacks systematically tries to destroy it. The 'Others' proceed in five 'waves': in the first wave, they release an EMP wave that takes out all electronics and lighting technology; in the second wave, they cause gigantic tsunamis and earthquakes that wipe out three billion people; in the third wave, they use birds as carriers of a deadly virus, and this plague claims 97 per cent of the remaining humans. In the fourth wave, the Others invent a way to take over a human body, so that not all humans are actually humans, and the surviving humans are now threatened also by living entities who appear and act like humans. These (non-)humans begin to capture the surviving human children and train them as perfect killers; children are being told by their trainers that the Others are preparing the last, fifth, wave of attack, and that they, the trained children, are the last defence against the Others. They equip the children with special helmets that supposedly enable them to identify the real Others and immediately eradicate them. In reality, those who are in this way identified as 'Others' are in fact the last surviving humans, so the children are unknowingly doing the dirty work for the Others – *they are themselves the fifth wave from which they think they are protecting humanity . . .*

Is not something homologous taking place in today's China? The pest that is engulfing China is, of course, the pest of global capitalism, and this pest is progressing in waves. First, the traditional network of solidarity is gradually eradicated, followed by the catastrophic disintegration of stable social relations. And was this not the real function of the Cultural Revolution? Some naive Leftists claim that the legacy of the Cultural Revolution and Maoism in general acts as a counter-force to unbridled capitalism, preventing its worst excesses, maintaining a minimum of social solidarity. What if, however, the exact opposite is the case? What if, in a kind of unintended, and for that reason all the more cruelly ironic, Cunning of Reason, the Cultural Revolution, with its brutal erasure of past traditions, was the 'shock' that created the conditions for the ensuing capitalist explosion? As has been demonstrated in detail by Naomi Klein, neo-liberal transition 'requires the mobilization of the state, at least for its initial *coup de force*'.[23] It is not a process of market forces and corporations winning over the state, but a process set in motion by the full mobilization of the state apparatus. The obvious example is the role of Pinochet's authoritarian rule in Chile's embrace of neo-liberalism – but what if China has to be added to Klein's list of states in which a natural, military or social catastrophe cleared the slate for a new capitalist explosion? The supreme irony of history is thus that it was Mao himself who created the ideological conditions for rapid capitalist development by tearing apart the fabric of traditional society. Incidentally, the commercial 'poisoning' of social relations that results from these waves is perfectly depicted in the work of Jia Zhangke, undoubtedly the greatest living Chinese film-maker.

But now comes the final trick: in order to combat this pestilence and disintegration caused by the Other/capital, the CCP mobilizes (especially young) cadres, teaching them how to identify the Others (enemies of communism) and how to crush the last wave of bourgeois counter-revolution. But, in reality, the Communist Party is itself this last wave of counter-revolution, and the communist cadre fighting for the Party are the executioners of this last wave of capitalism, like the trained children in *The 5th Wave*.

One often hears how Europe has systematically betrayed its own proclaimed 'values', inflicting unheard-of horrors on millions of its own and other people – from the Holocaust and the gulag to colonial slaughters in Congo. However, this obvious hypocrisy is precisely the point. Europe was betraying its own 'values' and was thus opening up the space for merciless self-critique: the very European 'values' provide the best tool for criticizing Europe. Others' 'values' cannot do the job – if we criticize Europe from the standpoint of, say, Chinese Confucian values (as Chinese ideologues are doing today), the result is that, since Europe has frequently violated its own proclaimed democratic principles, we should abandon democracy itself. The model of this critique is the good old Stalinist critique of bourgeois 'formal' democracy: it is just an empty form legitimizing and concealing ruthless exploitation, so . . . let's drop democracy itself. And, effectively, there is no democratic 'alienation' in today's China – not because democracy is non-alienated, but simply because there is no democracy *tout court*, alienated or not. To avoid a misunderstanding: of course the democratic form is not innocent here, of course the critique of the content legitimized by formal democracy should be radicalized into a critique of the form itself; however, this self-critique is thoroughly immanent to the democratic form, it is its own obverse.

One should be very precise here: what I am advocating is not the process of democratic self-purification by means of which we get rid of the dirty water (abuses of democracy) without losing the healthy baby (authentic democracy). The task is rather to trans-value the (democratic) values themselves, to throw out the baby (the democratic form) while keeping in the dirty water (of 'chaotic' popular participation, of large-scale 'authoritarian' decisions).

CHINA, RELIGION AND ATHEISM

The immanent tension of the Chinese social model emerges at its purest in the strangely twisted way that the dominant power relates to religion: it promotes 'patriotic' religions or cultures like Confucianism as a tool of social stability, but it avoids the last step of fully legitimizing them – members of the ruling Communist Party are (again) prohibited from participating in religious life. Why?

Recall Badiou's claim that democracy is our fetish. An exemplary case of this is provided by bestsellers and Hollywood blockbusters from *All the President's Men* to *The Pelican Brief*, in which a couple of ordinary guys discover a scandal that reaches up to the president, forcing him to step down. Even if the corruption is shown to reach the very top, ideology resides in the upbeat final message of such works: what a great democratic country is ours where a couple of guys like you and me can bring down the president, the mightiest man on Earth!

This is why the most inappropriate, stupid even, name for a new radical political movement is one that combines socialism and democracy: it effectively joins together the ultimate fetish of the existing world order with a term that blurs the key distinctions. Everyone can be a socialist today, right up to Bill Gates – it suffices to profess the need for some kind of harmonious unity of a society, for the common good, for the care of the poor and downtrodden.

An exemplary case of today's 'socialism' is China, where the CCP is now engaged in an ideological campaign of self-legitimization which promotes three theses: (1) only Communist Party rule can guarantee successful capitalism; (2) only the rule of the atheist Communist Party can guarantee authentic religious freedom; and, the most surprising one, (3) only a continuing Communist Party rule can guarantee that China will be a society of Confucian conservative values (social harmony, patriotism, moral order), as capitalism merges with local culture there, allowing it to thrive. Instead of dismissing these claims as nonsensical paradoxes, we should discern their reasons: without the stabilizing power of the Party (1) capitalist development would ignite into a chaos of riots and protests, (2) religious factional struggles would disturb social stability, and (3) unbridled hedonist individualism would corrode social harmony. The third point is crucial, since what lies in the background is the fear of the corroding influence of Western 'universal values' of freedom, democracy, human rights and hedonist individualism. The ultimate enemy is not capitalism as such, but Western rootless culture, which invades China through the free flow of the internet; and one has to fight it with Chinese patriotism – even religion should be 'sinicized' to ensure social stability. Xinjiang's CCP official Zhang Chunxian recently said that, while 'hostile forces' are stepping up their infiltration, religions must work under socialism to serve economic development, social harmony, ethnic unity and the unification of the country: 'Only when one is a good citizen can one be a good believer.'[24]

But even this sinicization (when non-Han Chinese societies come under Han influence; historically Korea, Vietnam and Taiwan) of religion is not enough: any religion, no matter how sinicized, is incompatible with membership of the Communist Party. An article in the newsletter of the Party's Central Commission for Discipline Inspection claims that, because of 'the founding ideological principle that Communist Party members cannot be religious', Party members don't enjoy any right to religious freedom: 'Chinese citizens have the freedom of religious belief, but Communist Party members aren't the same as regular citizens; they are fighters in the vanguard for a communist consciousness.'[25] But how does this exclusion of believers from the Party help religious freedom? Marx's analysis of the political *imbroglio* of the French revolution of 1848, touched on in the previous chapter, comes to mind again. The ruling Party of Order was the coalition of the two royalist wings, the Bourbons and the Orleanists. The two parties were, by definition, unable to find a common denominator at the level of royalism, since one cannot be a royalist in general, one has to support a particular royal house, so the only way for the two to unite was under the banner of the 'anonymous kingdom of the Republic' – in other words, the only way to be a royalist in general is to be a republican.[26] The same holds true for religion: one cannot be religious in general, one can only believe in some god(s) to the detriment of others, and the failure of all the efforts to unite religions proves that the only way to be religious in general is under the banner of the 'anonymous religion of atheism'. And, effectively, only an atheist regime can guarantee religious tolerance: the moment this neutral atheist frame disappears, factional struggle among different religions has to emerge. This is why, although fundamentalist Islamists attack the godless West, the greatest struggle goes on among them (ISIS focuses on killing Shia Muslims). There is, however, a much deeper fear at work in this forbidding of religious belief for CCP members:

> It would have been best for the Chinese Communist Party if its members were not to believe in anything, not even in communism, since numerous party members joined some of the churches (most of them the Protestant one) precisely because of their disappointment at how even the smallest trace of their communist ideals have disappeared from contemporary Chinese politics.[27]

In short, the biggest opposition to the Chinese leadership today are truly convinced communists, a group composed of old, mostly retired, Party cadres who feel betrayed by the unbridled capitalist corruption, and of the proletarian losers of the 'Chinese miracle', farmers who have lost their land, workers who have lost their jobs and wander around in search of the means of survival, workers exploited in Foxconn-like companies, all those who have suffered injustices and humiliations and have no one to turn to. They often participate in mass protests wearing posters with Mao quotes, and one can imagine how potentially explosive such a combination of experienced cadres and the poor who have nothing to lose is. China is not a stable country with an authoritarian regime guaranteeing harmony and thus keeping under control the capitalist dynamics: every year, thousands, tens of thousands even, of chaotic rebellions of workers, farmers, minorities, etc., have to be squashed by the police and the army. No wonder the official propaganda obsessively insists on the motif of the harmonious society: this very insistence bears witness to the opposite, to the threat of chaos and disorder. That is to say, one should apply here the basic rule of the Stalinist hermeneutics: since official media do not openly report on troubles, the most reliable way to detect them is to search for excessive positives in the state propaganda – the more harmony is celebrated, the more chaos and antagonisms there should be.

It is only against this background that one can understand the religious politics of the CCP: the fear of belief is effectively the fear of *communist* 'belief', the fear of those who remain faithful to the universal emancipatory message of communism. Significantly, one looks in vain in the ongoing ideological campaign for any mention of this basic class antagonism that is erupting daily in workers' protests. There is no talk about the threat of 'proletarian communism' – all the fury is directed against the foreign enemy:

> Certain countries in the West advertise their own values as 'universal values', and claim that their interpretations of freedom, democracy, and human rights are the standard by which all others must be measured. They spare no expense when it comes to hawking their goods and peddling their wares to every corner of the planet, and stir up 'colour revolutions' both before and behind the curtain. Their goal is to infiltrate, break down, and overthrow other regimes. At home and abroad certain enemy forces make use of the term 'universal values' to smear the Chinese Communist Party, socialism with Chinese

characteristics, and China's mainstream ideology. They scheme to use Western value systems to change China, with the goal of letting Chinese people renounce the Chinese Communist Party's leadership and socialism with Chinese characteristics, and allow China to once again become a colony of some developed capitalist country.[28]

There are some true points in the quoted passage, but they function as particular truths covering up a global lie. It is of course true that one cannot and should not naively trust the 'universal values' of freedom, democracy and human rights promoted by Western powers, that their universality is a false one, hiding a specific ideological bias. However, if Western universal values are false, is it enough to oppose them with a particular way of life like China's Confucian 'mainstream ideology'? Don't we need a different universalism, a different project of universal emancipation? The ultimate irony here is that 'socialism with Chinese characteristics' effectively means *socialism with a market economy (with capitalist characteristics)*, i.e., a socialism that fully integrates China into the global market. The universality of global capitalism is left intact – it is silently accepted as the only possible frame, and the project of Confucian harmony is mobilized only in order to keep under control the antagonisms that come from global capitalist dynamics. Mao repeatedly said that China can only progress if it moves away from Confucianism (and one should bear in mind the ambiguity of anti-Confucianism: it stands for legalist state terror but also for egalitarianism, anti-hierarchy, and revolutionary change – democracy and terror overlap in destroying traditional communal hierarchies). But do the last years not prove him wrong? Is the recent state-sponsored triumphant return of Confucianism not precisely the predominant ideological form of the ongoing wild capitalist development? Superficially, this is true, but at a deeper level, it isn't, since today's state-sponsored Confucianism is also a reactive formation, an attempt to control and regulate an explosive dynamic totally foreign to it.

All that remains of socialism are the Confucian five colours that should enable the Party to keep in check the antagonisms engendered by capitalist globalization. Such a socialism with national colours – a national socialism – is a socialism whose social horizon is the patriotic promotion of one's own nation, and the immanent antagonisms generated by capitalist development are projected on to a foreign enemy that poses a threat to social harmony. What the CCP aims at in its patriotic propaganda, when it talks about 'socialism with Chinese characteristics', is yet another version of 'alternative modernity': *capitalism without class struggle.*

If what goes on in China today can be characterized as 'capitalist socialism', what, then, to do with fundamentalist movements like Boko Haram? From the perspective of a traditional communal life, women's education is a key moment in the devastating effect of Western modernization: it 'liberates' women from family ties and trains them for becoming a part of the Third World cheap labour force. The struggle against women's education would thus seem to be a new form of what Marx and Engels, in *The Communist Manifesto*, called 'reactionary (feudal) socialism', the rejection of capitalist modernity on behalf of traditional forms of communal life. However, on a closer look, we can clearly see the limitation of applying this concept here: whatever Boko Haram is, it does not practise a return to pre-modern communal life, since it is (in its organizational form) an extremely modern organization that brutally imposes its universal model on traditional communal life in the territory it occupies. Boko Haram is run like a modern centralized terrorist/revolutionary organization, with leaders exerting total control, not as a tribal network where paternal chiefs meet to deliberate and decide on communal matters. It is thoroughly internationalist: it pursues a universal model, ignoring particular ways of life or particular ethnic identities. In short, Boko Haram is itself a form of perverted modernization: it obliterates traditional communal forms of life even more brutally than Western capitalist modernization.

What this means is that we should reject not only all manifestations of 'alternative modernity' (which amount to a 'capitalism without capitalism', without its destructive aspect), but also all attempts to rely on particular traditional life-worlds (local cultures) as potential 'sites of resistance' against global capitalism. The only path to freedom leads through the zero-point of the brutal loss of roots, i.e., the bringing to an end the disintegration of traditional ties set in motion by capitalism. When capitalism relies on traditional cultural roots it tries to contain its own destructive force.

ATHEISM, WHAT KIND OF ATHEISM?

The ambiguous attitude towards religion in modern China (it is tolerated, supported even, as an instrument of social stability and harmony, but nonetheless kept at a distance from the power structure proper) is far from being a Chinese local characteristic – we find its counterpart in the troubles with religion in the developed West. While a decade or two ago atheism became an acceptable option for a large part of the US public – we even find in some bookshops special shelves for 'atheism' – religion is more than persisting.

Richard Dawkins and Sam Harris recently dismissed 'regressive Leftists' who, while exposing to their scathing criticism all our sacred cows, from democracy to Christianity, from human rights to individual freedom, weirdly exempt Islam from this critique: even a soft attack on Islam is immediately rejected as 'Islamophobia', as intolerance towards another culture, as a brutal display of Western cultural imperialism. While there is a (very limited) point in this position, one should counter it with noticing how even the most ruthless rejections of religious faith are often secretly biased with regard to religion. For example, there is a deep necessity, not just a personal idiosyncrasy, in the fact that Sam Harris ends his scathing critique of religious faith (*The End of Faith*) with the anti-materialist concession (elaborated by David Chalmers) that consciousness may be a rudimentary phenomenon irreducible to material processes; plus he is quick to concede two exceptions to his overall condemnation of religion. First, he praises spiritual mysticism – spiritual experiences are a fact that should be closely studied. 'Mysticism is a rational experience. Religion is not.'[29] Second, a closer looks also renders visible Harris's covert Jewish bias:

> Judaism is a far less fertile source of militant extremism. Jews tend not to draw their identity as Jews exclusively from the contents of their beliefs about God. It is possible, for instance, to be a practising

Jew who does *not* believe in God. The same cannot be said for Christianity and Islam.[30]

In fact, the same goes for the majority of Christians today; and Islam even recognizes a distinction between private thoughts and public acts, and fully protects the private domain. As for how not-believing effectively functions, an interesting accident took place in New York in June 2015, when gay groups were publicly celebrating their great victory (the federal legalization of gay marriages), and some of their opponents organized counter-demonstrations. The Orthodox Jews of the Jewish Political Action Committee hired Mexican labourers to dress up as Jews and do the protesting for them, bearing signs that read things like 'Judaism prohibits homosexuality' and 'God Created Adam and Eve NOT Adam and Steve'. Heshie Freed, the group's representative, justified this act by claiming that the Mexicans were filling in for the Jews to protect them from moral corruption: 'The rabbis said that the yeshiva boys shouldn't come out for this because of what they would see at the parade.' As an acerbic critic commented, the Jewish boys were probably 'down in the street rockin' out with their cocks out' in the parade.[31] A wonderful new and unexpected vision of inter-passivity: I hire others to protest for me while I participate in the very thing I protest against through others.

Harris relies on an all too primitive notion of belief – as if 'believing' simply means 'taking (it) to be factually true'. What lurks in the background here is the standard Jewish argument for the unique character of Judaism: only Judaism keeps open the enigma of the Other, it doesn't obfuscate the anxiety when we encounter God – 'What does he want from us?' Christianity covers up this abyss by providing a soothing answer: God loves us, we can be sure of his care and mercy. We should imagine an interrogation of Christ similar to the final dialogue in Wilder's *Some Like It Hot*: 'You are a loser crucified by the establishment!' 'But I accepted my death for your benefit.' 'You cannot really help us!' 'But you have all my sympathy in your suffering.' 'What this means is that you are not a real God!' 'Well, nobody's perfect . . .' And even Christ's sympathy for us, the sinners, should not be sentimentalized – as for Christ forgiving us our sins, remember what Ford Maddox Ford wrote in *Parade's*

End: the true cruelty is to forgive someone without mercy. This is how Christ does it: just brutally forgiving us, with no sentimentality, no place for expressions of gratitude.

At the most basic level, Harris dismisses religious faith as epistemological nonsense out of sync with our present knowledge of the world: every religion involves accepting as truth statements that are clearly incompatible with what we know, i.e., statements that obviously could only have been generated in a society much more primitive than ours. When engaging in religious acts, we are thus obviously ready to suspend our normal standards of veracity: who, when dealing with everyday reality, would accept stories about water changing into wine, about birth without impregnation, etc.? In this discrepancy, Harris sees the main danger for the survival of humanity: the prospect of nuclear weapons in the hands of Muslim fundamentalists puts the means of our destruction at the disposal of people who mentally belong to the fourteenth century. The worst, for Harris, is the enlightened, 'tolerant' view that tells us that, in the name of religious freedom, we should not prevent others displaying any beliefs they want, and the concomitant claim that terrorist fundamentalism is a terrible perversion of the great authentic religions. Harris asks here the pertinent question: why then do we have only Muslim (and, to a smaller extent, Hindu) terrorists? The suffering of the Tibetans is no less terrible than the plight of Palestinians, for example, and yet there are no Tibetan terrorists . . . But is this true? Have we not encountered in the last decades alone Buddhist terror in (among other countries) Sri Lanka, Thailand and, in anti-Islamic form, in Burma/Myanmar?

There is another twist to be added to this story. When Harris writes, 'It is possible, for instance, to be a practising Jew who does *not* believe in God,' he fails to mention how the non-believer can nonetheless draw all practical consequences from this belief – for example, you might not believe in God yet nonetheless believe that God gave your people the land they claim as theirs:

> Deputy Foreign Minister Tzipi Hotovely told new members of the foreign ministry staff in a speech that Israel should no longer speak in veiled terms about possessing the land because God gave it to the

Jews. [Hotovely] quoted a medieval Jewish rabbi, Rashi, who wrote about the creation of the world. In that account, the rabbi suggested: 'For if the nations of the world should say to Israel, "You are robbers, for you conquered by force the lands of the seven nations [of Canaan]," they will reply, "The entire earth belongs to the Holy One, blessed be He; He created it (this we learn from the story of the Creation) and gave it to whomever He deemed proper when He wished. He gave it to them, and when He wished, He took it away from them and gave it to us."' According to Hotovely, Israel should be following the same policy today because it is time to 'tell the world we're right – and smart'.[32]

If such a direct legitimization of one's claim to land by reference to God's will is not religious fundamentalism, then one should wonder if this term has any meaning at all . . . However, one should note here the openly cynical twist introduced by the concluding predicate: 'we're right – and smart'. We're right in claiming God gave us this land, and smart in using this religious justification even though we know it's nonsense. The irony reaches its peak when we bear in mind that, according to some surveys, Israel is the most atheist state in the world (more than 60 per cent of Jews in Israel don't believe in God).

Unfortunately, the Israeli government has been sucked deeper and deeper into this mire. In his speech to the World Zionist Congress on 21 October 2015 in Jerusalem, Binyamin Netanyahu suggested that Hitler had wanted only to expel Jews, and that it was Haj Amin al-Husseini, the Palestinian grand mufti of Jerusalem, who somehow persuaded him instead to kill them. Netanyahu then described a supposed meeting between Haj Amin al-Husseini and Hitler in November 1941: 'Hitler didn't want to exterminate the Jews at the time; he wanted to expel the Jews. And Haj Amin al-Husseini went to Hitler and said: "If you expel them, they'll all come here [to Palestine]."' According to Netanyahu, Hitler then asked: 'What should I do with them?' and the mufti replied: 'Burn them.' Many leading Israeli Holocaust researchers immediately problematized these statements, pointing out that mass killings of Jews by SS mobile units were already under way when the two men met. Reacting to Netanyahu's comments, the opposition leader Isaac Herzog wrote: 'This is a dangerous historical distortion and I demand Netanyahu correct it immediately as it minimizes the Holocaust, Nazism and . . . Hitler's part in our people's terrible disaster.' He added that Netanyahu's remarks played into the hands of Holocaust deniers. The Zionist Union MP Itzik Shmuli called on Netanyahu to apologize to Holocaust victims: 'This is a great shame, a prime minister of the Jewish state at the service of Holocaust-deniers – this is a first.' Denouncing Netanyahu's comments, Erekat, the chief Palestinian peace negotiator, wrote: 'It is a sad day in history when the leader of the Israeli government hates his neighbour so much so that he is willing to absolve the most notorious war criminal in history, Adolf Hitler, of the murder of 6 million Jews during the Holocaust.' A spokesman for Angela Merkel also rejected Netanyahu's framing: 'All Germans know the history of the murderous race mania of the Nazis that led to the break with civilization that was the Holocaust. I see no reason to change our view of history in any way. We know that responsibility for this crime against humanity is German and very much our own.'[33]

We should be fully aware what such statements by Netanyahu mean: they are a clear sign of the regression of our public space. Things that were till now confined to the obscure underworld of racist obscenities are gaining a foothold in official discourse.

There is nonetheless one good thing about religious fundamentalisms: they also cannot tolerate *each other*, i.e., there is no danger of the 'united front' of Christian and Muslim fundamentalists in Europe (if one disregards minor events like their shared effort to criminalize 'disrespectful' writing about religion as hate speech). The European Muslim community confronts a paradoxical predicament: the only political force that does not reduce them to second-class citizens and allows them the space to deploy their religious identity are the 'godless' atheist liberals, while those who are closest to their religious social practice, their Christian mirror-image, are their greatest political enemies. The paradox is that not those who first published the Mohammed caricatures (Danish islamophobic conservatives) but those who, out of solidarity with freedom of expression, reprinted the caricatures (Leftists all around Europe), are their only true allies.

There is a kind of poetic justice in the fact that the all-Muslim outcry against godless Denmark was immediately followed by heightened violence between Sunnis and Shiites, the two Muslim factions in Iraq. The lesson of all totalitarianisms is writ large here: the fight against the external enemy sooner or later always turns into the fight against the inner enemy.

After all the recent arguments proclaiming the 'post-secular' return of the religious, the limits of disenchantment and the need to rediscover the sacred, perhaps what we truly need is a dose of good old atheism. One of the common ideas today is that reckless and cynical Western libertarians must learn their lesson: here are the limits of secular disenchantment. But is this really the lesson to be learned from the mob's killing, looting and burning on behalf of religion? For a long time, we have been told that, without religion, we are merely egotistical animals fighting for our lot, our only morality that of the wolf-pack, and that only religion can elevate us to a higher spiritual level. Today, as religion emerges as the main source of murderous violence around the world, one grows tired of the constant assurances that Christian, Muslim or Hindu fundamentalists are only abusing and perverting the noble spiritual message of their creed. Isn't it time to restore the dignity of atheism, perhaps our only chance of peace? As a rule, where religiously inspired violence is concerned, we put the blame on violence itself: it is the violent political agent who 'misuses' a noble religion, so the goal becomes to retrieve the authentic core of a religion from its political instrumentalization. What, however, if one should take the risk of inverting this relationship? What if what appears as a moderating force, compelling us to control our violence, is its secret instigator? Religious ideologists usually claim that, true or not, religion makes some otherwise bad people do good things; from today's experience, one should rather stick to Steve Weinberg's claim that, while, with or without religion, good people can do good things and bad people bad things, only religion can make good people do bad things.

WHITHER ZIONISM?

In July 2008, the Viennese daily *Die Presse* published a caricature of two stocky Nazi-looking Austrians, one of them holding in his hands a newspaper and commenting to his friend: 'Here you can see again how a totally justified anti-Semitism is being misused for a cheap critique of Israel!' This joke turns around the standard Zionist argument against the critics of the policies of the State of Israel: like every other state, the State of Israel can and should be judged and eventually criticized, but the critics of Israel misuse the justified critique of Israeli policy for anti-Semitic purposes. When today's Christian fundamentalist supporters of Israel reject Leftist critiques of Israeli policies, is their implicit line of argumentation not uncannily close to the caricature from *Die Presse*? Remember Anders Breivik, the Norwegian anti-immigrant mass murderer: he is anti-Semitic, but pro-Israel, since Israel is the first defence line against Muslim expansion – he even wants to see the Jerusalem Temple rebuilt. His view is that Jews are OK as long as there aren't too many of them – or, as he wrote in his 'Manifesto':

> There is no Jewish problem in Western Europe (with the exception of the UK and France), as we only have 1 million in Western Europe, whereas 800,000 out of these 1 million live in France and the UK. The US, on the other hand, with more than 6 million Jews (600 per cent more than Europe) actually has a considerable Jewish problem.

His figure thus realizes the ultimate paradox of a Zionist anti-Semite – and we find the traces of this weird stance more often than one would expect. Reinhardt Heydrich himself, the mastermind of the Holocaust, wrote in 1935:

> We must separate the Jews into two categories, the Zionists and the partisans of assimilation. The Zionists profess a strictly racial concept and, through emigration to Palestine, they help to build their own Jewish State [. . .] our good wishes and our official goodwill go with them.[34]

On his visit to France to commemorate the victims of the recent Paris killings, Netanyahu issued a call to France's Jewish community (which is the largest in Europe) to move to Israel for safety reasons. Even before his departure for Paris, Netanyahu announced that he planned to tell French Jews that they would be 'welcomed with open arms' in Israel. The headline in the main Polish daily *Gazeta wyborsza* tells it all: 'Israel wants France without Jews' . . . so do the French anti-Semites, one might add. How come we are now back at the starting place? The constitution of the State of Israel was, from the standpoint of Europe, the realized 'final solution' of the Jewish problem (getting rid of the Jews) entertained by the Nazis themselves. That is to say, was the State of Israel not, to turn Clausewitz around, the continuation of the war against Jews by other (political) means? Is this not the 'stain of injustice' that pertains to Israel?

26 September 1937 is a date anyone interested in the history of anti-Semitism should remember: on that day, Adolf Eichmann and his assistant boarded a train in Berlin in order to visit Palestine. Heydrich himself had given Eichmann permission to accept the invitation of Feivel Polkes, a leading member of Hagannah (the Zionist secret organization), to visit Tel Aviv and discuss there the coordination of Nazi and Zionist organizations to facilitate the emigration of Jews to Palestine. Both the Germans and the Zionists wanted as many Jews as possible to move to Palestine: Germans preferred them out of Western Europe, and Zionists themselves wanted the Jews in Palestine to outnumber the Arabs as fast as possible. (The visit failed because, owing to some violent unrest, the British blocked access to Palestine; but Eichmann and Polkes did meet days later in Cairo and discussed the coordination of activities.)[35] Is this weird incident not the supreme example of the Nazis and the radical Zionists sharing a common interest – in both cases, the purpose was a kind of 'ethnic cleansing', i.e., to change violently the ratio of ethnic groups in the population? (Incidentally, one should state clearly and unambiguously that, from the Jewish side, this deal with the Nazis is seen as an irreproachable act done in a desperate situation.)

Those whose memory extends at least a couple of decades back cannot avoid noticing how the entire frame of argumentation of those who defend Israeli policies towards Palestinians is changing. Till the late 1950s, Jewish and Israeli leaders were very honest about the fact that they have no full right to Palestine, and they even proudly declared their violent actions, even when they were described as 'terrorist' ones. Imagine we were to read the following statement in today's media:

> Our enemies called us terrorists ... People who were neither our friends nor our enemies ... also used this Latin name ... And yet, we were not terrorists ... The historical and linguistic origins of the political term 'terror' prove that it cannot be applied to a revolutionary war of liberation ... Fighters for freedom must arm; otherwise they would be crushed overnight ... What has a struggle for the dignity of man, against oppression and subjugation, to do with 'terrorism?'

One would automatically attribute this to an Islamic terrorist group and condemn it. However, the author of these words is none other than Menachem Begin, in the years when the Hagannah was fighting the British forces in Palestine.[36] It is almost attractive to see the first-generation Israeli leaders openly confessing the fact that their claims to the land of Palestine cannot be grounded in universal justice, that we are dealing with a simple war of conquest between two groups between whom no mediation is possible. Here is what David Ben-Gurion, Israel's first prime minister, wrote:

> Everyone can see the weight of the problems in the relations between Arabs and Jews. But no one sees that there is no solution to these problems. There is no solution! Here is an abyss, and nothing can link its two sides ... We as a people want this land to be ours; the Arabs as a people want this land to be theirs.'[37]

The problem with this statement today is clear: such an exemption of ethnic conflicts for land from moral considerations is simply no longer acceptable. Arthur Koestler, the great anti-communist convert, proposed a profound insight: 'If power corrupts, the reverse is also true; persecution corrupts the victims, though perhaps in subtler and more tragic ways.'

This is the fatal flaw in the one strong argument for the creation of a Jewish nation-state after the Holocaust: in creating their own state, the Jews would overcome the situation of being delivered up to the mercy of the diaspora states and the tolerance or intolerance of their nation's majority. Although this line of argument is different from the religious one, it has to rely on religious tradition to justify the geographic location of the new state. Otherwise, one finds oneself in the situation of the old joke about a madman looking for his lost wallet under the street light, and not in the dark corner where he has lost it, because one sees better under the light: because it was easier, the Jews took land from the Palestinians and not from those who caused them so much suffering and thus owed them a reparation.

Some time in the 1960s, and especially after the 1967 war, a new formula emerged: 'peace for land' (the return to the borders of the pre-1967 Israel in exchange for full Arab recognition of Israel) and the two-state solution (an independent Palestinian state on the West Bank and in Gaza). However, this solution, although officially endorsed by the UN, USA and Israel, was *de facto* gradually abandoned. What is replacing it is more and more openly signalled by big media. Caroline B. Glick (the author of *The Israeli Solution: A One-State Plan for Peace in the Middle East*) claimed in a *New York Times* article entitled 'There Should Be No Palestinian State' that those who propose to recognize Palestine as a state

know that in recognizing 'Palestine' they are not helping the cause of peace. They are advancing Israel's ruin. If they were even remotely interested in freedom and peace, the Europeans would be doing the opposite. They would be working to strengthen and expand Israel, the only stable zone of freedom and peace in the region. They would abandon the phony two-state solution, which [. . .] is merely double-speak for seeking Israel's destruction and its replacement with a terror state.

With strategic blindness and moral depravity now serving as the twin guideposts for European policy toward Israel, Israel and its supporters must tell the truth about the push to recognize 'Palestine'. It isn't about peace or justice. It's about hating Israel and assisting those who most actively seek its obliteration.[38]

What was (and still is) the official international policy is now openly denounced as a recipe for Israel's ruin. And it is clear that, far from standing for an extremist minority view, this stance just renders explicit the strategic orientation of the gradual colonization of the West Bank in the last decades: the disposition of new settlements (with a large number of them in the east, close to the Jordanian border) makes it clear that a West Bank Palestinian state is out of the question. (In some of his latest statements, Netanyahu himself has openly rejected the idea of an independent Palestinian state.) Furthermore, one cannot but note the irony of how, the stronger Israel gets, the more it presents itself as threatened. This rewriting of the past reached its peak in December 2016, when Benjamin Netanyahu warned New Zealand that the UN resolution it was co-sponsoring was a 'declaration of war' against Israel.[39] But this resolution (which called for Israel to stop building settlements on occupied Palestinian land, including East Jerusalem, declaring the settlements 'illegal') merely re-stated the old international position. So what was till now common policy is now an act of war. . .

The same shift – the expansion of the criteria of what counts as anti-Semitism – is also discernible in other domains. Here is what happened when the Metropolitan Opera recently staged again John Adams's *The Death of Klinghoffer*. At the first performance,

> men and women in evening attire walked through a maze of police barricades, while protesters shouted 'Shame!' and 'Terror is not art!' One demonstrator held aloft a white handkerchief splattered with red. Others, in wheelchairs set up for the occasion, lined Columbus Avenue. Political figures, including former Mayor Rudolph W. Giuliani, joined a rally, several hundred strong at Lincoln Center, to denounce an opera that has become the object of a charged debate about art, anti-Semitism and politics. *Klinghoffer*, considered a masterpiece by some critics, has long aroused passions, simply because of its subject matter: the murder of Leon Klinghoffer, an American Jewish passenger in a wheelchair, by members of the Palestine Liberation Front during the 1985 hijacking of the *Achille Lauro* cruise ship. One protester at the rally, Hilary Barr, 55, a pediatric nurse from Westchester County, said she believed the opera made excuses for terrorism. 'By putting this on a stage in the middle of Manhattan, the message is, "Go out, murder someone, be a terrorist and we'll write a play about you," she said.[40]

How come this opera, which was mostly accepted without problems at its premiere, is now denounced as anti-Semitic and pro-
terrorist? Another sign of the same shift: in a recent interview,
activist Ayan Hirsi Ali claimed that Israeli Prime Minister Bibi
Netanyahu should be awarded the Nobel Peace Prize for waging
the ongoing military campaign by the IDF against Hamas militants in Gaza. Asked whom she admired, Ali (who dismisses Islam
as a 'nihilistic cult of death') included Netanyahu on her list, saying that she admires him 'because he is under so much pressure,
from so many sources, and yet he does what is best for the people
of Israel, he does his duty [. . .] I really think he should get the Nobel
Peace Prize [. . .] In a fair world he would get it.'[41] Instead of dismissing this claim as ridiculous, we should detect cruel irony in its
partial truth: of course Israel is sincere in its striving for peace –
occupiers of a country by definition want peace in the region they
occupy . . . The real question is thus: is Israeli presence on the West
Bank an occupation, and is it legal for the inhabitants to resist
it, and with arms? In order to defend the right of Israel to hold
the West Bank, Jon Voight recently attacked Javier Bardem and
Penelope Cruz for their critique of the IDF bombing of Gaza – the
two of them

> are obviously ignorant of the whole story of Israel's birth, when in
> 1948 the Jewish people were offered by the UN a portion of the land
> originally set aside for them in 1921, and the Arab Palestinians were
> offered the other half.[42]

But who is here really ignorant? The passive form 'set aside'
obfuscates the key question: by whom? Voight is, of course, making an oblique reference to the Balfour declaration – a colonial
master (the British foreign secretary) promising to others land that
does not belong to his country. (Not to mention the fact that
Voight makes it appear as if all of it was 'set aside' for the Jewish
people who then graciously accepted only the half.) Plus Voight presents Israel as a peace-loving nation which merely defended itself
when attacked – but what about the 1956 Israeli occupation of the
entire Sinai peninsula (together with the British–French occupation

of the canal zone after its nationalization by Nasser)? Even the US condemned this act as an aggression and pressured Israel into withdrawal.

As for the claim that Jews have a historical right to the land of Israel since it was given to them by God – how? The Old Testament describes it in terms of ethnic cleansing. After their liberation from slavery in Egypt, the Israelites arrived on the edge of the Promised Land, where God then commanded them to destroy totally the people occupying these regions (the Canaanites): the Israelites were to 'save alive nothing that breatheth' (Deuteronomy 20:16). The book of Joshua records the carrying out of this command: 'they utterly destroyed all that was in the city, both man and woman, young and old, and ox and sheep, and ass, with the edge of the sword' (6:21). Several chapters later, we read that Joshua 'left none remaining, but utterly destroyed all that breathed, as the Lord God of Israel commanded' (10:40; 11:14). The text mentions city after city where Joshua, at God's command, puts every inhabitant to the sword, totally destroying the inhabitants and leaving no survivors (10:28, 30, 33, 37, 39, 40; 11:8). Does this mean that Jews are somehow guilty of an original act of ethnic cleansing? Absolutely not: in ancient (and not so ancient) times, more or less *all* religious and ethnic groups functioned like this, Buddhist ones included.[43] What one should do is not only unambiguously reject the direct use of these passages as a legitimization of contemporary politics; one should also not just ignore them, on the grounds that they are not essential to the religious edifice in question but merely secondary points conditioned by specific historical circumstances. The lesson is simply that every legitimization of a claim to land by reference to some mythic past should be rejected. In order to resolve (or contain, at least) the Israeli–Palestinian conflict, we should not dwell in the ancient past – we should, on the contrary, forget the past (which is in any case constantly reinvented to justify present actions). Another, even more crucial, lesson is that the Jewish people themselves will ultimately pay the price for the politics of ethnic fundamentalism that brings them uncannily close to anti-Semitic conservatism. It will push Jews towards becoming just another ethnic group craving for their particular *Blut und Boden*.

ISLAMOCENTRISM? NO, THANKS!

One should also submit to critical analysis the 'anti-eurocentrist' idea that Western modernity derives from the misapprehension of the insights of Muslim philosophy. There are many attempts to demonstrate this lineage – suffice it to mention Rasheed Araeen who, in response to the Western vision of Christianity as the peak of civilization, turns the cards around and elevates Islam to the peak of human history, proposing a progressive triad of Judaism, Christianity and Islam (note how he remains within the field of the 'religions of the book', dismissing all other religions as inferior) – an exemplary case of how critics of eurocentrism easily adopt the same stance they criticize their opponents for. In what, then, is this superiority of Islam grounded? To cut a long story slightly shorter, Rasheen proposes a rather simple progressive view of the evolution of human consciousness – here are some passages from his 'Language of Human Consciousness':[44]

Humanity's first self-awareness emerged from the consciousness which was primitive. It was the experience of the things seen by the EYE which created the first or primitive phase of consciousness, leading to the means by which humans began to express themselves through the images we can now see in the caves. This was the first expression of human consciousness, considered now as the first form of art, which then by passing through Mesopotamia, Egypt, Greece and the Romans, and developing into a language of art in which the human body or figure was central, became the basis of Christian art, ultimately becoming the basis of what was seen and imposed upon the world by the West as the most advanced civilization in which humanity's ultimate fulfilment and salvation were supposed to have lied.

Hegel also adopts this trajectory for his historical dialectic, involving a worldview which relegates other cultures or civilizations to an inferior or secondary status. In his view, they do not fully possess what he calls *self-consciousness*; which in fact is based on the sensuousness of the naked human body and its expression in art, which Hegel discovered in the beauty of Greek sculpture. He then historicizes it as the pinnacle of art's greatest achievement. Hegel's aesthetics

is based on the sensuousness of form, realized specifically from looking at and experiencing the human body, with the result Hegel is
unable to see any significance in what goes beyond and defies the
images produced by the primitive consciousness; and which in fact
leads him to his frivolous view about 'the ban on graven images' in
Islam. He is thus unable to understand that Islam had emerged in
opposition and defiance of what demanded the worship of these
images, and therefore it did not need the graven images for its representation. In fact, the concept of the Divine in Islam has no physical
form and it therefore cannot be represented through worldly images,
let alone the graven images which are perceived by and looked at by
the eye. It was therefore necessary for Islam to go beyond and confront what was and have remained trapped in the darkness of the
primitive consciousness.

It was actually not the question of ban on graven images which was
and is important, but the *liberation* of consciousness from these
images – a historically significant difference which Hegel failed to
grasp and recognize – which then enabled the Muslim mind to go
beyond the primitive consciousness, or what Lacan calls 'the mirror
stage', and penetrate the invisibility of things. From this had actually
emerged a form of geometry in art, whose complex multi-layered configurations created by the Arab/Muslim artists around more than a
thousand years ago had enabled humanity to see and think about
what was beyond the visible, what the consciousness of the eye could
not see or perceive, and offered not only an enlightened view of the
Divine but also what was historically an advance concept and understanding of the whole cosmos.

The first thing one should note here is that Araeen is offering an
utterly simplified scheme of human history, which runs in a direct
line from the 'primitive' fascination by corporeal sensual forms to
the contemporary society of the spectacle, similar to Adorno and
Horkheimer's dialectics of enlightenment, which runs in a direct line
from 'primitive' magic thought to contemporary technological
manipulation. In both cases, contemporary society (the administered
world, the society of spectacle) appears as the extreme point bringing
out the destructive potential that was latent at the very beginning.

The second thing to be noted is that Araeen's thesis on the liberation of consciousness from 'graven images' in Islam is strangely inconsistent. A true liberation would not have to rely on prohibition, it would not be traumatized by these images since it would entertain towards them a calm indifference. (Incidentally, this is why modernist abstract painting is thoroughly different from the abstract configuration of forms in the Islamic art praised by Araeen – modernist art is not the result of a prohibitive function.) The consequences of this inconsistency become apparent when Araeen applies his general principles to a concrete case, the murder of Qandeel Baloch by her brother Muhammad Waseem on 15 July 2016, of which Araeen says that it 'was indeed a sort of "honour killing", but what triggered this killing was not merely the moral codes of the tribe she came from whose violation can often lead to "honour killing"'. Here is his line of thought:

The role of mass-media, particularly of the TV, in Pakistan is enormous, particularly in defining and creating what is considered to be desirable modern life; and this role has now become supplemented by the so-called 'Social Media' [. . .] It was clear to Qandeel what she had to do to become famous and successful. She in fact called herself 'Pakistani Kim Kardashian', and justified it by also calling herself 'a modern feminist'. But when she presented herself in the Social Media, almost semi-naked, all hell broke loose. It wasn't so much a problem for the Pakistani public, as this kind of media spectacle is quite common now in Pakistan, as elsewhere in most of the Muslim world. It's in fact now considered to be an essential part of the modernity of the urban life of the bourgeoisie in Pakistan, which adopts and celebrates uncritically whatever comes from the West. But for a traditional Baloch family not everything was acceptable, as Qandeel had crossed the line.

A brief historical trajectory of Western art, from its beginning when images were created for worship and then their secularisation, their evolution first into photography and then cinema, and eventually their appearance in the private space of almost every home, and now their proliferation through the Social Media, can explain the connection, not only between the past and the present but also their underpinning, philosophically (Hegel, Clark, Gombrich . . .), based on what was conceived to be representable visually through a human form, which would then appear to the eye for worship or admiration. (Are the media images of celebrities not almost worshipped by the masses?)

[. . .] although this West's mission was largely accepted by the colonised world, including the Muslim world, there was also resentment, often hidden, against it, and in fact, in many cases an open revolt [. . .] this mission [. . .] has now evolved globally into the Media spectacles, particularly of TV and its extension into the Social Media, and its impact particularly on the Muslim world.

If I have been beating around the bush, let me say now what I actually wanted to say, clearly and conclusively. I have been trying to make a connection between the killing of Qandeel by her brother and what the ISIS is doing. I can in fact argue that the killing of Qandeel is the metaphor for the brutal violence of ISIS and its followers. However, the actual causes in both cases are not what they are generally perceived to be, particularly by the (Western) mass media and its propaganda against Islam. The issue here is not just the misrepresentation of Islam, but what deceives the masses, and what thus covers up the enormous violence of the dominant Western system, not against only Muslims but all people.

The conclusion is clear: while Araeen of course rejects the brutal violence of honour killings and of ISIS, he sees in it a (wrong and misdirected, true) reaction to the much more brutal violence of the dominant Western system and its regime of images of the human body, which culminates in the contemporary global culture of the spectacle, a culture that is inherently pornographic. This violence is properly metaphysical: it enslaves human beings and diverts them from the pursuit of spirituality. If we leave aside the question of to what extent the prohibition of images is itself an extremely violent gesture, one cannot avoid noting that the ultimate body 'image' is that of a naked woman, which is why it should be covered in order to prevent it exerting its fatal attraction on the public. Following Araeen's logic, should we not then say that *all* male violence against women, up to honour killings, is ultimately just a reaction to the more basic violence exerted by the public display of women's bodies?

But is Islamic iconoclasm not a clear case of the Hegelian 'abstract negation': do men not remain forever enslaved by the naked feminine body, unable to resist it? Recall the ridiculous Taliban prohibition of metal heels for women – as if, even if women are entirely covered with cloth, the clicking sound of their heels would still provoke men. The need to keep women veiled implies an *extremely sexualized* universe in which any encounter with a woman is a provocation that a man is unable to resist. Repression has to be so strong because sex itself is so strong – what a society is this in which the click of metal heels can make men explode with lust?

MUSLIM ROOTS OF MODERNITY?

One cannot finish without mentioning a conservative attempt to trace the common roots of the two extremes, Islamic fundamentalism and PC hedonist permissiveness. In the current decades, we are witnessing a revival of aggressive Catholic fundamentalism, which proposes a new global cognitive mapping of our situation. Islamic fundamentalism, with its clear definition of the (subordinate) role of women, and multicultural universalism (inclusive of gender theory and transgender demands which reduce sexual identity to a contingent cultural convention) are considered as two faces of the same coin. Even if they appear radically opposed, they both endeavour to destroy the Christian legacy that forms the core of European identity. This diagnosis is based on a two-level conspiracy theory. Gender theory is conceived as the ultimate offspring of 'cultural Marxism', whose main proponent is the Frankfurt School. The rise of the Frankfurt School followed the defeat of communist revolutions in western and central Europe in the 1920s. Communists came to the conclusion that they lost because they underestimated the tenacity of the basic Christian legacy, so they adopted a change in strategy – before engaging in a new revolutionary attempt, they should patiently work on undermining Christian family life, denouncing the patriarchal family as an instrument of oppression, advocating sexual freedoms, etc. Or, to quote a Slovene right-wing idiot (whose anonymity I should gracefully preserve), today's communist ideology does not survive 'in the orthodox form of Marxism and Leninism but in an essentially more treacherous and thereby dangerous form of the cultural Marxism of the Frankfurt school.' In short, the opposition between Western Marxism and the Stalinist orthodoxy is only apparent, and, according to some conspiracy-theorists, the Frankfurt School was established under the direct orders from the Stalinist Comintern . . .

So, on the other side of the coin, what is the link with Islam? Things get even crazier here in an interesting way. From the conservative Catholic standpoint, communism is the ultimate consequence of the nihilism of modern subjectivity, whose first flag-bearers are Cartesian philosophy and Protestantism; and the ultimate source of modern subjectivity is . . . yes, the misreading of Aristotle by medieval Muslim commentators like Avicenna and Averroes. (Such a view has some foundation: as in the case of the Haiti revolution, Islam can play an unexpected progressive role.[45]) While Christianity (with the exception of some evangelical sects) does not conceive of the scriptures as the direct word of God but as merely inspired by God and, as such, in need of proper interpretation, the Qur'an is for Muslims the direct word of God, to be read literally, with little room for interpretation. Epistemologically, this means that the divine truth is not an abyssal impenetrable Otherness but directly revealed to our mind (in the Qur'an). In other words, we do not have to explore the mystery of reality to gain access to the Absolute: the Absolute is already here for the believers, exempted from the meanderings of external reality. The key point here is that a gap opens up between our mind and external reality, one that persists even when we no longer strive for direct access to the Absolute. In this case, the gap turns into the one that characterizes nominalism, the gap between external reality and the names we give to things in that reality: universal notions are no longer grounded in objective reality (as they are in the Aristotelian ontology of Thomas Aquinas), but are instead free constructions formed on the basis of confused impressions. These universal notions are either contingent (which opens up the way to cultural relativism) or necessary (which opens up the way to Kantian transcendentalism) – in both cases, the gap between our universal notions and external reality is insurmountable.

We can see now how the same gap, the same break with Aristotelian realism, can lead to three different epistemological and ontological positions: (1) dogmatic ontological absolutism of truth (truth is directly accessible to our mind); (2) historical and cultural relativism (truth is a contingent cultural construct); (3) transcendental subjectivism (there is *a priori* necessary universal truth, but it is the truth of a transcendental subject that frames our access to reality, not the truth of reality itself). Furthermore, for an Aristotelian realist, it is easy to establish the logic of the passage from direct absolutism to nominalist relativism: since real knowledge is only possible through a long and arduous inquiry into reality, every direct assertion of absolute truth is ultimately an absolutized subjectivism, the elevation of a contingent construct into the absolute. This is why modernity oscillates between dogmatic objectivism (direct knowledge of objective reality) and subjectivist relativism – even today is our cognitive field not split between 'dogmatic' scientific objectivism (naturalist reductionism) and 'postmodern' cultural relativism?

From this standpoint, the original sin of modernity is the Cartesian primacy of epistemology over ontology: before getting to know reality, one should ascertain the foundation of our knowledge, its methods and its reliability. Such epistemology, which analyses the subject's cognitive capacities independently of objective reality, thus *de facto* functions as subjectivist ontology, grounding (our notion of) objective reality in the way the subject approaches it. Mind is thereby not grounded in reality – it is an external instrument that has a truth of its own. For neo-Thomists, the only way to break out of this circle is to return to Aquinas's realism, where universal notions are features that are immanent to external objective reality, and where the process of knowledge is a long and arduous penetration through particular objects to their universal essences. Sounds familiar? Of course it does: this kind of realism is uncannily close to the classic Soviet dialectical materialism, as was often recognized by many neo-Thomist historians of philosophy like Joseph M. Bochenski,[46] who praises dialectical materialism's realism and rationalism, its basic claim that reality exists outside our mind and that it is knowable, in contrast to subjective-idealist wild speculations or scepticism. He also praises the dialectical-materialist claim that reality is a complex interplay of different levels (mechanical, biological, social, spiritual), against all kinds of reductionist monism.

There is a supreme irony in the fact that the fundamentalist Catholic anti-communist vision relies on a philosophy that comes close to dialectical materialism, the most worthless aspect of orthodox Marxism. But this closeness is not as paradoxical as it may sound: both orientations, dialectical materialism and neo-Thomism, are ultimately traditionalist reactions to modernity. The question to be raised here is what then remains of paradigmatically modern notions like democracy, human rights and freedoms, etc., which are all grounded in modern subjectivity. Can one then imagine a common front of radical Islam and modern subjectivity directed against the alliance of Christian and dialectical-materialist orthodoxies? Yes, we can – but not without a radical transformation of both terms.

THE RETURN OF RELIGION?

In his analysis of today's return of religion as a political force, Boris Buden[47] rejects the predominant interpretation which sees this phenomenon as a regression caused by the failure of modernization. For Buden, religion as a political force is an effect of the post-political disintegration of society, of the dissolution of traditional mechanisms that guaranteed stable communal links: fundamentalist religion is not only political, it is politics itself, i.e. it sustains the space for politics. Even more poignantly, it is no longer just a social phenomenon but the very texture of society, so that in a way society itself becomes a religious phenomenon. It is thus no longer possible to distinguish the purely spiritual aspect of religion from its politicization: in a post-political universe, religion is the predominant space in which antagonistic passions return. What has happened recently in the guise of religious fundamentalism is thus not the return of religion in politics but simply *the return of politics as such.*

Why, then, is Islam the most politicized religion today? Judaism is the religion of genealogy, of matrilineal succession of generations. When, in Christianity, the son dies on the cross, this means that the father also dies (as Hegel was fully aware), and the patriarchal genealogical order as such dies; the Holy Spirit does not fit the family series, it introduces a post-paternal/familial community. In contrast to both Judaism and Christianity, Islam excludes God from the domain of the paternal logic: Allah is not a father, not even a symbolic one – God is neither born nor gives birth to creatures. *There is no place for a Holy Family in Islam.* This is why Islam emphasizes so much the fact that Muhammad himself was an orphan; this is why, in Islam, God intervenes precisely at the moments of the suspension, withdrawal, failure, 'black-out', of the paternal function (when the mother or the child is abandoned or ignored by the biological father). What this means is that God remains thoroughly in the domain of impossible-Real: he is the impossible-Real external to the father, so that there is a 'genealogical desert between man and God'.[48] This was the problem with Islam for Freud, since his entire theory of religion is based on the parallel of God with the father. Even more importantly, this inscribes politics into the very heart of Islam, since the 'genealogical desert' renders impossible the grounding of a community in the structures of parenthood or other blood-links: 'the desert between God and Father is the place where the political institutes itself.'[49] With Islam, it is no longer possible to ground a community, in the mode of *Totem and Taboo*, through the murder of the father and the ensuing guilt bringing brothers together – thence Islam's unexpected actuality. This problem is in the very heart of the (in)famous *umma*, the Muslim 'community of believers'; it accounts for the overlapping of the religious and the political (the community should be grounded directly in God's word), as well as for the fact that Islam is 'at its best' when it grounds the formation of a community 'out of nowhere', in the genealogical desert, as the egalitarian revolutionary fraternity. No wonder Islam succeeds when young men find themselves deprived of a traditional family safety network. This properly political dimension survives in Shia communities much more than in the Sunni majority. Khomeini stated clearly that the foundation of Islam is in politics: 'The religion of Islam is a political religion; it is a religion in which everything is politics, including its acts of devotion and worship.' Here is his most succinct formulation: 'Islam is politics or it is nothing.'[50]

Buden quotes Živko Kastić, a Croat Catholic-nationalist priest who declared that Catholicism is 'a sign that you are not ready to renounce your national and cultural heritage – the integral, traditional Croat being'.[51] What this quote makes clear is that it is no longer a question of belief, of its authenticity, but of Catholicism as a politico-cultural project. Religion is here just an instrument and a sign of our collective identity, of how much public space 'our' side controls, of asserting 'our' hegemony. That's why Kastić quotes approvingly an Italian communist who said '*Io sono cattolico ateizzato*' ('I am an "atheized" Catholic'); that's why Breivik, also an atheist, refers to the Christian legacy underpinning European identity – or, to quote Buden again: 'Belief appears now as culture, in its difference to another culture – either the culture of another confession or the culture of atheism in its modernist forms.'[52] One can see clearly how religious fundamentalists, who otherwise despise cultural relativism and historicism, already function within its horizon:

> The space of difference became now something exclusively cultural. In order for us to perceive political differences and divisions and to recognize them as such, they should first be translated into the language of culture and declare themselves as cultural identities [. . .] Culture thus became the ultimate horizon of historical experience.[53]

Our answer should be here the politics of Truth, a universalist politics which leaves behind every form of communitarian culturalism.

PART TWO

The Ideological Theatre of Shadows

4

The 'Terrorist Threat'

FORMS OF FALSE SOLIDARITY

When we are all in a state of shock after a brutal event like the killing spree in the *Charlie Hebdo* offices, it is the right moment to gather the courage to *think* – not later, when things calm down, as proponents of cheap wisdom try to convince us. The difficult thing is to combine the heat of a moment and the act of thinking. Thinking in the cold of the aftermath does not generate a more balanced truth – it rather normalizes the situation, allowing us to avoid the cutting edge of truth.

The first thing to reject is the formula of pathetic identification – 'I am . . .' (or 'We are all. . .') – which only functions within certain limits, beyond which it turns into obscenity. Yes, we can proclaim '*Je suis Charlie*', but things quickly start to crumble with examples like 'We all live in Sarajevo!' (during the early 1990s when Sarajevo was under siege) or 'We are all in Gaza!' (when Gaza was bombarded by the IDF): the brutal fact that we are *not* all in Sarajevo or Gaza is too strong to be covered up by a pathetic identification. Such identification becomes absurd in the case of 'Muslims' (*Muselmannen*, who have nothing to do with actual Muslims – they were the 'living dead' in Auschwitz, those who had lost the basic will to engage in life): it is not possible to say 'We are all Muslims!' (in order to show our solidarity with them), simply because in Auschwitz the dehumanization of victims went so far that identifying with them in any meaningful sense is impossible. 'Muslims' in Auschwitz were precisely excluded from the symbolic space of group-identification, which is why it would have been utterly obscene to proclaim pathetically, 'We are all

Muselmannen!' (And, in the opposite direction, it would also be ridiculous to assert one's solidarity with 9/11 victims by claiming 'We are all New Yorkers!' – millions in the Third World would emphatically say, 'Yes, we would love to become New Yorkers, give us a visa!') And the same goes for the *Charlie Hebdo* killings: while we can all easily identify with Charlie, it would have been much more difficult, uneasy even, to pathetically announce, 'We are all from Baga!' – there are simply not enough grounds for identification here. (For those who don't get it: Baga is a small town in the north-east of Nigeria where, after occupying it, Boko Haram executed all of its 2,000 residents.)

Thinking means to move beyond the pathos of universal solidarity that exploded in the days after the event and culminated in the Sunday 11 January spectacle of big political names from all around the world holding hands, from Cameron to Lavrov, from Netanyahu to Abbas – if there ever was an image of hypocritical falsity, this was it. When the Paris procession passed under his window, an anonymous citizen played Beethoven's 'Ode to Joy', the unofficial anthem of the European Union, adding a touch of political kitsch to the disgusting spectacle staged by the very leaders most responsible for the mess we are in. What about the obscenity of Russian Foreign Minister Lavrov joining the line of dignitaries protesting against the death of journalists? If he were to join such a protest in Moscow (where dozens of journalists have been murdered), he would be immediately arrested! What about the obscenity of Netanyahu pushing himself into the front line, when in Israel the very public mention of al-Nakbah (the 'catastrophe' of 1948 for Palestinians) is prohibited – where here is empathy with the Other's pain and suffering? And the spectacle was literally staged: the pictures shown in the media gave the impression that the line of political leaders was at the front of a large crowd walking along an avenue, thereby signalling their solidarity and unity with the people . . . except that the event was simply staged as a photo opportunity. A photograph taken of the entire scene from above clearly shows that behind the politicians there were just a hundred or so people, with a lot of empty space patrolled by police behind and around them. Really, the true *Charlie Hebdo* gesture would have been to publish on its front page a big caricature brutally and tastelessly mocking this event, with drawings of Netan-yahu and Abbas, Lavrov and Cameron, and other couples passionately embracing and kissing while sharpening knives behind their backs.

Although I am resolutely atheist, I think that this obscenity was too much even for God, who felt obliged to intervene with an obscen-ity of His own worthy of the spirit of *Charlie Hebdo*: while President François Hollande was embracing Patrick Pelloux, the doctor and columnist at *Charlie Hebdo*, in front of the magazine's offices, a bird defecated on Hollande's right shoulder, with the staff of the magazine trying to rein in their uncontrollable laughter – a truly divine answer of the Real to the disgusting ritual. Recall the Christian motif of a dove descending to deliver a divine message – plus, in some countries, when a bird shits on your head it's considered a sign of luck.

So, yes, the Paris terrorist attacks should be unconditionally con-demned. It is just that they should be *really* condemned, for which more is needed than the simple pathetic spectacle of the solidarity of all of us (free, democratic, civilized people) against the murderous Muslim Monster. We should, of course, unambiguously condemn the killings as an attack on the very substance of our freedoms, and condemn them without any hidden caveats ('*Charlie Hebdo* was pro-voking and humiliating the Muslims too much', 'the attacking brothers were deeply affected by the horrors of the American occu-pation of Iraq'; OK, so why didn't they attack some US military installation instead of a French satirical journal?). The problem with invoking the complex background is that it can just as well be used apropos, for example, Hitler: he also succeeded in mobilizing the injustice of the Versailles treaty, but it was nonetheless fully justified to fight the Nazi regime with all means at our disposal. The point is not whether the grievances which condition terrorist acts are true or not, the point is the politico-ideological project which emerges as a reaction against injustices. Rasheed Araeen's recent interventions in the cyberspace debate on refugees and terror are paradigmatic of this stance:

> Since the terror attack in Paris, in particular, everyone is busy talking about Islam and its extreme form of the ISIS, and how to defeat it. There is little talk or discussion about who or which created ISIS, that

it is a product of what was created by the American/Saudi imperialism to fight Soviets in Afghanistan, and then the invasion of Iraq by the combined Anglo-American military forces. Was it not the dismantling and disintegration of the Iraqi army that some of its army officers escaped to the north of Iraq and formed themselves into a group to resist and fight Anglo-American imperialism, which eventually became ISIS?[1]

Araeen emphasizes 'the absence of this in the public debate': what we get in the public media is 'complete garbage about Islam and Islamic extremism. No one ever mentioned the word "imperialism", that it is the continuing Western imperialism which is responsible for what is happening particularly in the Middle East, and the migration of people is its consequence.' The violent Muslim fundamentalism

> was created by the American/Saudi alliance in the 1980s in order to fight the Soviet presence in Afghanistan, which is now everywhere as Taliban or al-Qaeda and their offshoot ISIS [. . .] this spirit was created and was let out of the bottle by some powers of the West, and it doesn't matter whether you attribute it to Western imperialism or not, the responsibility for what happened as a result of this lies with the West. And therefore all this talk about Islamic extremism is humbug; if there is an Islamic extremism it is the result of what the West has been doing to the Muslim world particularly since 1980s.

This passage contains a whole series of problematic points. First, is it true that nobody talks about Western responsibility for the rise of ISIS? Isn't it widely debated? Second, what about the decline of the secular Left in Arab countries, which was very strong in the '50s and '60s (Mosadegh, Burgiba, Nasser . . .)? It is all too simple to blame the West for failed Arab modernization. (Significantly, the two states that recently disintegrated and became the main source of refugees are Iraq and Syria, the only two which were officially secular, where Islam was not the state religion.) Third, does the assertion of the sole responsibility of the West not involve a total passivization of Arabs as victims? Isn't it clear that Arab Muslims are now also engaged in a series of active political projects, from the expansion of

Islam into Europe to the conflict between Sunnis and Shias? Following Araeen's logic, one could say that the responsibility for Hitler is that of Western capitalism, so let's focus on that. While this is in some sense true (Max Horkheimer wrote in the 1930s that those who do not want to talk about capitalism should also keep silent about fascism), it didn't preclude the urgency to fight fascism with all means, Western democracies and the USSR together.

There is, furthermore, one feature of the recent events in France that seemed to pass mostly unnoticed: there were stickers and posters announcing not only *Je suis Charlie* but also *Je suis flic* ('I am the police')! The all-national unity celebrated and enacted in large public gatherings was not just the unity of the people reaching across all ethnic groups, classes and religions, but also (and perhaps above all) the unification of the people with the forces of order and control. France was till now the only country in the West (to my knowledge) where policemen were constantly the butt of brutal jokes portraying them as stupid and corrupt (a common practice in communist countries). Now, in the aftermath of the *Charlie Hebdo* killings, the police are applauded and lauded, embraced like protecting mothers – not just the police but also special forces (the CRS, which in '68 inspired the chant 'CRS: SS!'), secret services, the entire state security apparatus. No place for Snowden or Manning in this new universe; to quote Jacques-Alain Miller: 'Resentment against police is no longer what it was, except among the poor youth of Arab or African origins [. . .] an unprecedented event in the history of France.' What one does see occasionally around the world and in France is, in rare privileged moments, the ecstatic 'osmosis of a population with the national army which protects it from external aggressions. But the love of a population for the forces of *internal* repression?'[2] The terrorist threat thus succeeded in achieving the impossible: reconciling the generation of the '68 revolutionaries with their arch enemy, in something like a French popular version of the Patriot Act, enforced with popular acclamation, with people offering themselves to surveillance. In short, the ecstatic moments of the Paris manifestations gave body to a triumph of ideology: they united the people against an enemy whose fascinating presence momentarily obliterated all antagonisms. The public was offered a sad and depressing choice: you are either (part of the same body as) a *flic* or (in solidary with) a terrorist. So the question to be raised is: what do these choices obfuscate? What is it their function to obfuscate?

The reply to this question has nothing whatsoever to do with the cheap relativization of the crime ('Who are we in the West, perpetrators of terrible massacres in the Third World, to condemn such acts?'). It has even less to do with the pathological fear of many Western liberal Leftists of being guilty of Islamophobia. For these false Leftists, any critique of Islam is denounced as an expression of Western Islamophobia, Salman Rushdie was denounced for unnecessarily provoking Muslims and was thus (partially, at least) responsible for the *fatwa* condemning him to death, etc. The result of such a stance is what one can expect in such cases: the more the Western liberal Leftists probe into their guilt, the more they are accused by Muslim fundamentalists of being hypocrites who try to conceal their hatred of Islam. This constellation perfectly reproduces the paradox of the superego: the more you obey what the Other demands of you, the guiltier you are. It is as if the more you tolerate Islam, the stronger its pressure on you will be . . .

One of the after-effects of this superego stance is how our liberal media prefer to downplay sexual incidents with refugees and immigrants . Here are two cases. In 2015, a 'no-borders' activist woman was gang-raped by a group of Sudanese immigrants in an Italian refugee camp near the French border; however, her co-workers convinced her no to report the crime, arguing that the publicity would hurt the refugee and open-borders cause.[3] And after the New Year's Eve carnivalesque spectacle at Cologne railway station, an internal police memo detailed 'a request from the ministry' instructing police to 'cancel' the use of the word 'rape' in their reports.[4] Although this downplaying is understandable, the danger is that it feeds distrust of the media and thereby raises the visibility of the anti-immigrant right-wing press, which can be perceived as 'telling what others don't dare to say'. However, with a recent incident in Norway, the politically correct stance reached a new extreme.

In April 2016, it was reported that, a couple of years previously, Karsten Nordal Hauken, a young left-wing politician from Norway, a self-professed anti-racist and feminist, was anally raped at his home by a Somali refugee, who was then caught and sentenced to four years in prison. Having completed his sentence, the authorities intended to deport him back to Somalia. When Hauken learned about the deportation, he published a series of texts in which he explained that he now feels guilty and responsible: '[I] had a strong feeling of guilt and responsibility. I was the reason that he would not be in Norway any more, but rather sent to a dark uncertain future in Somalia.' Hauken also wrote that he sees his rapist 'mostly like a product of an unfair world, a product of an upbringing marked by war and despair'. Hauken in no way denies the traumatic impact of the rape on him; he admits that, in order to survive the crisis, he took refuge in alcohol and drugs:

> I feel forgotten and ignored. But I dare not talk about it, I'm afraid of attacks from all sides. I am afraid that no girls want me and that other men laugh at me. Afraid that I'll be perceived as anti-feminist when I say that young men who are struggling should get more attention. Men and boys must learn that it's okay to talk about their feelings. Boys and men are ignored. For me it resulted in years of depression, abuse, loneliness and isolation.[5]

It is easy to succumb here to the populist common sense, mocking the madness and masochism of political correctness brought to an extreme. So the first thing to do is to point out that the event raised so much interest because the crime was committed by an immigrant – there are rapes going on all the time that are ignored by the media. The second thing is that the law should be the same for all: no special treatment for immigrants, neither more severity nor more tolerance. Finally, one should commend how Hauken highlights the important topic of male victims of sexual violence and its consequences. The problem resides elsewhere: in Hauken's feeling of guilt and responsibility for what happened to his rapist. This stance embodies the extreme version of the axiom of political correctness: we (white Western men) are ultimately responsible even when horrible things are done to us, so we should feel responsible for the perpetrator when he is punished – the perpetrator is not really an agent but a passive victim of circumstances, his crime is 'a product of an unfair world, a product of an upbringing marked by war and despair' . . . I consider this stance an exemplary case of perverse pathology: if taken seriously, it can be expanded indefinitely. Are we not *all* victims of circumstances and upbringing? Does this not hold also for a paedophiliac priest who abuses dozens of children? Or for a rapist who brutally abuses women? So should his victim, the raped and beaten woman, also feel guilty and responsible? Hauken's stance is therefore not a weird eccentricity but the extrapolation of the politically correct stance.

We should follow here the basic axiom of psychoanalysis: what one is radically responsible for is the way one enjoys things – enjoyment means that nobody is merely a victim in this situation. What makes all perpetrators of sexual violence guilty is the way they subjectivize their predicament by reacting to it with an act of sexual violence – we are always fully responsible for the way we enjoy things, and enjoyment in this context should not be limited to direct sexuality, since it includes every form of humiliating the victim, of making him or her suffer. The starving Somali farmer who submits his daughter to cliterodectomy is no less responsible than a wealthy Western sadist who rapes sexual slaves.

IS FUNDAMENTALISM PREMODERN OR POSTMODERN?

This is why I also find insufficient calls for moderation along the lines of Simon Jenkins's claim[6] that our task is 'not to overreact, not to over-publicize the aftermath. It is to treat each event as a passing accident of horror'. The attack on *Charlie Hebdo* was not a mere 'passing accident of horror': it followed a precise religious and political agenda and was as such clearly part of a much larger pattern. Of course we should not overreact, if by this is meant succumbing to blind Islamophobia – but we should ruthlessly analyse this pattern. The best way to get an insight is to ask a simple question: are Muslim fundamentalists a premodern or a modern phenomenon? Things are much more ambiguous here. If one asks a Russian anti-communist which tradition is to be blamed for the horrors of Stalinism, one gets two opposed answers. Some see in Stalinism (and in Bolshevism in general) a chapter in the long history of Western modernization of Russia, a tradition that began with Peter the Great (if not before that, with Ivan the Terrible), while others put the blame on Russian backwardness, on the long tradition of Oriental despotism that predominated there. So while, for the first group, Western modernizers brutally disrupted the organic life of traditional Russia, replacing it with state terror, for the second group, the tragedy of Russia was that socialist revolution occurred at a wrong time and place, in a backward country with no democratic tradition. And are things not similar with the Muslim fundamentalism that finds its (hitherto) extreme expression in ISIS? Kevin McDonald has argued that Isis jihadis aren't medieval but rather are shaped by modern Western philosophy: we should look to revolutionary France if we want to understand the source of Islamic State's ideology and violence.

> When he made his speech in July at Mosul's Great Mosque declaring the creation of an Islamic state with himself as its caliph, Abu Bakr al-Baghdadi quoted at length from the Indian/Pakistani thinker Abul A'la Maududi, the founder of the Jamaat-e-Islami party in 1941 and originator of the contemporary term Islamic state [. . .] Central to [Maududi's] thought is his understanding of the French revolution, which he believed offered the promise of a 'state founded on a set of principles' as opposed to one based upon a nation or a people. For Maududi this potential withered in France; its achievement would have to await an Islamic state.
>
> In revolutionary France, it is the state that creates its citizens and nothing should be allowed to stand between the citizen and the state [. . .] This universal citizen, separated from community, nation or history, lies at the heart of Maududi's vision of 'citizenship in Islam'. Just as the revolutionary French state created its citizens, with the citizen unthinkable outside the state, so too the Islamic state creates its citizens [. . .]
>
> Don't look to the Qur'an to understand this – look to the French revolution and ultimately to the secularization of an idea that finds its origins in European Christianity: *extra ecclesiam nulla salus* (outside the church there is no salvation), an idea that became transformed

with the birth of modern European states into *extra stato nulla persona* (outside the state there is no legal personhood). This idea still demonstrates extraordinary power today: it is the source of what it means to be a refugee.

If Isis's state is profoundly modern, so too is its violence. Isis fighters do not simply kill; they seek to humiliate, as we saw last week as they herded Syrian reservists wearing only their underpants to their death. And they seek to dishonour the bodies of their victims, in particular through postmortem manipulations.[7]

Although there is a moment of truth in this comment, its basic thesis is nonetheless deeply problematic. It not only comes all too close to the politically correct self-blaming of the West. More importantly, the parallel between ISIS and the French Revolution is purely formal, like the parallel sometimes drawn between Nazism and Stalinism as two versions of the same 'totalitarianism': a similar set of extreme oppressive measures obfuscates not just a different social and ideological content but also a different functioning of the oppressive measures themselves (for example, there is nothing similar to Stalinist purges in Nazism). The moment of truth resides in the fact that the religious motif of man's total subordination to God (found, among other religions, in Islam), far from necessarily sustaining a vision of slavery and subordination, can also sustain a project of universal emancipation, as it does in Sayyid Qutb's *Milestones*, where he deploys the link between universal human freedom and human servitude to God:

A society in which sovereignty belongs exclusively to Allah and finds expression in its obedience to the Divine Law, and every person is set free from servitude to others, only then does it taste true freedom. This alone is 'human civilization', because the basis of human civilization is the complete and true freedom of every person and the full dignity of every individual in the community. On the other hand, in a society in which some people are lords who legislate and others are slaves who obey them, there is no freedom in the real sense, nor dignity for the individual [. . .]

In a society based on the concept, belief, and way of life originating from Allah, man's dignity is held inviolable to the highest degree: no one is a slave to another, as they are in societies in which the concepts, beliefs, and way of life originate from human sources. In the former society, man's noblest characteristics – both spiritual and intellectual – find fullest expression, while in a society based on colour, race, nationalism, or other similar bases, these degenerate into fetters for human thought and a means for suppressing nobler human attributes and qualities. All men are equal regardless of their colour, race, or nation, but when they are deprived of spirit and reason they are also divested of their humanity. Man is able to change his beliefs, thinking, and attitude toward life, but he is incapable of changing his colour and race, nor can he decide in what place or nation he is to be born. Thus it is clear that a society is civilized only to the extent that human associations are based on a community of free moral choice, and a society is backward in so far as the basis of association is something other than free choice.[8]

Qutb's underlying premise is that, insofar as we humans act 'freely' in the sense of just spontaneously following our natural inclinations, we are not really free but enslaved to our animal natures – we find this same line of reasoning earlier, in Aristotle, who, referring to slavery to illustrate a general ontological feature, wrote that, left to themselves, slaves are 'free' in the sense that they just do what they want, while free men follow their duty – and it is this very 'freedom' that makes slaves slaves:

> all things are ordered together somehow, but not all alike – both fishes
> and fowls and plants; and the world is not such that one thing has
> nothing to do with another, but they are connected. For all are ordered
> together to one end, but it is as in a house, where the freemen are least
> at liberty to act at random, but all things or most things are already
> ordained for them, while the slaves and the animals do little for the
> common good, and for the most part live at random; for this is the
> sort of principle that constitutes the nature of each.[9]

Qutb thus envisages universal (also social and economic) freedom as the absence of any masters: my servitude to God is the negative guarantee of the rejection of all other (earthly, human) masters – or, as we can put it more daringly, the only positive content of my sub-ordination to God is my rejection of all earthly masters. Note, however, the symptomatic absence of one term in this series of natural properties of a human being: true, one cannot change colour, race or nation; but one also cannot change *sex*, so why does his free society not require the equality of men and women? Through such details we can discern the unbridgeable gap that separates Qutb's project from the Western emancipatory project of equality based on people's sovereignty, without a guarantee in any form of the big Other.

In spite of all that is deeply problematic in the quoted passage, is there not a grain of truth in it, i.e., does this characterization of slaves not describe today's consumerist slavery, where I am allowed to act at random and 'do what I want', but remain as such enslaved to the stimuli of commodities? Back to Aristotle and Qutb, Aristotle's advantage is (from our standpoint, at least) that he refers to the sense of ethical duty, not subordination to God, as the agency that constrains our animal freedom; however, the advantage of Qutb is that he envisages universal (also social and economic) freedom, a universal absence of any masters. What Qutb proposes is a kind of symbolic exchange homologous to the one described in the famous lines from Racine's *Athalie*: *Je crains Dieu, cher Abner, et je n'ai point d'autre crainte* ('I fear God, my dear Abner, and have no other fear'). All fears are exchanged for one fear; it is the very fear of God that makes me fearless in all worldly matters. Once again, for Qutb, my sole master is God, so my servitude to God means that I reject all other earthly masters. [10]

A more general point to be made here is that resistance to global capitalism should not rely on premodern traditions, on the defence of their particular life-forms – for the simple reason that such a return to premodern traditions is impossible since globalization already shapes the forms of resistance to it. Those who oppose globalization on behalf of traditions threatened by it do this in a form which is already modern: they already speak the language of modernity. Their content may be ancient, but their form is ultra-modern. So instead of seeing in ISIS a case of extreme resistance to modernization, one should rather conceive of it as yet another case of perverted modernization and locate it in the series of conservative modernizations that began with the Meiji restoration in Japan (rapid industrial modernization assumed the ideological form of 'restoration', of the return to the full authority of the emperor). The well-known photo of Baghdadi, the ISIS leader, with an exquisite Swiss watch on his arm, is here emblematic: ISIS is well organized in web propaganda, financial dealings, etc., although these ultra-modern practices are used to propagate and enforce an ideologico-political vision that is not so much conservative as a desperate move to impose clear hierarchic delimitations, principal among them those that regulate religion, education and sexuality. In short, we should not forget that even this image of a strictly disciplined and regulated fundamentalist organization is not without its ambiguities: is religious oppression not (more than) supplemented by the way local ISIS military units seem to function? While the official ISIS ideology lambasts Western permissiveness, the daily practice of the ISIS gangs includes full carnivalesque orgies (gang rapes, torture and murder, robberies of the infidels).

The unheard-of radicality of ISIS resides in the fact that it does not mask its brutality but openly displays it: media-transmitted beheadings, sex slavery admitted to and justified, and so on.[11] Let's take an extreme version of this phenomenon, the Nigerian Boko Haram movement. The name can be roughly and descriptively translated as 'Western education is forbidden', specifically the education of women. How, then, do we account for the existence of a sociopolitical movement whose main programmatic item is the hierarchic regulation of the relationship between the two sexes? The enigma is thus: why do some Muslims, who were undoubtedly exposed to the exploitation, domination, and other destructive and humiliating aspects of colonialism, target in their response what is (for us, at least) the best part of the Western legacy, our egalitarianism and personal freedoms, inclusive of a healthy dose of irony and mocking of all authorities? The obvious answer would have to be that their target is well-chosen: what makes the liberal Western powers so unbearable is that they not only practise exploitation and violent domination, but that, to add insult to injury, they present this brutal reality in the guise of its opposite, of freedom, equality and democracy.

COLONIAL FEMINISM,
ANTI-COLONIAL ANTI-FEMINISM

It has become a commonplace to observe that the rise of ISIS is the latest chapter in the long story of the anti-colonial re-awakening (the arbitrary national borders imposed by the great powers after the First World War are being redrawn) and simultaneously a chapter in the struggle against the way global capital undermines the power of nation states. But what causes fear and consternation is another feature of the ISIS regime: the public statements of the ISIS authorities make it clear that, for them, the principal task of state power is not the regulation of the welfare of its population (health, the fight against hunger); what really matters is religious life, ensuring that all public life obeys religious laws. This is why ISIS remains more or less indifferent towards humanitarian catastrophes within its domain – their motto is 'take care of religion and welfare will take care of itself'. Therein resides the gap that separates the notion of power practised by ISIS from the modern Western notion of what Michel Foucault called 'bio-power', which regulates individuals' lives to protect general welfare: the ISIS caliphate totally rejects the notion of bio-power.

It is therefore not enough to invoke the antagonisms of global capitalism: there is a basic socio-cultural rift behind ISIS's attacks on the West. Decades ago, Ayatollah Khomeini made it clear why an attack like that on *Charlie Hebdo* could be considered appropriate: 'We're not afraid of sanctions. We're not afraid of military invasion. What frightens us is the invasion of Western immorality.'[12] Is *Charlie Hebdo* not the epitome of 'Western immorality'? When Khomeini talks about fear, about what a Muslim should fear most in the West, we should take it literally. Muslim fundamentalists really don't have any problems with the brutality of economic and military struggles; their true enemy is not the West's economic neo-colonialism and military aggressiveness but its 'immoral' culture.

The same holds for Putin's Russia, where the conservative nationalists define their conflict with the West as cultural, focusing in the last resort on sexual difference: apropos the victory of Conchita

Wurst, the bearded Austrian drag queen, at the Eurovision song contest, Putin told a dinner in St Petersburg: 'The Bible talks about the two genders, man and woman, and the main purpose of union between them is to produce children.'[13] As usual, the rabid nationalist Zhirinovsky was more outspoken:

> [Zhirinovsky] called this year's result 'the end of Europe', saying: 'There is no limit to our outrage [. . .] There are no more men or women in Europe, just *it*' [. . .] Vice premier Dmitry Rogozin isued a scathing tweet claiming the Eurovision result 'showed supporters of European integration their European future – a bearded girl'.[14]

There is a certain quasi-poetic, uncanny beauty in this image of the bearded lady (for a long time a standard feature of cheap circus freakshows) as the symbol of a united Europe – no wonder Russia refused to transmit the Eurovision contest to its TV public, with calls for a renewed cultural Cold War. Note the same logic as Khomeini's: the truly feared object is immoral depravity, the threat to sexual difference – Boko Haram just brought this thinking to its logical end.

In many African and Asian countries, gay movements are also perceived as an expression of the cultural impact of capitalist globalization and of its undermining of traditional social and cultural forms; consequently, the rejection of gay liberation appears as an aspect of the anti-colonial struggle. Does the same not hold for Boko Haram? For its members, the liberation of women appears as the most visible feature of the destructive cultural impact of capitalist modernization.

Sexual difference as a set of fixed features that define the role of each gender of course implies strong hierarchy and divided responsibility. The soft attitude towards rape in Muslim countries is clearly based on the premise that a man who has raped a woman must have been secretly seduced (provoked) by her into doing it. In the autumn of 2006, Sheik Taj Din al-Hilali, Australia's most senior Muslim cleric, caused a scandal when, after a group of Muslim men had been jailed for gang rape, he said: 'If you take uncovered meat and place it outside on the street [. . .] and the cats come and eat it . . . whose fault is it – the cats' or the uncovered meat? The uncovered meat is the problem.'[15] The scandalous nature of this comparison between a woman who is not veiled and raw, uncovered meat distracted attention from another, much more surprising, assumption underlying al-Hilali's argument: if women are held responsible for the sexual conduct of men, does this not imply that men are totally helpless when faced with what they perceive as sexual provocation, that they are simply unable to resist it, that they are totally enslaved to their sexual hunger? In contrast to this presumption of a complete lack of male responsibility for their own sexual conduct, the emphasis on public female eroticism in the West relies on the premise that men *are* capable of sexual restraint, that they are not blind slaves to their sexual drives. This total responsibility of the woman for the sexual act is confirmed by the weird legal regulations in Iran, where, on 3 January 2006, a 19-year-old girl was sentenced to death by hanging after admitting having stabbed to death one of three men who tried to rape her. Here is the deadlock: what would have been the result if she had not decided to defend herself? If she had allowed the men to rape her, she would have been subjected to 100 lashes under Iranian laws on chastity; if she had been married at the time of the rape, she would likely have been found guilty of adultery and sentenced to death by stoning. So whatever happens, the responsibility is fully *hers*. What, then, should she have done? The answer is simple and clear: *stay at home*, never going out alone.

Such an attitude is in no way limited to Islam – it is just an extreme expression of a stance found all around us. In her article 'In Russia and Ukraine, Women are Still Blamed for Being Raped', Anastasiya Melnychenko wrote:

> Throughout the post-Soviet world, people immediately start to question what the woman did wrong. Maybe she was wearing a short skirt? Maybe she was walking home too late? Or maybe she was drunk? The suggestion is that a woman is guilty simply because she is a woman.[16]

The same thesis is heard in the cinema version of *The Handmaid's Tale*: 'Men can't resist. But we're different. We can resist.' So while in one part of the world, abortion and gay marriage are endorsed as a clear sign of moral progress, in other parts, homophobia and anti-abortion campaigns are exploding. In June 2016, al Jazeera reported that a 22-year-old Dutch woman told the police that she had been raped after being drugged in an upmarket nightclub in Doha – and the result was that she was convicted by a Qatari court of having illegitimate sex and given a one-year suspended sentence. (At the opposite end, what counts as harassment in the PC environment is also getting extended. There was a case reported of a woman walking on a street with a bag in her hand, and a black man walking fifteen yards behind her; becoming aware of it, the woman (unconsciously, automatically?) tightened her grip on the bag, and the black man reported that he experienced the woman's gesture as a case of racist harassment . . .)

When we are dealing with the oppressive atmosphere in Muslim countries, we should not forget to compare it to the (no less oppressive) atmosphere in the American Bible Belt.[17] We should also remember that the concept of the 'politically suspicious' religion is not reserved exclusively for Islam. In the US during the Second World War, owing to the large number of Buddhists within the Japanese minority, Buddhism – which is today celebrated in the West as the model of tolerant spirituality – occupied the place of the 'politically suspicious' religion in a way similar to the role played by Islam today.[18] There are other surprising parallels awaiting us. According to Islamic State's ideological narrative,

> Islam's final showdown with an anti-Messiah will occur in Jerusalem after a period of renewed Islamic conquest [. . .] An anti-Messiah, known in Muslim apocalyptic literature as Dajjal, will come from the Khorasan region of eastern Iran and kill a vast number of the caliphate's fighters, until just 5,000 remain, cornered in Jerusalem. Just as Dajjal prepares to finish them off, Jesus – the second-most-revered prophet in Islam – will return to Earth, spear Dajjal, and lead the Muslims to victory.[19]

Sounds familiar? Of course it does: it is the slightly reformulated Armageddon story regularly used by American Christian fundamentalists . . . so good to see Christian and Muslim fundamentalists moving in the same direction and relying on the same ideological fantasies even when they pretend to hate each other.

In July 2016, it was reported that a leading religious figure, referring to ancient sacred texts, was claiming that raping captured enemy women can be justified in wartime. Was this yet another crank Muslim priest close to ISIS? No, it was the newly appointed chief rabbi of the Israel Defense Forces, who got himself in trouble with comments that seemed to condone raping non-Jewish women in wartime.[20] The lesson of this scandal is not just that religious authorities should apply today's moral standards in their effort to make traditional religious sources relevant – we all know that ancient sacred texts are monuments to barbarian brutality. A much more important lesson concerns the unexpected (perhaps) proximity of 'civilized' Israeli hardliners and 'barbarian' Muslim fundamentalists.

'BÊTE ET MÉCHANT'

How did the notion of human rights and freedoms, which provokes such antagonism in Muslim countries, arise from the Christian tradition? It is only in the space created by the distance between God and the law that the modern notion of human rights could have emerged: human rights can be conceived of only when the law is not the last word of God, when obeying the law is supplemented by a different dimension (of love, grace). It is crucial to bear in mind the interconnection between the Decalogue and human rights, the latter being the modern obverse of the former. As the experience of our liberal-permissive society amply demonstrates, human rights ultimately express, in their essence, simply the right to violate the Ten Commandments. 'The right to privacy' – the right to adultery, done in secret, when no one sees me or has the right to probe into my life. 'The right to pursue happiness and to possess private property' – the right to steal (to exploit others). 'Freedom of the press and of the expression of opinion' – the right to lie, slander and humiliate. 'The right (in the US, at least!) of free citizens to possess weapons' – the right to kill. And, ultimately, 'freedom of religious belief' – the right to celebrate false gods. Of course, human rights do not directly condone the violation of the Commandments, they just keep open a marginal 'grey zone' out of reach of (religious or secular) power. In this shady zone, I can violate the Commandments, and if power probes into it, catching me with my pants down and trying to prevent my violations, I can cry, 'Assault on my basic human rights!' The point is thus that it is structurally impossible for power to draw a clear line of separation and prevent only the 'misuse' of a human right without infringing upon its proper use, i.e. a use that does *not* violate the Commandments.[21]

It is in this grey zone that the brutal humour of *Charlie Hebdo* belongs. We should recall that *Charlie Hebdo* began in 1970 as a successor to *Hara-Kiri*, a magazine banned for mocking the death of General de Gaulle. After an early reader's letter accused *Hara-Kiri* of being 'dumb and nasty' (*'bête et méchant'*), the phrase was taken up as the official slogan of the magazine and made it into everyday language. This is the grey zone of *Charlie Hebdo*: not a benevolent satire but, quite literally, dumb and nasty, so that it would have been much more appropriate for the thousands to proclaim *'Je suis bête et méchant'* rather than the flat *'Je suis Charlie'*. As it was, the Paris manifestations of solidarity effectively were *bête et méchant*!

Refreshing as it could be in some situations, the *'bête et méchant'* stance enacted by *Charlie Hebdo* is clearly constrained by the fact that laughter is not in itself liberating, but deeply ambiguous. Recall the contrast between the solemn aristocratic Spartans and the merry, democratic Athenians, which is part of our common view of Ancient Greece. This view, however, misses how the Spartans, who prided themselves on their severity, placed laughter at the centre of their ideology and practice – they recognized communal laughter as a power helping us to increase the glory of the state. (Athenians, on the contrary, legally constrained such brutal and excessive laughter as a threat to the spirit of respectful democratic dialogue, where no humiliation of the opponent should be permitted.) The Spartan type of laughter – the brutal mocking of a humiliated enemy or slave, making fun of their fear and pain from the position of power – survives today: we find it, among other places, in Stalin's speeches, where he scoffs at the panic and confusion of the 'traitors', in a torturer jeering at the confused rambling of his half-dead victim, or in a well-mannered gentleman poking fun at the clumsy attempts of his less-educated servant to imitate his manners. (Incidentally, this brutal laughter is to be distinguished from another mode of the laughter of those in power, the cynical derision that signals that they don't take seriously their own ideology.) The problem with the *Charlie Hebdo* humour was not that it went too far in its irreverence, but that it was a harmless excess perfectly fitting the hegemonic cynical functioning of ideology in our societies. It posed no threat whatsoever to those in power; it merely made their exercise of power more tolerable. Upton Sinclair wrote that it is difficult to get a man to understand something when his job depends on not understanding it. How does this work? Not as a direct psychotic foreclosure of a part of the subject's knowledge but more in the guise of a fetishist denial: while the subject understands the thing very well, he *suspends the symbolic efficiency of his understanding.*

One can risk the hypothesis that what is missing from Islam (and Judaism) is the carnivalesque mocking of divinity that is part of European religious tradition itself, starting with the Ancient Greek ritualistic ridiculing of the gods of Olympus. There is nothing subversive or atheist here: this mocking is an inherent part of religious life. As for Christianity, we must not forget the moments of carnivalesque irony in Christ's parables and riddles. Even the crucifixion contains its own mocking, blasphemous spectacle in the donkey-riding King who is Christ, his crown a matter of thorns.

Islam, of course, has its own carnivalesque underside, but it functions in a different way. When the media were preoccupied by the Cologne event, either demonizing it as the brutal intrusion of Muslim barbarism or desperately trying to downplay it, a key feature was almost totally ignored: during the big anti-Mubarak protests at Tahrir Square, similar incidents were going on all the time – groups of protesters would dance around a woman, intruding into her privacy, touching her obscenely, sometimes even raping her. (The large majority of Western reporters decided to ignore the numerous incidents of this type they were witnessing, out of sympathy for the protesters and afraid of being perceived as pro-Mubarak. Similar things are regularly going on in the West Bank and in other places in the Middle East.) A proof if one is needed is that the Cologne incident was part of the Middle Eastern carnival tradition that ignores women's plight.

It is against this background that one should approach the sensitive topic of the multiple ways of life. While in Western liberal-secular societies state power protects public freedom and intervenes in the private space (for instance when it suspects child abuse), such 'intrusions into domestic space, the breaching of "private" domains, is disallowed in Islamic law, although conformity in "public" behaviour may be much stricter [. . .] for the community, what matters is the Muslim subject's social practice – including verbal publication – not her internal thoughts, whatever they may be'.[22] Although, as the Qur'an says, 'let him who wills have faith, and him who wills reject it' (18:29), this 'right to think whatever one wishes does not [. . .] include the right to express one's religious or moral beliefs publicly with the intention of converting people to a false commitment'.[23] This is why, for Muslims, it is 'impossible to remain silent when confronted with blasphemy': their reaction is so passionate because, for them, 'blasphemy is neither "freedom of speech" nor the challenge of a new truth but something that seeks to disrupt a living relationship'.[24] From the Western liberal standpoint, there is, of course, a problem with both terms of this neither/nor: what if freedom of speech should include acts that disrupt a living relationship? And what if a 'new truth' may also have the same disruptive effect? What if a new ethical awareness makes the existing living relationship appear unjust?

Yasri Khan, a Muslim member of the Swedish Green Party, refused to shake hands with a female journalist, claiming that the act is 'too intimate'; when he was criticized, he said that this criticism reflected ethnocentric prejudices that abound even in the Green Party, which otherwise advocates cultural diversity. 'How do you combine diversity and [freedom of] religion with an ethnocentric and prejudiced idea of gender equality?'[25] Although Khan's act may be justified (partially, at least), his defence points towards the core of the problem: can gender equality, which must include the shaking of hands between men and women in public, really be dismissed as 'an ethnocentric and prejudiced idea'? And the obverse, can submission of women be defended as a component of a particular cultural identity we are obliged to respect? Where do we set the limit here?

If, for Muslims, it is not only 'impossible to remain silent when confronted with blasphemy', but also impossible to remain inactive, to do nothing – and this action may include violent and murderous acts – then the first thing to do is to locate this attitude in its contemporary context. Does exactly the same not hold for the Christian anti-abortion movement? For them it is also 'impossible to remain silent' in the face of hundreds of thousands of foetuses killed every year, a slaughter they compare to the Holocaust. It is here that true tolerance begins – the tolerance of what we experience as 'impossible-to-bear' ('*l'impossible-à-supporter*', as Lacan put it) – and at this level Left-liberal political correctness comes close to religious fundamentalism with its own list of 'impossible to remain silent when confronted with . . .': our own 'blasphemies' of (what is perceived as) sexism, racism, and other forms of intolerance. It is easy to mock the Islamic regulation of everyday life (a feature Islam shares with Judaism, incidentally), but what about the politically correct list of seduction moves that can be considered verbal harassment, of jokes that are considered racist or sexist or even 'speciesist' (if one makes too much fun of other species of animals)? What one should emphasize here is the immanent contradiction of the Left-liberal stance: the libertarian stance of universal irony and mocking, making fun of all authorities, spiritual and political (the stance embodied in *Charlie Hebdo*), tends to slip into its opposite, an excessive sensitivity to the other's pain and humiliation.

It is because of this contradiction that most of the Left's reactions to the Paris killings followed the predictable pattern: while they correctly suspected that something is deeply wrong in the spectacle of liberal consensus and solidarity with the victims, they were able to condemn the killings only after long and boring qualifications of the 'we are also guilty' type. This fear that, by clearly condemning the killings, we somehow court the danger of Islamophobia is politically and ethically totally wrong. There is nothing 'Islamophobic' in thoroughly condemning the Paris killings, in the same way that there is nothing anti-Semitic in thoroughly condemning Israeli policies towards Palestinians. The moment one searches for any kind of 'balance' here, the ethico-political fiasco arrives.

What this also means is that, when approaching the Israeli–Palestinian conflict, one should stick to ruthless and cold standards, suspending the urge to try to 'understand' the situation: one should unconditionally resist the temptation to 'understand' the Arab anti-Semitism (where we really encounter it) as a 'natural' reaction to the sad plight of the Palestinians, or to 'understand' the Israeli measures as a 'natural' reaction to the background memory of the Holocaust. There should be no 'understanding' for the fact that in many, if not most, Arab countries, from Saudi Arabia to Egypt, Hitler is still considered a hero, or the fact that, in primary-school textbooks, all the traditional anti-Semitic myths, from the notorious forged 'Protocols of the Elders of Zion' to the claims that Jews use the blood of Christian (or Arab) children for sacrificial purposes, are repeated. To claim that this anti-Semitism articulates, in a displaced mode, resistance against capitalism in no way justifies it: displacement is not here a secondary operation, but the fundamental gesture of ideological mystification. What this claim *does* involve is the idea that, in the long term, the only way to fight anti-Semitism is not to preach liberal tolerance, etc., not to interpret or judge singular acts 'together', but to excise them from their historical texture. When any public protest against the Israel Defense Forces' activities in the West Bank is denounced as an expression of anti-Semitism, and – implicitly, at least – put in the same category as denial of the Holocaust, that is to say, when the shadow of the Holocaust is permanently evoked in order to neutralize any criticism of Israeli actions, it is not enough to insist on the difference between anti-Semitism and the critique of particular measures of the State of Israel; one should go a step further and claim that it is the State of Israel that, in this case, is desecrating the memory of the Holocaust victims, ruthlessly manipulating them, instrumentalizing them into a means to legitimize present political decisions. What this means is that one should reject the very notion of any logical or political link between the Holocaust and the present Israeli–Palestinian tensions: these are two thoroughly different phenomena, one being part of the European history of Rightist resistance to the dynamics of modernization, the other being one of the last chapters in the history of colonialism. On the other hand, the difficult task for the Palestinians is to accept that their true enemy are not Jews but those Arab regimes that themselves manipulate their plight in order, precisely, to prevent that shift, i.e., a political radicalization in their own midst. Part of today's situation in Europe is effectively the growth of anti-Semitism – for example, in Malmö an aggressive minority of Muslims harasses Jews so that they are afraid to walk in the streets in their traditional dress. Such phenomena should be clearly and unambiguously condemned: the struggle against anti-Semitism and the struggle against Islamophobia should be viewed as two aspects of the *same* fight.

So, again, the obvious tolerant solution (mutual respect for another's sensitivities) no less obviously doesn't work: if Muslims find it 'impossible to bear' our blasphemous images and reckless humour (which we consider a part of our freedoms), Western liberals also find 'impossible to bear' many practices (the subordination of women, etc.) that are part of the Muslim 'living relationship'. In short, things explode when members of a religious community experience as blasphemous injury and a danger to their way of life not a direct attack on their religion, but *the very way of life of another community* – as was the case with attacks on gays and lesbians in the Netherlands, Germany and Denmark, or as is the case with those Frenchmen and Frenchwomen who see a woman covered by a burka as an attack on their French identity, which is why they also find it 'impossible to remain silent' when they encounter such a covered woman in their midst. The origins of liberalism are not to be looked for in some overblown individualism; originally, it was rather a reply to the problem of what to do in such a situation, when two ethnic or religious groups are living close to each other but have incompatible ways of life.

TERRORISTS WITH A HUMAN FACE

A closer look at some of the 'terrorists' provides another surprise. Mohamed Lahouaiej-Bouhlel, the 31-year-old French man of Tunisian descent who, on the evening of 14 July 2016, drove a rented truck into a crowd celebrating Bastille Day in Nice and killed eighty-four people, was known to police only in connection with common-law crimes such as theft and violence – intelligence services held no record of any radical Islamist links. Working as a delivery driver, he acted as if he was fully integrated into normal daily and professional life, when, all of a sudden, his life began to disintegrate, and a descent into petty crime and violence led to the self-destructive terrorist act. Other cases follow a similar pattern – just recall Hasna Aitboulahcen, the woman who was supposed to be one of the perpetrators of the Paris attacks: she also led a 'modern', secular life and converted to hard Islam only in the last three months before the attacks.

The most outstanding case in this series is Salah Abdeslam, the Paris terror suspect who was arrested in March 2016 in Brussels. The first thing that strikes the eye is that he is no Mohammed Atta, no figure of solemn and austere 'inhuman' fanaticism, but fully 'human' in the usual meaning of the word: he displays all ordinary weaknesses (he is reported to cry often) and is a kind person, smiling a lot, fond of music and dance, drinking and other aspects of *joie de vivre*. Born in Belgium, Abdeslam is a French citizen of Moroccan descent who was employed by STIB-MIVB (the Brussels public transport company) as a mechanic from September 2009 to 2011; it is not clear why he was sacked (perhaps it was due to repeated absences, or criminal acts), but from December 2013 Abdeslam was the manager of a bar in Molenbeek that was frequented by Maghrebian customers and was a centre of drug dealing. In short, Abdeslam comes from a fully integrated family, had a permanent job, and was taking part in ordinary daily life – so why did he radicalize himself? His life story forms a kind of Hegelian triad: ordinary working citizen, descent into drugs and criminal subculture, then final descent/ ascent into religious terror . . . Is the reason provided by another terrorist shot in Paris, Abdelhamid Abaaoud, who, in a video clip promoting ISIS, addresses his viewers with a simple question: are you satisfied with your life? Is this all you want, or do you strive for something more, a more profound engagement that would make your life not only meaningful but also more dynamic, adventurous, fun even? (Incidentally, that's why the solution is not to establish refugee communities in our big cities. Terrorists as a rule come from such places; they stand for the second generation rebellion of children against their well-integrated parents. Their problem is not a lack of integration: they react to integration into Western society as such, a society they consider decadent.)

We should here avoid falling for the cheap socio-psychological concept of an alienated generation that cannot find proper life-fulfilment in our consumerist society. Even worse is to seek a parallel between Right and Left violence, the standard motif of the Liberal centre. There is violence and there is violence, and the point is not to *a priori* disqualify any mode of violence, but to inquire into what mode of violence we are dealing with. Recall the 2008 student protests in Greece, which were threatening to spread all over Europe, from Croatia to France. Many observers have noted as a key feature their violent nature – not violent in the sense of killing people, but violent in the sense of disturbing public order and destroying (well-selected) objects of private and state property, with the goal of disrupting the smooth running of the state and capitalist machinery. The wager of Leftist political terrorism (the RAF in Germany, the Red Brigades in Italy, Action Directe in France) was that, in an epoch in which the masses are totally immersed in capitalist ideological sleep, so that the standard critique of ideology is no longer operative, only a resort to the raw Real of direct violence – '*l'action directe*' – can awaken the masses. While one should reject without ambiguity the murderous way this insight was acted upon, one should not be afraid to endorse the insight itself. Today's post-political 'silent majority' is not stupid, but it is cynically resigned. The limitation of post-politics is best exemplified not only by the success of Rightist populism, but by the UK elections of 2005. In spite of the growing unpopularity of Tony Blair (he was regularly voted the most unpopular person in the UK), there was no way for this discontent to find a politically effective expression, and so Labour was re-elected with Blair at the helm. Something is obviously very wrong here – it is not that people 'do not know what they want', but, rather, that cynical resignation prevents them acting upon it, so the result is the weird gap between what people think and how they act (vote). Such a frustration can foment dangerous extra-parliamentary explosions, which the Left should not bemoan; rather, it should take the risk of using them to 'awaken' the people. In clear contrast to this (wrong and morally unacceptable) strategy, the Muslim acts of terror – and this holds generally for Rightist terror, from Breivik to the US fundamentalists – are not intended to 'awaken' Europeans to their reality and mobilize them, but to terrorize them.

And the series goes on: the seventeen-year-old Afghani refugee who attacked passengers with an axe on a train in Southern Germany had been specially selected for foster care because he seemed to be adjusting well to his new life. The question of integration is much more complex than the simplistic notion that the indigenous majority in a Western country is not ready to accept immigrants. Sloterdijk was right: whereas we Europeans were 'discovering' other continents from the sixteenth century onwards, the people of the Third World are now 'discovering' Europe.[26]

Ali Sonboly, the eighteen-year-old man with German-Iranian citizenship, a 'bullied teen loner obsessed with mass killings',[27] who shot and killed nine people at a shopping centre in the suburbs of Munich, got engaged in a short conversation (or, rather, a shouting match) just before his shooting spree – here is a condensed version:

Man on balcony: 'You fucking asshole you.'
Ali: 'Because of you I was bullied for seven years . . .'
Man: 'You asshole you. You're an asshole.'
Ali: '. . . And now I have to buy a gun to shoot you.'
Unknown speaker: 'Shit/fucking Turks!'
Man: 'Shit/fucking foreigners!'
Ali: 'I am German [. . .] Yeah what, I was born here.'
Man: 'Yeah and what the fuck you think you're doing?'
Ali: 'I grew up here in the Hartz 4 [unemployment benefits in Germany] area.'

The obvious meaning of 'I am German . . . I was born here' would be that, although formally a German citizen, he wasn't really accepted and recognized as one but was treated as a marginal outcast living off unemployment benefits – but the question remains: what was his desire? Did he really want to become German? And what kind of German? Furthermore, Ali's reference to his social position which made him what he is ('I grew up here in the Hartz 4 area') sounds all too reflexive, recalling the mantra about the neglect of social programmes and integration efforts having deprived the younger immigrant generation of any clear economic and social prospects: violent outbursts are their only way to articulate their dissatisfaction. So instead of indulging

ourselves in revengeful fantasies, we should make the effort to understand the deeper causes of the violent outbursts: can we even imagine
what it means to be a young man in a poor and racially mixed suburb,
a priori suspected and harassed by the police, living in high poverty and
broken families, not only unemployed but often unemployable, with no
hope of a future? The moment we take all this into account, the reasons
why people are taking to the streets become clear . . . The problem with
this account is that it only lists objective conditions for the violence,
ignoring the subjective dimension: to riot is to make a subjective statement, to implicitly declare how one relates to one's objective conditions,
how one subjectivizes them. We live in an era of cynicism where we can
easily imagine a protester who, when caught looting and burning a
store and pressed for the reasons for his violence, would suddenly start
to talk like social workers, sociologists and social psychologists, quoting diminished social mobility, rising insecurity, the disintegration of
paternal authority, the lack of maternal love in his early childhood – he
knows what he is doing, and he is nonetheless doing it, as in the famous
number 'Gee, Officer Krupke' from *West Side Story*, which contains
the statement 'Juvenile delinquency is purely a social disease':

> Gee, Officer Krupke, we're very upset;
> We never had the love that ev'ry child oughta get.
> We ain't no delinquents,
> We're misunderstood.
> Deep down inside us there is good!
>
> My father is a bastard,
> My ma's an S.O.B.
> My grandpa's always plastered,
> My grandma pushes tea.
> My sister wears a mustache,
> My brother wears a dress.
> Goodness gracious, that's why I'm a mess!
>
> Officer Krupke, you're really a slob.
> This boy don't need a doctor, just a good honest job.
> Society's played him a terrible trick,
> And sociologic'ly he's sick!

The young delinquents are not only a social disease, they declare themselves to be one, ironically staging different accounts of their predicament (how a social worker, a psychologist, a judge might describe it). In order to get this point, one should discern in a kind of spectral analysis the different modes of contemporary racism. First, there is the old-fashioned unabashed rejection of the (despotic, barbarian, orthodox, corrupt, oriental) Muslim Other on behalf of authentic (Western, civilized, democratic, Christian) values. Then there is the 'reflexive' politically correct racism: the multiculturalist perception of Muslims as the terrain of ethnic horrors and intolerance, of primitive irrational war passions, to be opposed to the post-nation-state liberal-democratic process of solving conflicts through rational negotiations, compromises and mutual respect. Racism is here as it were elevated to the second power: it is attributed to the Other, while we occupy the convenient position of a neutral benevolent observer, righteously dismayed at the horrors going on down there. Finally, there is the reverse racism: it celebrates the exotic authenticity of the Muslim Other who, in contrast to the inhibited, anemic Western Europeans, still exhibits a prodigious lust for life. This brings us to another key feature of this reflected racism: it turns around the distinction between cultural contempt towards the Other and straight racism. Usually, racism is considered the stronger, more radical version of cultural contempt: we are dealing with racism when the simple contempt of the other's culture is elevated into the notion that the other ethnic group is, for inherent (biological or cultural) reasons, inferior to ours. However, today's 'reflected' racism is paradoxically able to articulate itself in the terms of the direct respect for the other's culture: was not the official argument for apartheid in the old South Africa that the black cultures should be preserved in their uniqueness, and not dissolved in the Western melting pot? Do not even today's European racists like le Pen emphasize how what they ask for is only the same right to cultural identity that Africans and others ask for themselves? It is all too simple to dismiss such arguments with the claim that the respect for the other is here simply 'hypocritical'. The mechanism at work is rather that of the disavowal that is characteristic of the fetishistic split: 'I know very well that the Other's culture is worthy of the same respect as mine, but nonetheless . . . (I despise them passionately).'

The more general point to be made here is the Hegelian lesson that the global reflexivization/mediatization generates its own brutal immediacy, best captured by Étienne Balibar's notion of excessive, non-functional cruelty as a feature of contemporary life:[28] a cruelty whose figures range from 'fundamentalist' racist and/or religious slaughter to the 'senseless' outbursts of violence performed by adolescents and the homeless in our megalopolises, a violence one is tempted to call Id-Evil, a violence grounded in no utilitarian or ideological reasoning. All the talk about foreigners stealing work from us, or about the threat they represent to our Western values, should not deceive us: under closer examination, it soon becomes clear that this talk provides a rather superficial secondary rationalization. The answer we ultimately obtain from a skinhead is that it makes him feel good to beat up foreigners, that their presence disturbs him . . . What we encounter here is indeed Id-Evil, i.e., Evil structured and motivated by the most elementary imbalance in the relationship between the ego and *jouissance*, by the tension between pleasure and *jouissance* in the very heart of the foreign body. Id-Evil thus stages the most elementary 'short-circuit' in the relationship of the subject to the primordially missing object-cause of his desire: what 'bothers' us in the 'other' (Jew, Japanese, African, Turk) is that he appears to entertain a privileged relationship to the object – the Other either possesses the object-treasure, having snatched it away from us (which is why we don't have it), or he poses a threat to our possession of the object. What one should propose here is the Hegelian 'infinite judgement', asserting the speculative identity of these 'useless' and 'excessive' outbursts of violent immediacy, which display nothing but a pure and naked ('non-sublimated') hatred of the Otherness, with the global reflexivization of society. Perhaps the ultimate example of this coincidence is the fate of psychoanalytic interpretation: today, the formations of the unconscious (from dreams to hysterical symptoms) have definitely lost their innocence and are thoroughly reflexivized. The 'free associations' of a typical educated analysand consist for the most part of attempts to provide a psychoanalytic explanation of their disturbances, so that one is quite justified in saying that we have not only Jungian, Kleinian, Lacanian interpretations of the symptoms, but symptoms themselves which are Jungian, Kleinian, Lacanian, i.e. whose reality involves implicit reference to some psychoanalytic theory. The unfortunate result of this global reflexivization of the interpretation (everything becomes interpretation, the unconscious interprets itself) is that the analyst's interpretation itself loses its performative 'symbolic efficiency' and leaves the symptom intact in the immediacy of its idiotic *jouissance*.

What happens in psychoanalytic treatment is strictly homologous to the response of the neo-Nazi skinhead who, when really pressed for the reasons for his violence, suddenly starts to talk like a social worker, sociologist or social psychologist, citing diminished social mobility, rising insecurity, the disintegration of paternal authority, the lack of maternal love in his early childhood. The unity of practice and its inherent ideological legitimization disintegrate into raw violence and its impotent, inefficient interpretation. This impotence of interpretation is also one of the necessary obverses of the universalized reflexivity hailed by the risk-society-theorists: it is as if our reflexive power can flourish only insofar as it draws its strength and relies on some minimal 'pre-reflexive' substantial support which eludes its grasp, so that its universalization comes at the price of its inefficiency, i.e. by the paradoxical re-emergence of the brute Real of 'irrational' violence, impermeable and insensitive to reflexive interpretation. So the more today's social theory proclaims the end of nature and/or tradition and the rise of the 'risk society', the more implicit references to 'nature' pervade our daily discourse: even when we do not speak of the 'end of history', do we not put forward the same message when we claim that we are entering a 'post-ideological' pragmatic era, which is another way of claiming that we are entering a post-political order in which the only legitimate conflicts are ethnic/cultural conflicts? Typically, in today's critical and political discourse, the term 'worker' has disappeared from the vocabulary, substituted and/or obliterated by 'immigrants/immigrant workers': Algerians in France, Turks in Germany, Mexicans in the USA. In this way, the class problematic of workers' exploitation is transformed into the multiculturalist problematic of the 'intolerance of the Otherness', etc., and the excessive investment of the multiculturalist liberals in protecting immigrants' ethnic rights clearly draws its energy from the 'repressed' class dimension. Although Francis Fukuyama's thesis on the 'end of history' quickly fell into disrepute, we still silently presume that the liberal-democratic capitalist global order is somehow the finally found 'natural' social regime, we still implicitly conceive of conflicts in developing countries as a subspecies of natural catastrophe, as outbursts of quasi-natural violent passions, or as conflicts based on the fanatic identification with one's ethnic roots (and what is 'the ethnic' here if not again a codeword for 'nature'?). And, again, the key point is that this all-pervasive renaturalization is strictly correlative to the global reflexivization of our daily lives. For that reason, when confronted with ethnic hatred and violence, one should reject thoroughly the standard multiculturalist idea that, against ethnic intolerance, one should learn to respect and live with the Otherness of the Other, to develop tolerance for the different lifestyles, and so on. The way to fight ethnic hatred effectively is not through its immediate counterpart, ethnic tolerance; on the contrary, what we need is *even more hatred*, but the proper political hatred, the hatred directed at the common political enemy.

And should we not put into the same series even Andreas Lubitz, the co-pilot of the Germanwings flight who crashed his plane into the French Alps and killed all 150 people on board, himself included? Since he definitely had no ties to any political or ideological/ religious group or organization, so-called experts have tried to attribute his actions to psychological issues, depression and so on – but the fact remains that he was a perfectly hard-working, modern, non-ideological liberal man, getting up at 5 o'clock every morning for a five kilometre jog, having good relations with friends, living a very disciplined life . . .[29]

So, perhaps, instead of searching in the far recesses of Islam, another approach is needed, and we should bring into focus the nihilism proper to our own societies: something must be wrong with us if young people who appeared integrated regress into terrorism, so where does their hatred come from? Recall the French suburban riots of autumn 2005, when we saw thousands of cars burning and a major outburst of public violence. We are dealing here with the standard reversal of frustrated desire into aggressiveness that is described by psychoanalysis, and Islam simply provides the form to ground this (self-)destructive hatred. Frustration and envy get radicalized into a murderous and self-destructive hatred of the West, and people become involved in violent revenge. This violence can only culminate in acts of orgiastic (self-)destruction, without any serious vision of an alternative society. There is no emancipatory potential in fundamentalist violence, however anti-capitalist it claims to be: instead it is a phenomenon inherent in the global capitalist universe.

CIACCO'S RESPONSE, OR, STRANGERS IN A STRANGE LAND

Jacques Lacan wrote that, even if what a jealous husband claims about his wife (that she sleeps around with other men, say) is all true, his jealousy is still pathological – why? The real question is not 'Is his jealousy well-grounded?' but 'Why does he need jealousy to maintain his self-identity?' Along the same lines, one could say that, even if most of the Nazi claims about the Jews were true (they exploit Germans, they seduce German girls), their anti-Semitism would still be (and was) pathological, since it represses the true reason why the Nazis *needed* anti-Semitism in order to sustain their ideological position.

And is it not exactly the same with the growing fear of refugees and immigrants? To extrapolate it to the extreme: even if most of our prejudices about them were proven to be true (they are hidden fundamentalist terrorists, they rape and steal), the paranoiac talk about the immigrant threat is still an ideological pathology that reveals more about us Europeans than about immigrants. The central issue is not 'Are immigrants a real threat to Europe?' but 'What does this obsession with the immigrant threat tell us about the weakness of Europe?'

So there are two dimensions here which should be kept apart. One is the atmosphere of fear, of the struggle against the Islamization of Europe, with its own obvious absurdities: refugees who flee terror are equated with the terrorists they are escaping from. And thus the obvious fact that there are among the refugees also terrorists, rapists, criminals, etc., while the large majority are desperate people looking for a better life, is given a paranoiac twist – immigrants appear (or pretend) to be desperate refugees, while in reality they are the spearheads of a new Islamic invasion of Europe; and, above all, as is usually the case, the responsibility for problems that are immanent to modern global capitalism is projected onto an external intruder.

A suspicious gaze always finds what it is looking for; 'proofs' are everywhere, even if half of them are soon proven to be fakes. One should especially emphasize this point today when, all around Europe, the fear of the refugees' invasion is reaching truly paranoiac proportions. People who haven't seen a single actual refugee react aggressively to the very proposal of establishing a refugee centre in their proximity; stories about incidents catch the imagination, spread like wildfire and persist even after they are clearly proven false. This is why the worst reaction to the racist anti-immigrant paranoia is to ignore actual incidents and problems with immigrants, arguing that every critical mention of immigrants only feeds the racist enemies. Against this reasoning, one should point out that it is such silence that really helps our racist enemies – it directly feeds the distrust of ordinary people ('You see, they are not telling us the truth!'), boosting the credibility of racist rumours and lies.

The other dimension is the tragi-comic spectacle of endless self-culpabilization of Europe which allegedly betrayed its humanity, of a murderous Europe leaving thousands of drowned bodies at its borders – a self-serving exercise with no emancipatory potential whatsoever. Furthermore, the accent on humanitarian catastrophe deftly de-politicizes the situation. No wonder Angela Merkel, referring to the refugee crisis, recently said: 'Do you seriously believe that all the euro states that last year fought all the way to keep Greece in the eurozone – and we were the strictest – can one year later allow Greece to, in a way, plunge into chaos?'[30] This statement clearly expresses the basic lie of her humanitarian position: it is part of a stick-and-carrot approach, with humanitarian help as a bonus for politico-economic surrender.

We should apply to the humanitarians who bemoan 'the end of Europe' the great Hegelian lesson: when someone is painting a picture of Europe's overall and utmost moral degeneration, the question to be raised is in what way such a stance is complicit in what it criticizes. No wonder that, with the exception of humanitarian appeals to compassion and solidarity, the effects of such compassionate self-flagellation are nil.

When Leftist liberals endlessly vary the motif of how the rise of terrorism is the result of Western colonial and military interventions in the Middle East, their analysis, although pretending to be respectful towards others, stands out as a blatant case of patronizing racism that reduces the Other to a passive victim and deprives it of any agenda. Along these lines, one can even read the extreme brutality of ISIS as a desperate attempt to assert one's full agency, so that the message of their actions is: 'Allow us at least to be autonomous agents of Evil!', to which they are getting the Left-liberal reply from the West: 'No way! Sorry, the more you are violent, the more you are an effect of Western imperialism!' What such a view fails to see is how Arabs are in no way just passive victims of European and American neo-colonial machinations. Their different courses of action are not just reactions, they are different forms of active engagement in their predicament: expansive and aggressive push towards Islamization (financing mosques in foreign countries, etc.), open warfare against the West, and so on. All these are ways of actively engaging in a situation with a well-defined goal.

What the European emancipatory legacy should be defended from is thus primarily Europeans themselves, namely the anti-immigrant populists who see Europe threatened by the over-tolerant multicultural Left. It is easy to say that Muslim immigrants who violate our rules should be thrown out and sent back where they come from – but what about those among ourselves who violate our emancipatory legacy? Where should they be thrown? One should be more attentive to the hidden proximity between them and fundamentalist Islamists, especially in view of the sudden discovery of women's and gay rights by anti-immigrant populists, who oppose these rights in their own community but defend them when women or gays are attacked by Muslim fundamentalists, using the Muslim fundamentalists' hatred of women and gays as another argument against them. The obscenity of the situation is breathtaking: the very people who, in our countries, continuously mock and attack abortion rights and gay marriages are now reborn as defenders of Western freedoms.

This is why there is no place for a negotiated compromise here, no point at which the two sides may agree ('OK, anti-immigrant paranoiacs exaggerate, but there are some fundamentalists among the refugees . . .'): even the minimal accuracy of the anti-immigrant racist's claims does not serve as a true explanation of his paranoia, and, on the opposite side, the humanitarian self-culpabilization is thoroughly narcissistic, closed to the immigrant Neighbour. Everything 'bad' about the other is dismissed either as our (Western racist) projection onto the other or as the result of our (Western imperialist) mistreatment (colonial violence) of the other; what lies beyond this closed circle of ourselves and our projections (or, rather, the projections of our 'repressed' evil side onto the other), what, within this perspective, we encounter as the 'authentic' other when we truly open ourselves up to them, the good innocent other, is, again, our ideological fantasy. Is this reversal of the alleged utmost objectivity ('what the immigrant really is') into utmost subjectivity not an exemplary case of what Hegel discerned as the secret of the Kantian *Ding-an-sich*? The 'thing-in-itself', the way it is independently of how we relate to it, is a pure *Gedankending*, 'creature of our mind'.

So who or what is the real Other? In today's market, we find a whole series of products deprived of their malignant property: coffee without caffeine, cream without fat, beer without alcohol . . . One should definitely add to this series *smell*: perhaps the key difference between the lower class and middle class concerns the way they relate to smell. For the middle class, lower classes smell, their members do not wash regularly – or, to quote the proverbial answer of a middle-class Parisian as to why he prefers to ride the first-class cars in the metro: 'I wouldn't mind riding with workers in second class – it is only that they smell!' This brings us to one of the possible definitions of what a neighbour means today: a neighbour is the one who by definition *smells*. This is why today deodorants and soaps are crucial – they make neighbours at least minimally tolerable. I am ready to love my neighbours . . . provided they don't smell too badly. A little while ago, scientists in a laboratory in Venezuela added a further element to these series: through genetic manipulation, they succeeded in growing beans that, upon consumption, do not generate bad-smelling and socially embarrassing winds! So, after decaf coffee, fat-free cakes, diet cola and alcohol-free beer, we now get wind-free beans . . .

So the task is to talk openly about all unpleasant issues without a compromise with racism, i.e., to reject the humanitarian idealization of refugees that dismisses every attempt to confront openly the difficult issues of the cohabitation of different ways of life as a concession to the neo-fascist Right. What disappears in this way is the true encounter with a real neighbour in his or her specific way of life. Descartes, the father of modern philosophy, noted that, when he was young, foreign people's manners and beliefs appeared to him ridiculous and eccentric; but then he asked himself, what if our own manners also appear to them ridiculous and eccentric. The outcome of this reversal is not a generalized cultural relativism, but something much more radical and interesting: we should learn to experience ourselves as eccentric, to see our customs in all their weirdness and arbitrariness. In his *Everlasting Man*, G. K. Chesterton imagines the monster that man might have seemed to the merely natural animals around him:

> The simplest truth about man is that he is a very strange being; almost in the sense of being a stranger on the earth. In all sobriety, he has much more of the external appearance of one bringing alien habits from another land than of a mere growth of this one. He has an unfair advantage and an unfair disadvantage. He cannot sleep in his own skin; he cannot trust his own instincts. He is at once a creator moving miraculous hands and fingers and a kind of cripple. He is wrapped in artificial bandages called clothes; he is propped on artificial crutches called furniture. His mind has the same doubtful liberties and the same wild limitations. Alone among the animals, he is shaken with the beautiful madness called laughter; as if he had caught sight of some secret in the very shape of the universe hidden from the universe itself. Alone among the animals he feels the need of averting his thought from the root realities of his own bodily being; of hiding them as in the presence of some higher possibility which creates the

mystery of shame. Whether we praise these things as natural to man or abuse them as artificial in nature, they remain in the same sense unique.[31]

Is a 'way of life' not precisely such a way of being a stranger on the earth? A specific 'way of life' is not just composed of a set of abstract (Christian, Muslim) 'values', it is something embodied in a thick network of everyday practices: how we eat and drink, sing, make love, how we relate to authorities . . .

Islam (as any other substantial religion) is a name for an entire way of life – in its Middle East version, it relies on a large family with strong authority held by parents and brothers (which is not specifically Muslim but more Mediterranean), and when young members, especially girls, from such families get involved with their peers from more individualist Western families, this almost inevitably gives rise to tensions. We 'are' our way of life, it is our second nature, which is why direct 'education' is not able to change it. Something much more radical is needed, a kind of Brechtian 'extraneation', a deep existential experience by means of which it all of a sudden strikes us how stupidly meaningless and arbitrary our customs and rituals are – there is nothing natural in the way we embrace and kiss, in the way we wash ourselves, in the way we behave while eating . . .

The point is thus not to recognize ourselves in strangers, not to gloat in the comforting falsity that 'they are like us', but to recognize a stranger in ourselves – therein resides the innermost dimension of European modernity. Communitarianism is not enough: a recognition that we are all, each in our own way, weird lunatics provides the only hope for a tolerable co-existence of different ways of life. *Stranger in a Strange Land*, Robert A. Heinlein's sci-fi classic from 1961, tells the story of a human who comes to Earth in early adulthood after being born on Mars and raised there by Martians. Maybe, this is the situation for all of us.

Does this mean that we should resign ourselves to a co-existence of isolated groups of lunatics, leaving it to the public law to maintain some kind of minimal order by imposing rules of interaction? Of course not, but the paradox is that we should go through this zero-point of 'de-naturalization' if we want to engage in a long and difficult process of universal solidarity, of constructing a Cause that is strong enough to traverse different communities. If we want universal solidarity, we have to become universal in ourselves, relate to ourselves as universal by acquiring a distance towards our life-world. Hard and painful work is needed to achieve this, not just sentimental ruminations about migrants as a new form of 'nomadic proletariat'.

So, to raise Lenin's old question, what is to be done? To begin with, what about a couple of totally feasible pragmatic measures? Short-term: the EU should establish receiving centres in the nearest-possible safe locations (northern Syria, Turkey, the Greek islands . . .), and then organize a direct transport of accepted refugees to their European destination (via ferries and air bridges), thereby putting out of business the smugglers turning around billions of dollars, as well as ending the humiliating misery of thousands wandering on foot through Europe. Mid-term: apply all means, public and secret, from WikiLeaks-style information wars to economic blackmail (of Saudi Arabia, for example), to stop the wars or at least to expand conflict-free zones. The only long-term solution is, of course, communism, but this is another story. . .

To conclude, let us reach back to one of our great classics. In Canto VI of *Inferno* (lines 77–89), Dante asks the glutton Ciacco (who, it is interesting to note, is not ready to assume his name: instead of saying 'I am Ciacco,' he says, 'You citizens called me Ciacco') about the fate of the men of good reason, men who dedicated their life to the good of the city:

> And I continued thus: 'Still would I learn
> More from thee, further parley still entreat.
> Of Farinata and Tegghiaio say,
> They who so well deserved; of Giacopo,
> Arrigo, Mosca, and the rest, who bent
> Their minds on working good. Oh! tell me where
> They bide, and to their knowledge let me come.
> For I am prest with keen desire to hear
> If Heaven's sweet cup, or poisonous drug of Hell,
> Be to their lip assign'd.' He answer'd straight:

'These are yet blacker spirits. Various crimes
Have sunk them deeper in the dark abyss.
If thou so far descendest, thou mayst see them.'

Imagine we were to visit Dante's Hell now and find there in the Third
Circle today's Ciacco, a gluttonous Western European who ignores
the plight of migrants, focused as he is on continuing his consumption undisturbed. If we were to ask him, 'But tell me, where are all
those humanitarians who bent their minds on working good?', would
he not snap back: 'You will have to descend much deeper, their souls
are much blacker than mine!' Why? Is this not a too cruel reaction?
The point is that, self-critical as it may appear to be, the humanitarian reaction almost imperceptibly transforms a politico-economic
problem into a moral one of 'refugee crisis' and of 'helping the victims'. Instead of attacking the silent lower-class majority as racist
and ignorant of the immigrants' plight, or, at best, as stupid victims
of racist media propaganda, it should address their actual concerns,
which express themselves in a racist way.

Furthermore, does the advocacy of unrestrained acceptance of
immigrants not involve a weird mixture of ethics and pragmatic reasoning? It is our duty to receive refugees . . . plus it will profit us since
the European population is diminishing due to low birth rates . . .
But why should the diminishing population be a problem? Aren't
there already too many people on the earth? Instead of political
intervention proper, we thus get the old couplet of morality ('open
you heart to those who suffer') and biology ('Europe needs new
young blood to rejuvenate itself'). This paradox mirrors another,
much deeper, reversal of the standard political coordinates, where
the Left is politicizing the conflicts and the Right naturalizing/depo-
liticizing them: in today's populist Right, the topic of immigrants is
not 'depoliticized', it is on the contrary extremely politicized, presented as a well-orchestrated enemy action, and 'it is the traditional
political left that seems to be forced to take recourse to depoliticized
vocabulary: immigrants are simply human beings who need our help
(very much like in the case of natural disasters)'.[32]

The basic premise of our approach to refugees should thus be literally *anti-humanist*: humans are in general not good but *perverted*

egotists. Even when they seem to sacrifice their egotist interests for a higher common goal, this is more often than not part of a strategy to gain a perverted satisfaction. The task is therefore not to idealize refugees but to accept them the way they are, equal to ourselves not in their humanity but in their unprincipled opportunism and petty perversions.

5

The Sexual is (Not) Political

THE TRAPS OF POLITICAL CORRECTNESS

People often ask themselves if a person can really imagine what it is to be another person; what a psychoanalyst would add is that we also cannot imagine what it is to be ourselves – or, more precisely, we (only) imagine that we are ourselves without really being it. Here is an example of this impossibility to be oneself.

In the Spring of 2015, UK media extensively reported on Grace Gelder, a middle-aged photographer who, after practising Indian meditation and upon hearing Bjork singing in one of her songs the line 'I am married to myself', decided to do precisely that: she organized the full ceremony of self-marrying, proclaimed her vows to herself, put on a wedding ring and kissed herself in a mirror . . . Far from being an idiosyncratic eccentricity, the idea of self-dating and self-marrying circulates more and more on the web. Technical details on how to proceed with self-dating abound: the prospective self-lover should leave loving messages all around his or her apartment; when one decides on a self-date, one should put one's apartment in order, prepare a nice table with candles, put on one's best clothes, inform one's friends that one has an important meeting with oneself . . . The goal of self-dating is to gain a deep knowledge of oneself, of what one really is and wants, so that, by taking a vow to my deeper self, I can achieve self-acceptance and self-harmonization, and this will enable me to lead a deeply satisfied life . . . won't it?

Before we collapse into laughter at this idea and dismiss it as an extreme expression of contemporary pathological narcissism, we should ascertain its moment of truth: the idea of self-dating and self-marrying presupposes that I am not directly one with myself. I can marry myself only if I am not directly myself, so that my self-unity has to be registered by the big Other, performed in a symbolic ceremony, made 'official'. Here, however, problems arise: how does this inscription into the symbolic order, in the eyes of which I am then 'married to myself', relate to my direct self-experience? What if the result of my probing into myself is that I discover that I don't like what I find there at all? What if all I find is the filth of envy, sadistic fantasies and disgusting sexual obsessions? What if the much-celebrated 'inner wealth' of my personality is inherently excremental – *vulgari eloquentia*, what if I am really full of shit? In short, what if I discover that I am my own neighbour in the strict biblical sense (the abyss of an impenetrable X totally foreign to my official self), and what if I search for contact with others precisely to escape from myself? They say that in order to love others, you have to love yourself – truly? What if the opposite holds, at two levels: I love others to escape myself, and I can only love myself insofar as I am able to love others? Self-marrying presupposes that I've found peace with myself – but what if I cannot reconcile myself with myself? And what if I fully discover this only after I get married to myself? Should I enact a formal self-divorce? Should this divorce be permitted for Catholics? This is why, apropos of the injunction to love your neighbour as yourself, Lacan acerbically noted 'the impossibility of responding to this sort of challenge in the first person; no one ever supposed that to this "Thou shalt love thy neighbour as thyself", an "I love my neighbour as myself" could answer, because obviously the weakness of this formulation is clear to everyone.'[1]

Therein resides the problem with the well-known motto 'Be yourself' ... Which self? Insofar as the self whom I marry when I self-marry is my ideal ego, 'the best in me', the idealized image of myself, relaxed self-identification and self-acceptance imperceptibly turn into radical self-alienation, and the fear that I am not true to my 'true self' haunts me forever. And exactly the same question – which self? – haunts the latest politically correct obsession whose commercial expression is the so-called 'Affirmative Consent Kit' offered online by the Affirmative Consent Project for only $2: a small bag (available in faux-suede or canvas version) filled with a condom, a pen, some breath mints, and a simple contract stating that both participants freely consent to a shared sexual act. The suggestion is that a couple ready to have sex either takes a photo holding the contract in their hands, or that they both date and sign it. Although the 'Affirmative Consent Kit' addresses a very real problem, it does it in a way which is not only silly but directly counter-productive – why?

The underlying idea is that a sex act, if it to be cleansed of any suspicion of coercion, has to be declared in advance as the result of a free, conscious decision taken by both participants – to put it in Lacanian terms, it has to be registered by the big Other, inscribed into the symbolic order. As such, the kit is just an extreme expression of an attitude that is growing all around the US – for example, the state of California has passed a law requiring all colleges that accept state funding to adopt policies requiring all students to obtain affirmative consent (which it defines as 'affirmative, conscious, and voluntary agreement to engage in sexual activity' that is 'ongoing' and not given when too drunk) before engaging in sexual activity, or else risk punishment for sexual assault.

'Affirmative, conscious, and voluntary agreement' – by whom? The first thing to do here is to mobilize the Freudian triad of Ego, Superego and Id (in a simplified version: my conscious self-awareness, the agency of moral responsibility enforcing norms on me, and my deepest half-disavowed passions). What if there is a conflict between the three? Under the pressure of the Superego, my Ego say 'no', but my Id resists and clings to the denied desire? Or (a much more interesting case) the opposite: I say 'yes' to the sexual invitation, surrendering to my Id passion, but in the midst of performing the act, my Superego triggers an unbearable guilt feeling? So, to bring things to the absurd, should the contract be signed by the Ego, Superego and Id of each party, so that it is valid only if all three say 'yes'? Plus, what if the male partner also uses his contractual right to step back and cancel the agreement at any moment in the sexual activity? Imagine that, after obtaining the woman's consent, when the prospective lovers find themselves naked in bed, some tiny bodily detail (an unpleasant sound like a vulgar belching) dispels the erotic charm and makes the man withdraw? Is this not in itself an extreme humiliation for the woman?

The ideology that sustains this promotion of 'sexual respect' deserves a closer look. The basic formula is: 'Only yes means yes!' – it has to be an explicit yes, not just the absence of a no. No 'no' does not automatically amount to a 'yes': if a woman who is being seduced does not actively resist it, this still leaves the space open for different forms of coercion. Here, however, problems abound: what if a woman passionately desires it but is too embarrassed to openly declare so? What if, for both partners, ironically playing coercion is part of the erotic game? And a 'yes' to what, precisely, to what types of sexual activity, is a declared 'yes'? Should then the contract form be more detailed, so that the principal consent is specified: a 'yes' to vaginal but not anal intercourse, a 'yes' to fellatio but not swallowing the sperm, a 'yes' to light spanking but not harsh blows . . . One can easily imagine a long bureaucratic negotiation killing all desire for the act, but it could also get libidinally invested in itself. Not to mention the opposite possibility: an enforced 'yes'. In one of the most painful and troubling scenes in David Lynch's *Wild at Heart*, Willem Dafoe exerts sexual pressure on Laura Dern in a lonely motel room: he touches and squeezes her, invading the space of her intimacy and repeating in a threatening way, 'Say "Fuck me!" ', i.e. extorting from her words that would signal her consent to a sexual act. The ugly, unpleasant scene drags itself on, and when, finally, the exhausted Dern utters a barely audible 'Fuck me!', Dafoe abruptly steps away, assumes a nice, friendly smile and cheerfully retorts: 'No, thanks, I don't have time today, I've got to go; but on another occasion I would do it gladly . . .' The uneasiness of this scene, of course, resides in the fact that the shock of Dafoe's final rejection of Dern's forcefully extracted offer gives the final pitch to him: his unexpected rejection is his ultimate triumph, and while rape would of course be worse, in a way this outcome is more humiliating to her. He has attained what he really wanted: not the act itself, just her consent to it, her symbolic humiliation.

These problems are far from secondary. They concern the very core of erotic interplay from which one cannot withdraw into a neutral position of meta-language and declare one's readiness (or unreadiness) to engage in it: any such declaration is part of the interplay and either de-eroticizes the situation or gets eroticized itself.

There is something in the very structure of erotic interplay that resists the direct formal declaration of consent or intent. In the English working-class drama *Brassed Off*, the hero accompanies home a young woman who, at the entrance to her flat, tells him: 'Would you like to come in for a coffee?' To his answer – 'There is a problem: I don't drink coffee' – she retorts with a smile: 'No problem: I don't have any . . . ' The immense direct erotic power of her reply resides in how, through a double negation, she pronounces an embarrassingly direct sexual invitation without ever mentioning sex: when she first invites the man in for a coffee and then admits she has no coffee, she does not cancel her invitation, she just makes it clear that the first invitation for a coffee was a stand-in (or pretext), indifferent in itself, for the invitation to sex. So what should the man do here to obey 'sexual respect'? Should he tell the girl: 'Wait a minute, let us make it clear: since you invited me to a cup of coffee in your flat without having any coffee, this means you want sex – yes?' One can imagine how such an '(Only a) yes means yes' approach would not only ruin the encounter but would also be perceived by the girl (in a fully justified way) as an extremely aggressive and humiliating act.

We can imagine here multiple levels, beginning with direct communication: 'I would like you to come to my flat and fuck me.' 'I would also love to fuck you, so let's just go up and do it!' Then, the direct mention of the detour as a detour: 'I would like you to come to my flat and fuck me, but I am embarrassed to ask for it directly. So I will be polite and ask if you want to come up with me for a coffee.' 'I don't drink coffee, but I would also love to fuck you, so let's just go up and do it!' Then, the idiot's answer: 'Would you like to come up to my flat for a cup of coffee?' 'Sorry, I don't drink coffee.' 'Idiot, it's not about coffee, it's about sex, coffee was just a pretext!' 'Oh, I get it, yes, let's go up and do it!' Then a version with direct jumps between levels: 'Would you like to come up to my flat for a cup of coffee?' 'Yes, I would love to fuck you!' (Or, 'Sorry, I am now too tired for sex.') And the inverted version: 'Would you like to come up to my flat and fuck me?' 'Sorry, I am not in the mood for coffee right now.' (This retreat into politeness is, of course, again an act of extreme aggression and humiliation.) We can also imagine a version along the lines of 'coffee without. . .': 'I'm tired tonight, so I would love to come up to your place just for a cup of coffee, no sex.' 'I have my period now, so I cannot give you coffee without sex – but I have a good DVD to watch, so what about coffee without DVD?' Up to the ultimate self-reflexive version: 'Would you like to come up to my place?' 'I am not sure if I want sex or to watch a movie, so how about we just go up and have a cup of coffee?'

Why does the direct invitation to sex not work? Because the true problem is not that coffee is never fully coffee, but that sex is never fully sex, that there is no sexual relationship, which is why the sexual act needs a fantasmatic supplement. So it's not just polite censorship that prevents a direct invitation – 'Let's go up and have sex!' – coffee or something like that has to be mentioned to provide the fantasmatic frame for sex. In other words, what is primordially repressed in the scene from *Brassed Off* is not sex (which, for this reason, has to be replaced in the explicit text by coffee), but what is missing in sex itself, the inherent impossibility/failure of sex. The replacement of sex by coffee is a secondary repression whose function is to obfuscate the primordial repression.

The 'yes means yes' sexual rule is an exemplary case of the narcissistic notion of subjectivity that predominates today. A subject is experienced as something vulnerable, something that has to be protected by a complex set of rules, warned in advance about all possible intrusions that may disturb him or her. Upon its release, *ET* was banned in Sweden, Norway and Denmark: its non-sympathetic portrayal of adults was considered dangerous for the relation between children and their parents. (An ingenious detail confirms this accusation: for the first 10 minutes of the film, all adults are seen only below their belts, like the adults in cartoons who threaten Tom and Jerry. . .) From today's perspective, we can see this prohibition as an early sign of the politically correct obsession with protecting individuals from any experience that may hurt them in any way. Not only real-life experiences but even fiction can be censored, as we can see in a recent request by Columbia University's Multicultural Affairs Advisory Board (MAAB) to put 'trigger warnings' on canonic works of art. (A proof that, sometimes, fictions are to be taken more seriously than reality.) What triggered this request was a complaint by a student, a victim of sexual assault, who was 'triggered' by the vivid depictions of rape in Ovid's *Metamorphoses*, which she had been instructed to read. Since the professor dismissed the student's complaint, the MAAB also proposed 'sensitivity training classes' for professors teaching them how to deal with attack survivors, persons of colour or those from a low-income background. Jerry Coyne is right to claim that

the pathway of such trigger warnings – not just for sexual assault but for violence, bigotry, and racism – will eventually lead to *every* work of literature being labelled as potentially offensive. There goes the Bible, there goes Dante, there goes Huck Finn (*loaded* with racism), there goes all the old literature written before we realized that minorities, women, and gays weren't second-class people. And as for violence and hatred, well, they're everywhere, for they're just as much parts of literature as parts of life. *Crime and Punishment?* **Trigger warning:** brutal violence against an old woman. *The Great Gatsby?* **Trigger warning:** violence against women (remember when Tom Buchanan broke Mrs Wilson's nose?). *The Inferno?* **Trigger warning:** graphic violence, sodomy, and torture. *Dubliners?* **Trigger warning:** Pedophilia [. . .] In the end, anybody can claim offence or triggering about anything: liberals about conservative politics, pacifists against violence, women against sexism, minorities against bigotry, Jews against anti-Semitism, Muslims against any mention of Israel, creationists against evolution, religionists against atheism, and so on.[2]

And the list can go on indefinitely – recall the proposal to digitally delete smoking from Hollywood classics ... And it is not only low-income people who may feel hurt – what about the rich people who cocoon themselves to avoid getting 'triggered' by close encounters with actual lower classes? Is not isolation in cocooned 'safe spaces' precisely the strategy of the rich? But the case of religion is especially interesting. In Western Europe, Muslim representatives are leading a campaign to impose a legal prohibition on blasphemy and disrespect of religion(s). OK, but should we not apply this prohibition also to religious texts themselves, prohibiting or totally rewriting in PC style the complete Bible and Qur'an? (Not to mention that we should also prohibit disrespecting atheism.) And – the ultimate inescapable paradox – would quite a lot of people not feel hurt by such universalized trigger warnings, experiencing it as an oppressive regime of total control? What we should reject here is the basic MAAB premise: 'Students need to feel safe in the classroom . . .' No, they don't need to feel safe, they need to learn how to openly confront all the humiliations and injustices of life and to fight against them. The entire MAAB vision of life is wrong: 'It's time for students to learn that Life is Triggering [. . .] Cocooning oneself in a Big Safe Space for four years gets it exactly backwards.'[3] One should be taught to step out of the cocooned Big Safe Space, enter the dangerous unsafe life outside and intervene there. One should be taught that we do *not* live in a safe world – we live in a world with multiple catastrophes, from environmental ones and new prospects of war to rising social violence.

'If you can't face Hiroshima in the theatre you'll eventually end up in Hiroshima itself.' This statement (by Edward Bond) provides the best argument against those who oppose graphic descriptions of sexual violence and other atrocities, dismissing them as participating in the same violence that these descriptions pretend to critically analyse and reject. For example, in a (very) critical review of my intervention at the 'Benjamin in Ramallah' conference, the writer claims that I enumerate

> a detailed list of ritualized sexual violences taking place *outside* of the Islamic world, thus showing his willingness to accompany 'honour killings' with matching atrocities. He was each time rhetorically apologetic about his descriptions ('It is really hard to talk about this but I must tell you') and each time came back with more obscene, bloody and graphic details. This suffices to grasp the pointlessness (and ambivalence) of his intervention: displaying concerns about sexual violence *by subjecting* the watchful audience to the violence of crude images of heinous sexual practices.[4]

This is the prototype of a politically correct line of argument that I not only reject but consider extremely dangerous. In order to really grasp sexual violence one has to be shocked, traumatized even, by it – if we constrain ourselves to aseptic technical descriptions we do exactly the same as those who refer to torture as 'enhanced interrogation technique' or to rape as 'enhanced seduction technique'. It is only the taste of the thing itself that effectively vaccinates us against it. And we can already see the consequences of such a stance: when, at the beginning of September 2016, Facebook censored the iconic 'napalm girl' photograph of a terrified 9-year-old naked Vietnamese girl running away from napalm bombs, it hypocritically justified it as a defence against displaying child nudity, which can be construed as child pornography, ignoring the obvious political dimension. What this image could 'trigger' is clearly not sexual arousal but the awareness of the horror of war against civilian population. (The big public outcry quickly forced Facebook to reinstate the picture.) Along these lines, Nikki Johnson-Huston described eloquently how 'white Liberals have hijacked the conversation about diversity, political correctness and what topics we should be outraged about':

> My problem with Liberalism is that it's more concerned with policing people's language and thoughts without requiring them to do anything to fix the problem. White liberal college students speak of 'safe spaces', 'trigger words', 'micro aggressions' and 'white privilege' while not having to do anything or, more importantly, give up anything. They can't even have a conversation with someone who sees the world differently without resorting to calling someone a racist, homophobic, misogynistic, bigot and trying to have them banned from campus, or ruin them and their reputation. They say they feel black people's pain because they took a trip to Africa to help the disadvantaged, but are unwilling to go to a black neighbourhood in the city in which they live. These same college students will espouse the joys of diversity, but will in the same breath assume you are only on campus because of affirmative action or that all black people grew up in poverty.[5]

Therein resides the political problem with political correctness: to paraphrase Robespierre, it admits the injustices of actual life, but it wants to cure them with a 'revolution without revolution': it wants social change with no actual change. So it's not just the question of balancing the two extremes, of finding the right point between political correctness, which aims at prohibiting forms of speech that may hurt others, and general freedom of speech, which should not be constrained – the PC attempt to regulate speech is false in itself, since it obfuscates the problem instead of trying to resolve it.

A further consequence of the PC attitude to speech is the spreading prohibition of irony: when one makes a remark considered non-PC, it is less and less possible to save oneself by claiming it was meant ironically. Here, opposites coincide again: at the beginning of September 2016, media reported that

> North Korea has forbidden people from making sarcastic comments about Kim Jong-un or his totalitarian regime in their everyday conversations. Even indirect criticism of the authoritarian government has been banned [. . .] Residents were warned against criticizing the state in a series of mass meetings held by functionaries across the country [. . .] Officials told people that sarcastic expressions such as 'This is all America's fault' would constitute unacceptable criticism of the regime.[6]

Such a strategy ultimately cannot but fail, for a simple reason: in such circumstances, the official jargon itself more and more functions as its own ironic commentary.

UNITED AGAINST HETEROSEXISM

I fully experienced the truth of these lines in the afternoon of Sunday 31 July 2016, sitting in a hotel room in Vancouver watching the live coverage of the Vancouver Pride Parade where, as the main media put it, 'the power of love shined'. Everyone was there, hundreds of thousands of people, either in the procession (headed, as expected, by none other than the Canadian PM Justin Trudeau, with his entire family, who stole the show) or among the public observing the parade and warmly applauding it. (Such love, of course, has nothing whatsoever to do with the violent passion of authentic love, with the exclusive fixation on a singular being that totally derails our immersion in the rhythms of ordinary daily life. The 'love' that shined at the parade was the stupid all-inclusive 'oceanic feeling' for which Freud had no sense, a feeling that is ideology embodied, a feeling that obliterates all struggle and antagonism.) This big and all-inclusive display of 'unity in diversity' of course needed an enemy – 'heterosexism' was constantly evoked by the TV commentators who, of course, didn't mean to thereby attack heterosexuality as such but merely the privileging of heterosexuality into a universal norm that reduces other sexual orientations to a secondary deviation. (Although this critical view of heterosexism pretends to be non-normative, open to every orientation, it in fact subtly privileges non-heterosexual orientations – at least as less prone to ideological appropriation and more 'subversive' with regard to hegemonic ideology.) To paraphrase Mao, hundreds of flowers were blossoming: the parading groups encompassed not just queer and LGBT organizations but also libraries and bookstores, restaurants, theatres, lawyers, ecological groups, industrial and agricultural companies, up to a nightclub 'always open to gays and trans'. Here is the official self-presentation of the organizers:

> There are approximately 150 parade entries – floats, dancers, marching groups and more – that make for a constant stream of entertainment along the three-hour route. Prepare to be wowed, amazed and inspired with sights such as four-foot-high headdresses, pink fire engines, more rainbow flags than you can count and signs conveying messages of hope and change. One of the most memorable parts of the parade are the costumes, which are so elaborate and outrageous that they make a feather boa and go-go boots look tame.

Young men danced in small tights accentuating the contours of their penises, interrupting their dance only to passionately embrace and kiss; overweight boys and girls displayed layers of fat hanging from their bellies (thereby subverting the sexist norms of beauty) . . . We were far from the situation decades ago when gays lived in the shadowy underground, at best politely tolerated and ignored. (One should nonetheless note that this marginalization and exclusion from public space gave birth to a surplus-enjoyment of its own: all the thrill of living in the half-forbidden shadowy space, of transgressing the predominant rules ... We find among some in the LGBT community a contradictory desire of gaining full legitimacy in the public space and simultaneously enjoying the thrill of transgression.) Such joyful public display is justified since heterosexism is still present in our everyday lives: by way of proudly displaying their orientation, queer people not only overcome their own reticence, they also make us, the observers, aware of our persisting prejudices, confirmed by our uneasiness in observing their display.

The irony of this parade is that the situation from decades ago is almost symmetrically inverted: now it is heterosexuality that is tolerated, but it is expected that the heterosexual majority not display their orientation with too much pride, since such display would instantly qualify as heterosexist – heterosexuality is (not explicitly but subtly) perceived as a limitation, as a sexual orientation that is opportunistically satisfied with the old established patterns and avoids the risks of exploring new liberating possibilities, as an impassive submission to the libidinal order imposed by the structure of social domination. 'LGBT+' thus provided the specific colour of the entire field: although LGBT+ probably comprises no more than 10 per cent of the population, they determined the colour of the entire field; all were united under their banner. (If we limit the population to those who effectively reject the two options of the standard gender identity and thus exclude lesbians and gays who still experience themselves as women or men, we get around 1% of the population – and how can one not recall the Occupy Wall Street famous slogan of 99% against the 1% privileged wealthy? In the case of transgender people, (not legal but ethical) justice is on the side of the 1% against the 99% at ease with their gender identity.)

So 'we are all queer', although some are more so than others. Such unity is by definition ideology at its purest, and we should immediately ask two questions: what is the form of subjectivity that underlies this unity, and who or what was *de facto* excluded (left unmentioned, ignored) from this bouquet of a hundred flowers blossoming or directly refused to participate? Many ethnic groups declined to take part, in solidarity with Black Lives Matter Vancouver's protest against the Pride parade's inclusion of a police float; many Indigenous people are members of BLM and thus *de facto* did not participate.[7] Queer

Muslim group Salaam and queer South Asian group Trikone were also sitting out this year's pride parade; Salaam stated that 'because of the racist backlash [. . .] we need to have our own march [. . .] Pride is not talking to us. The city is not talking to us.'[8] These absences signal precisely the sites of social antagonisms, and we should include in this picture those transgender individuals whose life is full of anxieties and social uncertainties and is far from the image of happy painted young men dancing half-naked and kissing.

For all these reasons, watching the Vancouver Pride Parade left a bitter taste in my mouth (but also in many LGBTQ people) – it reminded me of many similar parades that I watched in my youth in communist Yugoslavia, working-day parades where different collectives presented themselves celebrating their 'unity in diversity' under the shared umbrella of the ruling ideology (brotherhood and unity of all nations in the self-management and non-aligned socialist Yugoslavia). Even the subtle boredom and bureaucratic jargon of the Vancouver TV commentators with their politically correct predictability (they were careful to designate the parade's ideological umbrella with a version of the complex formula 'LGBTQIA+') reminded me of the similar jargon of the communist commentators, where every irony was prohibited.

As for the underlying form of subjectivity, we are clearly dealing with the sexualized version of the so-called post-traditional 'protean subject': today, the hegemonic form of subjectivity is no longer the autonomous subject subordinated to the paternal Oedipal Law that guarantees his (moral) freedom, but the fluid subject that experiences itself as permanently reinventing and reconstructing itself, joyfully experimenting with combinations of different identities. The paradigmatic theorist of this new form of subjectivity is Judith Butler, and although she insists on its 'subversive' character, it is easy to demonstrate that such a subjectivity rejecting any fixed identity and obsessed with permanent playful discursive reinvention fits perfectly contemporary consumerist and commodified society. This is why the obsessive attacks on patriarchy and Oedipal order sound so false and desperate: they attack an enemy that is in full retreat, reacting to something new which is already hegemonic. In short, the problem with this vision of a new fluid subjectivity is not that it is utopian but that it is already predominant – yet another case of the hegemonic ideology presenting itself as subversive and transgressive of the existing order. (The consequence to be drawn from all this is, of course, not to advocate a return to paternal symbolic authority as the only way out of the self-destructive deadlock of the late-capitalist narcissistic protean self, but to invent a new notion of subject, a subject which is really not so new since it is already here in philosophical modernity, from the Cartesian *cogito* and Kant's transcendental I. One should also doubt the accuracy of the clinical category of the post-Oedipal 'protean subject' – does it really move beyond Oedipus or does it continue to rely on the Oedipal logic?)

A more general remark on the fate of sexual liberation seems appropriate here. Graham Harman quotes a perspicuous remark on the 1960s – 'You have to remember that the 1960s really happened in the 1970s' – and comments on it: 'an object somehow exists "even more" in the stage following its initial heyday. The marijuana smoking, free love, and internal violence of the dramatic American 1960s were in some ways even better exemplified by the campy and tasteless 1970s.'[9] If, however, one takes a closer look at the passage from the 1960s to the 1970s, one can easily see the key difference: in the '60s, the spirit of permissiveness, sexual liberation, counter-culture and drugs was part of a utopian political protest movement, while in the 1970s this spirit was deprived of its political content and fully integrated into the hegemonic culture and ideology. Consequently, the 'even more' (which means: integration into the hegemonic ideology) was paid for with a 'much less' (i.e., depoliticization), and although one should definitely raise the question of the limitation of the spirit of the '60s that rendered this integration so easy, the repression of the political dimension remains a key feature of the popular culture of the '70s.

For this reason, the idea of conceiving of transgender identity as a *sinthom*, a constellation of signifiers that circulate around an empty centre, in Lacan's sense, is of no great use – it is either too general or too narrow. On the one hand, *sinthom* is for (late) Lacan the most elementary 'formula' of enjoyment, providing the minimum of consistency to the libidinal edifice of every human being. On the other hand, Lacan reads Joyce's literary texts as a *sinthom*, a synthetic formation which allowed him to avoid psychosis, i.e., which served him as a formation that supplemented the missing Name-of-the-Father – but I don't think transgender individuals are potential psychotics who avoided psychosis by creating a *sinthom* . . . The ethical greatness of transgender subjects resides precisely in the fact that they reject 'depersonalization' and remain subjects, assuming the deadlock of subjectivity even more radically than other more 'normalized' subjects. Transgender subjects in no way subtract their space of enjoyment from intersubjectivity and practise their search for enjoyment in direct dealings with objects; their anxieties seem to concern precisely their position in social space. On the contrary, today's consumerist capitalism does this subtraction quite well: instead of sex with persons, we have more and more sex with what Lacan calls *lathouses*, technologically created partial objects, all the 'things that did not exist' prior to the scientific intervention into the real, from mobile phones to remote-controlled toys, from air conditioners to artificial hearts.

A CASE OF PSEUDO-STRUGGLE

The struggle between fundamentalism and permissiveness reached a new height (or, rather, low) when some French municipal authorities prohibited 'burkinis' (a swimsuit that fully covers the body) on their beaches. Three reasons were quoted: (1) the burkini is a hygienic threat to the water at the beach; (2) it is a security risk, since it can hide weapons; (3) it is incompatible with French secular culture. In reaction to this 'threat', the French Prime Minister Manuel Valls praised the bare breasts of Marianne, the symbol of the French Republic and an icon of liberty and reason, as the opposite of the burkini: 'Marianne has a naked breast because she is feeding the people! She is not veiled, because she is free! That is the republic!' In short, Muslim women who wear the veil are not free, so the veil is anti-French, while bare breasts are emblematic of France: 'French PM suggests naked breasts represent France better than a headscarf', ran one headline.[10] The barely covered obscenity of this line of argumentation was soon noted: is the attraction of Marianne with a bared breast (recall the famous Delacroix painting *Liberty Leading the People*) really grounded in the perception that she is feeding the people?

As expected, the US engaged in this celebration of the alleged emancipatory potential of naked breasts in a more organized grass-roots way – feminist groups in big cities from San Francisco to New York organized 'GoTopless Day protests', where hundreds of women walked along the streets with bared breasts to demand full equality, i.e., to display their rejection of yet another form of sexual segregation (men can walk around topless while women cannot):

> GoTopless Day always falls at the Sunday closest to Women's Equality Day, Aug 26. It is indeed on Aug 26, 1920 that women earned their right to vote on the basis of Gender Equality. In 1971, the US Congress made Aug. 26 into a nationally recognized date and named it 'Women's Equality Day'. The president of the United States is summoned to commemorate this date each year. It is only logical that GoTopless Day protests (or celebrations depending on the legal status of your city) would fall around Women's Equality Day since the right to go topless for women is based on gender equality as their right to vote once was. On Sunday Aug. 28, people in cities around the world are invited to stand up for women's right to go topless in public. Please contact us if you would like to organize an event in your area so we can list your venue on our 'Boob Map' 2016.[11]

These parades promote 'gender equality and women's rights to bare their breasts in public' – as if the second is a natural implication of the first . . . and it goes without saying that if many of the women protesters were old and fat, and the display of their sagging bared breasts didn't meet the established norms of beauty, this only added another point to the protest, the rejection of the norms of beauty that objectify women. However, this go-topless movement should be analysed as part of a specific ideological constellation and not universalized into an emancipatory gesture. A couple of years ago, I was visiting some US campuses and giving talks there together with Mladen Dolar; the following incident happened at a dinner following our presentations. The professor informally chairing the event proposed that we all (a dozen or so people) briefly introduced ourselves, stating our professional position, the field of our work, and our sexual orientation. Our American colleagues did this as the most normal and obvious thing, while Dolar and I simply sidestepped the last issue. I was tempted to propose adding other features to this self-presentation: how much one earns per year and how much wealth one possesses (I am sure my US friends would find this much more intrusive than the question of sexual orientation. . .). In his own wonderful comment on this incident, Dolar recalls another experience:

> Some years ago, when some American friends were visiting Slovenia in the summer, I took them to a beach on the Adriatic coast. It was a public and very crowded beach, and my friends were rather perplexed when they saw that the women, in large part, freely took their bras off, as is commonly done in this part of the world, wandering around with bare breasts, while nobody made anything of it. My friends said this would never happen on a public beach in America (I have never been to one, so I take their word for it). They were rather embarrassed, despite their Leftist-liberal persuasions, feeling discomfort at what they saw as an edge of a deliberate public display and sexual provocation – as a European lack of reticence and discretion. It was almost like invoking a caricature ghost of Puritanism in the midst of this age of permissiveness. This gave rise to some musings about the question of the neighbour, that strange creature next to us whom we are supposed to love, but who causes embarrassment and mortification the moment s/he comes too close, intruding upon our private space, crossing the bar of discretion, exposing us, as it were, by exposing him/herself, exposing his or her intrusive privacy which thus cannot be kept at a proper distance.[12]

(Incidentally, in the last decade or so, the number of topless women on beaches worldwide has diminished considerably – now, they are found only exceptionally. However, it would be wrong to read this change as a sign of conservative regression.) Far from being opposed or incompatible, the two features (declaring one's sexual orientation and keeping one's body covered) supplement each other within the universe of US Puritanism, which is, as we can see, alive and kicking. That is to say, the way to account for such paradoxes is to bear in mind how the very indiscretion, the surprising openness, can function as a tool of discretion, of withdrawal.

We are thus in the midst of another pseudo-struggle: burkini or bared breasts – *this* choice should definitely be depoliticized, left to the domain of the idiosyncrasy of personal preference. That is to say, in spite of the emancipatory potential of the struggle for sexual freedoms, one should nonetheless become suspicious when the personal is declared political in the wrong way: when the direct display of one's intimate preference becomes the ultimate political act. Authentic politics is never about publicly asserting what one is in the intimacy of one's desires and fantasies. In other words, the GoTopless movement is something like the Kardashians' show in progressive politics. The Kardashians brought the notion of fame to its self-referentiality: basically, they are thoroughly ordinary people who are famous for being famous. Even when their TV show touches a potentially hot political topic (as happened with their visit to Cuba), their comments are strictly reduced to common-sense platitudes, like waving a hand at a passing child and shouting 'Hi, Cuba!' or commenting on how in Cuba people know how to disconnect and enjoy peaceful life, while in the US they are all the time trying to achieve something.

However, one should be a little careful with Kim Kardashian. After she was tied up and robbed of her jewellery in a posh Paris hotel, the famed designer Karl Lagerfeld criticized her for being too flashy with her money. So she was partly to blame for the heist: she was 'too public – we have to see in what time we live. You cannot display your wealth then be surprised that some people want to share it. If you are that famous and you put all your jewellery on the net you go to hotels where nobody can come near to the room.' Although I consider Kim Kardashian to be a public figure of embarrassing tastelessness, I find Lagerfeld's comment disgusting – he is basically reproaching her for mixing with ordinary people, for not staying isolated from them. But if there is a redeeming feature of Kim, it is precisely her way of going out and mixing with her public. It is all too easy to make fun of the poor Kim – she is vulgar, her spontaneity is utterly faked, she is not just herself (what she really is), she rather *plays herself* (an ideal image of herself). It is all too easy to point out how her fame lacks any substance – but is it not that she just brings out a feature which is common to all 'famous people' in our consumerist societies? Take someone who may appear to be the opposite of Kim, Angelina Jolie, with all her humanitarian engagements directed at saving these or those victims. While Kim is mocked, Jolie is respectfully received by big political figures, and in 2017 she will even teach at the prestigious London School of Economics (as a visiting professor on a graduate course called Women, Peace and Security). If anything, I find Jolie more problematic: while both Kim and Jolie participate in the culture of celebrity, Jolie wants to have her cake and eat it. She fully exploits the celebrity culture *and* tries to obfuscate this fact by acting as an agent of 'higher' causes. The true obscenity is not Kim's shameless self-display, the true obscenity is Jolie offering herself as an authentic ethico-political figure. Making fun of Kim makes us forget that the stupidity projected into her is our shared substance. But what is the obscenity of poor Kim compared to the obscenity that pervades the big humanitarian celebrities? So, what if despising Kim is an immanent part of her celebrity? What if the ideal consumer of her shows and news is not a naive believer in her but a self-conscious consumer who knows very well how vulgar she is, goes on avidly swallowing news about her, while enjoying the feeling of superiority that this knowledge gives him or her?

SEXUAL DIFFERENCE, HIERARCHY OR ANTAGONISM?

The oppressive religious atmosphere in Muslim countries is a fact that has to be confronted – but how? There is a struggle going on in Palestinian social media, ignored in the West. Two figures are at its centre: Mohammed Assaf and Tamer Nafar. Assaf is a pop singer from Gaza, wildly popular not only among Palestinians but in all Arab countries and even in parts of Europe, and he is supported by Hamas in Gaza and by the Palestinian Authority, which proclaimed him the cultural ambassador of Palestine. He sings, with a beautiful voice, tender ballads and patriotic songs arranged in a popular style. Politically, he is a unifying figure, above political divisions except in his support for Palestinian freedom. In March 2016, Assaf declared in an interview that, as part of keeping 'tradition', he would not allow his sister to sing in public. Tamer Nafar, the Palestinian rap artist who is the main actor and co-writer of Udi Aloni's movie *Junction 48*, responded to Assaf in this touching open letter:

> If any other pop artist said: 'According to our tradition women are not allowed to sing, and on a personal level I cherish these traditions so I cannot allow my sister to sing,' I would protest and hurt him, but since it's Assaf, our Cinderella from Gaza, saying these words, I still will have rage, but mainly I am hurt.
>
> Like the Palestinians who were united for the first time in the streets of Gaza, the West Bank, the Diaspora, the Refugee Camps and inside of '48 to support Muhammad Assaf, we ask Assaf to join us on the same streets to encourage that girl from Yemen, Gaza, Morocco, Jordan and al Lyd – that girl who is dreaming to sing, dance, write and perform in *Arab Idol*! We as Palestinians must fight the Israeli Apartheid and the Gender Apartheid. My dream is to march hand in hand, a woman holding a man's hand against any separation wall. It is not reasonable to walk separately and ask for unity at the same time!
>
> You want to talk about traditions? From personal experience, I used to be an angry kid in the ghettos of Lyd. I wouldn't calm down unless my mom sang to me a Fairuz song. That is the tradition i want to cherish! So, my dear Arab sisters (Hawwa), sing as loud as you can, break the borders so we can calm down. Freedom for all or freedom for none![13]

Udi Aloni's *Junction 48* deals with the difficult predicament of the young 'Israeli Palestinians' (Palestinians descended from the families that remained within Israel after the 1948 war), whose everyday life involves a continuous struggle on two fronts: against both Israeli state oppression and the fundamentalist pressures from within their own community. In his songs, Nafar mocks the tradition of 'honour killings' of girls in Palestinian families, for which he has been attacked also by Western PC Leftists. A strange thing happened to him during a recent visit to the US. After he performed his song protesting against honour killings at the Columbia University campus in New York, some anti-Zionist students attacked him for dealing with the topic – their reproach being that, in this way, he promotes the Zionist view of Palestinians as barbaric primitives (adding that, if there are indeed any honour killings, Israel is responsible for them because the Israeli occupation keeps Palestinians in primitive conditions and prevents their modernization). Here is Nafar's dignified reply: 'When you criticize me you criticize my own community in English to impress your radical professors. I sing in Arabic to protect the women in my own 'hood.'

Nafar's point is that Palestinians do not need the patronizing help of Western liberals; even less do they need the silence about honour killing that is part of the Western Leftist's 'respect' for the Palestinian way of life. These two aspects – the imposition of Western values as universal human rights, and respect for different cultures independently of the horrors that can be part of these cultures – are two sides of the same ideological mystification. A lot has been written about how the universality of universal human rights is twisted, how they secretly give preference to Western cultural values and norms (the priority of the individual over his/her community, and so on). But we should also add to this insight that the multiculturalist anti-colonialist defence of the multiplicity of ways of life is also false: it covers up the antagonisms within each of these particular ways of life, justifying acts of brutality, sexism and racism as expressions of a particular culture that we have no right to judge by foreign Western values.

This polemic between Assaf and Nafar is part of a big struggle for sexual difference, which gives a new twist to the old 1968 motto 'The sexual is political.' The destructive effects of this struggle are discernible all around the world. The fate of Attawapiskat, a remote aboriginal community in northern Ontario, which drew the attention of the media in early 2016, exemplifies the way the Canadian aborigines remain a broken nation unable to find the minimal stability of a life pattern:

Since autumn there have been more than 100 suicide attempts in Attawapiskat, which has a population of just 2,000. The youngest person to attempt suicide was 11 years old, the oldest 71. After 11 people tried to take their own lives on Saturday evening, exhausted leaders declared a state of emergency. On Monday, as officials scrambled to send crisis counsellors to the community, 20 people – including a nine-year-old – were taken to hospital after they were overheard making a suicide pact. 'We're crying out for help,' said Attawapiskat chief Bruce Shisheesh. 'Just about every night there is a suicide attempt.'

In searching for the reasons for this terrible toll, one should look beyond the obvious (overcrowded houses riddled with mould, drug abuse and alcoholism, etc.); the principal among the systemic reasons is the devastating legacy of the residential school system, which disrupted continuity between generations:

for decades, more than 150,000 aboriginal children were carted off in an attempt to forcibly assimilate them into Canadian society. Rife with abuse, the schools aimed to 'kill the Indian in the child', as documented by a recent truth commission. Thousands of children died at these schools – the absence of dietary standards in the schools left many undernourished and vulnerable to diseases such as smallpox, measles and tuberculosis – with hundreds of them hastily buried in unmarked graves next to the institutions. In nearly a third of the deaths, the government and schools did not even record the names of the students who had died.[14]

(One should note here that the sexual exploitation of children in residential schools is widespread.) For millions of people all around the world, a similar kind of hell is the reality of what sociologists call the process of modernization, of the dissolution of traditional family ties: what they get is just the destructive aspect, which they are unable to 'sublate' into post-traditional individuality. Jacqueline Rose recently made a key point when she dealt with the question: is the widespread talk about violence against women in our mainstream media an indication that there is more of this violence in real life, or is it just that this violence has become more visible because, on account of growing feminist awareness, we apply higher ethical standards, which qualify as violence that which was before considered part of a normal state of things? Rose points out that this higher visibility is profoundly ambiguous: it signals the fact that feminist awareness has penetrated general culture, but it also neutralizes the impact of violence against women, rendering it tolerable and standardized – we see it all around, we protest against it, and life goes on ... The Boko Haram way is no solution to this deadlock because it does not enact an actual return to traditional communal life but merely counteracts destruction with an even more (self-)destructive 'totalitarian' group identification.

Boko Haram simply brings the logic of normative sexual difference to its extreme. (Incidentally, Lacan's point is that the true threat is not polymorphous perversion, which destabilizes, sometimes even ignores, sexual difference, but this difference itself in its antagonistic dimension.) The notion of sexual difference that prescribes to each of the two sexes a specific role to play thereby imposes a symbolic norm destined to guarantee sexual relationships, to provide the coordinates of 'normal' sex. An exemplary case of such (mis)use of sexual difference is provided by Suheyb Öğüt in his comment 'The Butch Lesbians and the HDPKK':[15]

According to psychoanalysis every relationship is sexual. But this doesn't mean that every relation in everyday life smells of sexuality. On the contrary, this means that in every relationship – whatever it is, political, social or economic – agents occupy a sexual position which is either the position of a man or that of a woman. Indeed, even if the type of relationship is not a conventional one but the one unusual for the majority of the population, this rule is valid. It is exactly for this reason that even in 'queer' relations – like in heterosexual relations – there is a male (master, dominant) role and a female (servant, submissive) role which is enacted. Otherwise the relationship is an impossible one.

For example, lesbians: fundamentally there are two types of lesbians: butch (male role) and femme (female role). When we observe the butch lesbians, it seems impossible to distinguish them from males. Their body language (seating, walking, gestures, mimics, clothes, even their tattoos) is macho. They look very brave and good.[16] They are much more aggressive and 'if punch, knock down' type of people than an average man. If you engage in a fight with a butch you should probably immediately run away. This macho 'image' is also enacted in their relationship with their partners: they are very dominant and they ask partners to behave towards them in a very submissive way. So when you observe this type of relationship, you notice the same phallic enjoyment as that of a man enjoying the submissiveness[17] of his partner.

But in reality the situation is exactly the opposite one. Butch doesn't occupy a position of phallic manhood, for sure. The macho-male mask – witnessing her symbolic castration – that she wears in everyday life doesn't allow her to derive from it any sort of phallic enjoyment. It is rather the enjoyment of the Big Other which defines her macho manhood. This is because a butch lesbian is desperately obliged to use some artificial tool as the substitution for the real-natural organ that she lacks, and also because she waives her own pleasure in order to really possess her partner like a man would do. This kind of pleasure found in waiving her own bodily pleasure, a pleasure found in merely serving painfully the Other's pleasure, corresponds to female enjoyment. Behind their macho appearances butches are therefore nothing but the usual obedient 'good girls'. However, this situation of which they are unconsciously aware doesn't disturb them much as long as they look macho from the view of the Other, as long as they can keep on hiding their 'good girl' in their inside.

Never mind, these HDP+PKK's look like butches who act like a macho, challenging the State and the majority of people by way of using dildo-like external weapons. There is a 'good girl' woman behind this mask. There is a pathetic servant behind those who work for the Big Other's enjoyment (of secularism, of Israel, of Kemalism). What, then, makes them endure the pain of masking their castrated submissive femme, of leaving behind their original 'good girl' femininity? Here is the answer, the same as the butch lesbian's answer: they endure the pain in order to be able to be seen and approved of as a disobedient (leftist) and roughneck (secular) master by the Big Other. That's it.[18]

This brief comment (which appeared in a popular Turkish newspaper), a theoretical and political nightmare, enacts a blatant misuse of Lacanian psychoanalysis. It offers sexual difference in the traditional sense (master and servant, active and passive . . .) as a framework that defines the specific agencies 'for manhood and for womanhood', and then universalizes it as a model for all human relations, 'political, social or economic'; even when a sexual relation is not the standard one, as is the case with lesbians, there has to be the dominant masculine position and the submissive feminine position (butch and femme). This framework is supposed to function as a kind of formal *a priori*, a condition of possibility, of any relationship – 'otherwise the relationship is an impossible one' . . . But Lacan's point is precisely this, namely that sexual relationship *is* an impossible one: *Il n'y a pas de rapport sexuel.* Every other (not directly sexual) interhuman relation can be sexualized precisely because 'there is no sexual relationship': sexuality affects other domains not because of its overpowering strength but because of its weakness. For Lacan, 'there is no sexual relationship' means (among other things) precisely that no symbolic opposition (like active/passive, master/servant, etc.) can adequately determine sexual difference.

Things then take an even worse turn: a lesbian relationship is explained in terms of the opposition between the 'natural-real' sexual organ (penis) and an artificial external dildo: butch lesbians lack a real penis, so they have to rely on the artificial dildo in order to impress some figure of the big Other (their Ego Ideal) with their masculinity. One should also note the political dimension of Öğüt's text: written in order to support the official policy of the Turkish government (which denounces Kurdish opposition as terrorists), it is meant to slander one of the greatest aspects of the Kurdish struggle in Syria, the women-fighters who proved to be very efficient against ISIS (we should also note the late turn towards feminism of Ocalan, the imprisoned leader of PKK). The idea is that these women-fighters are like butch lesbians: they fake their masculinity by way of displaying their dildos (masculine guns) in order to impress the figure of their Zionist-secular (i.e., anti-Turkish) big Other. There is a slight problem here. For Lacan, the phallus (which defines masculinity) is not the penis but a signifier, the signifier of castration, which means precisely an external supplement, 'structured like a dildo' (to paraphrase Lacan's famous formula 'the unconscious is structured like a language'). So the situation described by Öğüt as a lesbian diversion is for Lacan a normal one: what defines the masculinity of a man is not his possession of a penis but the way he relates to some external phallic signifier on which his authority relies, and he does this in order to be noted by a figure of the big Other that confers on him his authority. Consequently, would Öğüt be ready to say that Erdogan is also a butch, a weak guy who displays his dildo in order to impress the big Other (Turkey, Islam)?

THE IMPASSES OF TRANSGENDER

In 'The Instance of the Letter in the Unconscious, or Reason According to Freud', Lacan, correcting Saussure, illustrates the relationship between signifier and signified by way of emphasizing the differential character of the signifier. He presents the image of a signifying couple, GENTLEMEN and LADIES, and, under each of the two terms, beneath a bar, he draws an identical image of a toilet door – with the clear point that sexual difference is not a matter of nature (biology, meaning) but a matter of signifier: the signified is the same. Lacan comments:

> Here we see that, without greatly extending the scope of the signifier involved in the experiment – that is, by simply doubling the nominal type through the mere juxtaposition of two terms whose complementary meanings would seem to have to reinforce each other – surprise is produced by the precipitation of an unexpected meaning: the image of two twin doors that symbolize, with the private stall offered Western man for the satisfaction of his natural needs when away from home, the imperative he seems to share with the vast majority of

primitive communities that subjects his public life to the laws of urinary segregation.[19]

The notion of sexual difference that prescribes to each of the two
sexes a specific role to play thereby imposes a symbolic norm that
extends up to the domain of urinary segregation. The irony is that
segregated toilet doors are today at the centre of a big legal and ideological struggle, especially in the US. On 29 March 2016, a group of
eighty predominantly Silicon Valley-based business executives,
headed by Facebook CEO Mark Zuckerberg and Apple CEO Tim
Cook, signed a letter to North Carolina Governor Pat McCrory
denouncing a law prohibiting transgender people from using the
public facilities of the opposite sex. 'We are disappointed in your
decision to sign this discriminatory legislation into law,' the letter
says. 'The business community, by and large, has consistently com-
municated to lawmakers at every level that such laws are bad for our
employees and bad for business.' (The law says a person must use
segregated public facilities such as bathrooms and showers according
to biological sex, not gender identity. A transgender person would
have to have his sex legally changed on a birth certificate to use the
facilities of his preferred gender.) So it is clear where big capital
stands. Tim Cook can easily forget about hundreds of thousands
of Foxconn workers in China assembling Apple products in slave
conditions – he makes his big gesture of solidarity with the underprivileged by demanding the abolition of gender segregation . . . As is
often the case, big business stands here proudly united with politically correct theory.

So what is 'transgenderism'? It occurs when an individual experiences a discord between his or her biological sex (and the corresponding gender, male or female, assigned to him by society at
birth) and his subjective identity. As such, it does not concern only
'men who feel and act like women' and *vice versa* but a complex
structure of additional 'genderqueer' positions: bi-gender, trigender,
pangender, genderfluid, up to agender. The ultimate vision of social
relations that sustains transgenderism is so-called postgenderism: a
social, political and cultural movement whose adherents advocate a
voluntary abolition of gender rendered possible by recent scientific

progress in biotechnology and reproductive technologies. The proposal doesn't only concern scientific possibility but is also ethically grounded: the premise of postgenderism is that the social, emotional and cognitive consequences of fixed gender roles are an obstacle to full human emancipation. A society in which reproduction through sex is eliminated (or in which other versions are possible: a woman can also 'father' her child, etc.) will open unheard-of new possibilities of freedom, social and emotional experimentation. It will eliminate a distinction that sustains all later social hierarchies and exploitations . . . One can argue that postgenderism is the truth of transgenderism: the universal fluidification of sexual identities unavoidably reaches its apogee in the cancellation of sex as such. This ambiguity characterizes the conjunction of sexuality and freedom throughout the twentieth century: as attempts to liberate sexuality become more radical, the more they get close to their self-overcoming and turn into attempts to enact a liberation *from* sexuality:

> If part of the twentieth century's revolutionary programme to create a radically new social relation and a New Man was the liberation of sexuality, this aspiration was marked by a fundamental ambiguity: is it sexuality that is to be liberated, delivered from moral prejudices and legal prohibitions, so that the drives are allowed a more open and fluid expression, or is humanity to be liberated from sexuality, finally freed from its obscure dependencies and tyrannical constraints? Will the revolution bring an efflorescence of libidinal energy or, seeing it as a dangerous distraction to the arduous task of building a new world, demand its suppression? In a word, is sexuality the object of or the obstacle to emancipation?[20]

The oscillation between these two extremes is clearly discernible in the first decade after the October Revolution, when feminist calls for the liberation of sexuality were soon supplemented by gnostic-cosmological calls for a New Man who would leave sexuality itself behind as the ultimate bourgeois trap. The first thing to note here is that transgenderism goes together with the general tendency in today's predominant Left-liberal ideology to reject any particular 'belonging' and to celebrate the 'fluidification' of any identity.

Thinkers like the French social theorist and public figure Frédéric Lordon recently demonstrated the inconsistency of 'cosmopolitan' anti-nationalist intellectuals who advocate a 'liberation from belonging' and, *in extremis*, tend to dismiss every search for roots and every attachment to a particular ethnic or cultural identity as an almost proto-fascist stance. Lordon contrasts this self-proclaimed rootlessness with the nightmarish reality of refugees and illegal immigrants who, deprived of basic rights, desperately search for some kind of belonging (such as a new citizenship). Lordon is quite right here: it is easy to note how the 'cosmopolitan' intellectual elites, despising local people who cling to their roots, themselves belong to their own quite exclusive circles of rootless elites, and thus how their cosmopolitan rootlessness is the marker of a deep and strong belonging. (This is why it is an utter obscenity to propose an equivalence between elite 'nomads' flying around the world and refugees desperately searching for a safe place where they could belong – the same obscenity as that of putting together a dieting upper-class Western woman and a starving refugee woman.) This properly Hegelian paradox was at work throughout history: within each particular community (nation), today's universal class of CEOs and university elites appears as a particular group isolated from the majority by their entire lifestyle – a humanities professor in New York has much more in common with a humanities professor in Paris or even Seoul than with a worker who lives on Staten Island. Today's universal class which reaches across particular nations – CEOs, intellectuals – is simultaneously within every nation an extremely particular group separated from all others by its lifestyle – it is a universality that divides a particular identity from within.

Furthermore, we encounter here the old paradox: the more marginal and excluded one is, the more one is allowed to assert ethnic identity and an exclusive way of life. This is how the politically correct landscape is structured: people far from the Western world are allowed to fully assert their particular ethnic identity without being proclaimed essentialist racist identitarians (native Americans, blacks. . .). The closer one gets to the notorious white heterosexual males, the more problematic making this assertion becomes: Asians are still OK, Italians and Irish maybe, with Germans and

Scandinavians it is already problematic . . . However, prohibiting the assertion of the particular identity of White Men (as the model of oppression of others), although it presents itself as the admission of their guilt, nonetheless confers on them a central position: this very prohibition makes them into the universal-neutral medium, the place from which the truth about the others' oppression is accessible. The imbalance weighs also in the opposite direction: impoverished European countries expect the developed West European ones to bear the full burden of multicultural openness, while they can afford patriotism. Although asserting the identity of a marginal, oppressed minority is of course not the same thing as asserting the identity of a privileged white nation, we should nonetheless not lose sight of the formal identity between the two: 'the nationalist right has simply taken over the identity politics. They are saying: "Not you (gays, blacks . . .), we are the real victims here, we are the minority, nobody cares about us. . ." '[21] (Incidentally, something similar happened with the anti-abortion movement, which also presents itself as the simple and logical expansion of the anti-racist fight: first, the fight was to include blacks and other races into the set of those who are fully human, and now we just want to extend this fight to those who are not yet born . . .)

And it is easy to detect a similar tension in transgenderism. Transgender subjects who appear as transgressive, defying all prohibitions, simultaneously behave in a hyper-sensitive way; they feel oppressed by enforced choice ('Why should I decide if I am man or woman?'), they need a place where they can fully recognize themselves. If they so proudly insist on their 'trans-', beyond all classification, why do they display such an urgent demand for a proper place? Why, when they find themselves in front of gendered toilets, don't they act with heroic indifference – 'I am transgendered, a bit of this and that, so I can well choose whatever door I want!'? Furthermore, do 'normal' heterosexuals not have a similar problem, do they not also often find it difficult to recognize themselves in prescribed sexual identities? One could even say that man (or woman) is not a certain identity but more a certain mode of avoiding an identity . . . And we can safely predict that new anti-discriminatory demands will emerge: why not marriages among multiple persons?

What justifies the limitation to the binary form of marriage? Why not even a marriage with animals – after all, we already know about the finesse of animal emotions?

This deadlock of classification is clearly discernible in the need to expand the formula: the basic LGBT (Lesbian, Gay, Bisexual, Transgender) becomes LGBTQIA (Lesbian, Gay, Bisexual, Transgender, Questioning, Intersex, Asexual) or even LGBTQQIAAP (Lesbian, Gay, Bisexual, Transgender, Queer, Questioning, Intersex, Asexual, Allies, Pansexual).[22] To resolve the problem, one often simply adds a +, which serves to include all other groups associated with the LGBT community, as in LGBT+. This, however, raises the question: is + just a stand-in for the missing positions, like 'and others', or can one be directly a +? The properly dialectical answer is: yes – in the series, there is always one exceptional element that clearly does not belong to it and thereby gives body to +. It can be 'allies' ('honest' non-LGBT individuals), 'asexuals' (negating the entire field of sexuality) or 'questioning' (floating around, unable to adopt a determinate position). (Especially suspicious is here the category of 'allies': why should heterosexuals who have a sympathy for transgender people count as a special category of sexual identity? Is their sympathy not a fact of their morality, which has nothing to do with their sexuality? The hidden normativity of transgenderism is clearly perceptible here: heterosexuality is silently conceived as 'lower' than a transgender position, as immanently linked to oppression, so 'allies' are 'honest enemies' in almost the same sense in which historians of Nazism like to discover an 'honest Nazi', a Nazi who admits the criminal nature of Nazism . . .)

Consequently, there is only one solution to this deadlock, the one we find in another field of waste-disposal, that of trash bins. Public trash bins are more and more differentiated today: there are special bins for paper, glass, metal cans, cardboard, plastic, etc. Here already, things are getting complicated: if I have to dispose of a paper bag or a notebook with a tiny plastic band, where does it belong, to paper or to plastic? No wonder that we often get on the bins detailed instructions beneath the general designation: PAPER – books, newspapers, etc., but *not* hardcover books or books with plasticized cover, etc. In such cases, to properly dispose of one's waste would take half an hour or more of detailed reading and analysing. To make things easier, we then get a supplementary trash bin for GEN-ERAL WASTE, where we throw everything that doesn't meet the specific criteria of other bins – as if, apart from paper trash, plastic trash, etc., there is trash as such, universal trash. And should we not do the same with toilets? Since no classification can satisfy all identities, should we not add to the two usual gender slots, MEN, WOMEN, a door for GENERAL GENDER? Is this not the only way to inscribe into an order of symbolic differences its constitutive antagonism? Lacan pointed out that the 'formula' of the sexual relationship as impossible/real is 1+1+a, i.e., the two sexes plus the 'bone in the throat' that prevents its translation into a symbolic difference. This third element does not stand for what is excluded from the domain of difference, it stands for (the real of) the difference as such.

The reason for this failure of every classification that tries to be exhaustive is not the empirical wealth of identities that defy classification but, on the contrary, the persistence of sexual difference as real, as 'impossible' (defying every categorization) and simultaneously unavoidable. The multiplicity of gender positions (male, female, gay, lesbian, bi-gender, transgender, etc.) circulates around an antagonism that forever eludes it. Gays are men, lesbians women, transsexuals enforce a passage from one to another, cross-dressing combines the two, bi-gender floats between the two ... whichever way we turn, the 'two' lurks beneath.

This brings us back to what one could call the primal scene of anxiety that defines transgenderism: I stand in front of the standard bi-gender toilets with two doors, LADIES and GENTLEMEN, and I am caught in anxiety, not recognizing myself in either of the choices. Again, do 'normal' heterosexuals not have a similar problem, do they also not often find it difficult to recognize themselves in pre-scribed sexual identities? Which man has not caught himself in a momentary doubt: 'Do I really have the right to enter GENTLEMEN? Am I really a man?'? We can now see clearly what the anxiety when confronted with the choice LADIES or GENTLEMEN really amounts to: the anxiety of (symbolic) castration. Whatever choice I make, I will lose something, and this something is *not* what the other sex has – both sexes together do not form a whole since something is irretrievably lost by the very division of sexes. We can even say that, in making the choice, I assume *the loss of what the other sex doesn't have*, i.e., I have to renounce the illusion that the Other has that X which would fill in my lack. And one can well guess that trans-genderism is ultimately precisely an attempt to avoid (the anxiety of) castration: a flat space is created in which the multiple choices that I can make do not bear the mark of castration – or, as Alenka Zupančič puts it:

> One is usually timid in asserting the existence of two genders, but when passing to the multitude this timidity disappears, and their existence is firmly asserted. If sexual difference is considered in terms of gender, it is made – at least in principle – compatible with mechanisms of its full ontologization.[23]

Therein resides the crux of the matter: although the LGBT trend is right in 'deconstructing' the standard normative sexual opposition, in de-ontologizing it, in recognizing in it a contingent historical construct full of tensions and inconsistencies, it however reduces this tension to the fact that the plurality of sexual positions is forcefully reduced to the normative straitjacket of the binary opposition of masculine and feminine, with the idea that, if we get rid off this straitjacket, we will get a fully blossoming multiplicity of sexual positions (LGBT etc.), each of them with a full ontological consistency. Once we get rid of the binary straitjacket, I can fully recognize myself as gay, bisexual, or whatever. From the Lacanian standpoint, however, the antagonistic tension is irreducible, it is constitutive of the sexual as such, and no amount of classificatory diversification and multiplication can save us from it.

Although LGBT+ perceives itself as undermining the normativity of the heterosexual binary opposition, one should never forget that it involves a normativity of its own: since 'binary' heterosexuality is perceived as the violent imposition of a model onto the plurality of sexual forms and practices, it is clear that practices which reject the standard heterosexuality are normatively preferred to it, i.e., that there is also an ethical edge to opposing the heterosexual norm. Judith Butler deploys this superiority in her theory of the rise of heterosexuality: the first libidinal object of a child is his/her parent of the same sex, and when, under the pressure of heterosexual normativity, the child is compelled to drop this libidinal object, s/he identifies with what s/he was forced to abandon – a small boy becomes a man by way of identifying with his father as his primordial libidinal object, and the same goes for girls. (Butler refers here to Freud's thesis according to which our ego is composed of identifications with lost libidinal objects.) However, homosexuals refuse to abandon the primordial object: boys and girls continue with their libidinal attachment to the same-sex objects. This is also why the difference between homosexuality and heterosexuality corresponds to that between melancholy and mourning: heterosexuals successfully conclude the work of mourning for the lost object, while homosexuals remain faithful to it, which means that heterosexuality is based on a radical betrayal . . .

FAILED INTERPELLATION

The underlying structure is here that of a failed interpellation. In the case of interpellation, Althusser's own example contains more than his own theorization gets out of it. Althusser evokes an individual who, while carelessly walking down the street, is suddenly addressed by a policeman: 'Hey, you there!' By answering the call – that is, by stopping and turning towards the policeman – the individual recognizes-constitutes himself as the subject of Power, of the big Other-Subject. Ideology

> 'transforms' the individuals into subjects (it transforms them all) by that very precise operation which I have called interpellation or hailing, and which can be imagined along the lines of the most commonplace everyday police (or other) hailing: 'Hey, you there!'
>
> Assuming that the theoretical scene I have imagined takes place in the street, the hailed individual will turn round. By this mere one-hundred-and-eighty-degree physical conversion, he becomes a subject. Why? Because he has recognized that the hail was 'really' addressed to him, and that 'it was really him who was hailed' (and not

someone else). Experience shows that the practical transmission of hailings is such that they hardly ever miss their man: verbal call or whistle, the one hailed always recognizes that it is really him who is being hailed. And yet it is a strange phenomenon, and one which cannot be explained solely by 'guilt feelings', despite the large numbers who 'have something on their consciences'.

Naturally for the convenience and clarity of my little theoretical theatre I have had to present things in the form of a sequence, with a before and an after, and thus in the form of a temporal succession. There are individuals walking along. Somewhere (usually behind them) the hail rings out: 'Hey, you there!' One individual (nine times out of ten it is the right one) turns round, believing/suspecting/knowing that it is for him, i.e. recognizing that 'it really is he' who is meant by the hailing. But in reality these things happen without any succession. The existence of ideology and the hailing or interpellation of individuals as subjects are one and the same thing.[24]

The first thing that strikes the eye in this passage is Althusser's implicit reference to Lacan's thesis on a letter that 'always arrives at its destination': the interpellative letter cannot miss its addressee since, on account of its 'timeless' character, it is only the addressee's recognition/acceptance that constitutes it as a letter. The crucial feature of the quoted passage, however, is the double denial at work in it: the denial of the explanation of interpellative recognition by means of a 'guilt feeling', as well as the denial of the temporality of the process of interpellation (strictly speaking, individuals do not 'become' subjects, they 'always-already' are subjects).[25] This double denial is to be read as a Freudian denial: what the 'timeless' character of interpellation renders invisible is a kind of atemporal sequentiality that is far more complex than the 'theoretical theatre' staged by Althusser on behalf of the suspicious alibi of 'convenience and clarity'. This 'repressed' sequence concerns a 'guilt feeling' of a purely formal, 'non-pathological' (in the Kantian sense) nature, a guilt which, for that very reason, weighs most heavily upon those individuals who 'have nothing on their consciences'. That is to say, of what, precisely, does the individual's first reaction to the policeman's 'Hey, you there!' consist? It consists of an inconsistent mixture of two elements: (1) why me, what does the policeman want from me? I'm innocent, I was just minding my own business and strolling around . . .; however, this perplexed protestation of innocence is always accompanied by (2) an indeterminate Kafkaesque feeling of 'abstract' guilt, a feeling that, in the eyes of Power, I am *a priori* terribly guilty of something, although it is not possible for me to know of what precisely I am guilty, and for that reason – since I don't know what I am guilty of – I am even more guilty; or, more pointedly, it is of this very ignorance of mine that my true guilt consists.[26]

What we have here is thus the entire Lacanian structure of the subject split between innocence and abstract, indeterminate guilt, confronted with a non-transparent call emanating from the Other ('Hey, you there!'), a call where it is not clear to the subject what the Other actually wants from him (*'Che vuoi?'*). In short, what we encounter here is interpellation prior to identification. Prior to the recognition in the call of the Other by means of which the individual constitutes himself as 'always-already'-subject, we are obliged to acknowledge this 'timeless' instant of the impasse in which innocence coincides with indeterminate guilt: the ideological identification by means of which I assume a symbolic mandate and recognize myself as the subject of Power takes place only as an answer to this impasse. So what remains 'unthought' in Althusser's theory of interpellation is the fact that prior to ideological recognition we have an intermediate moment of obscene, impenetrable interpellation without identification, a kind of vanishing mediator that has to become invisible if the subject is to achieve symbolic identity, i.e., to accomplish the gesture of subjectivization. In short, the 'unthought' of Althusser is that there is already an uncanny subject that precedes the gesture of subjectivization. And the same goes for sexual interpellation: my identification as 'man' or 'woman' is always a secondary reaction to the 'castrative' anxiety of what I am.

This is why the obvious solution of drawing a line of distinction between the legal aspect and the psychological turmoil of being transgender is all too easy. The problem with this approach (ending the segregation in toilets (and similar measures) is just an external legal measure that should be adopted on behalf of social justice but which in no way helps to cancel the psychic turmoil and anxiety of being transgender) is that one precisely cannot draw such a line since (as we have surely learned from Kafka) the legal domain is inherently a domain of intense libidinal investments, of anxieties, perverse satisfactions, etc. Having a toilet 'room of one's own' can easily turn into an even stronger segregation than having no room of one's own, and imposing a neutral toilet for all will continue to function as a denial of basic antagonisms.

In Lacan's precise sense of the term, the third element (the Kierkegaardian chimney sweeper) effectively stands for the phallic element – how? Insofar as he stands for pure difference: officer, maid and chimney sweeper are the masculine, the feminine, *plus their difference as such*, as a particular contingent object – again, why? Because not only is difference differential, but, in an antagonistic (non-)relationship, it precedes the terms it differentiates: not only is woman not-man and *vice versa*, but woman is what prevents man from being fully man and *vice versa*. It is like the difference between the Left and the Right in the political space: their difference is the difference in the very way difference is perceived. The whole political space appears differently structured if we look at it from the Left or from the Right; there is no third 'objective' way (for a Leftist, the political divide cuts across the entire social body, while for a Rightist, society is a hierarchic whole disturbed by marginal intruders). Difference 'in itself' is thus not symbolic/differential, but real-impossible – something that eludes and resists the symbolic grasp. This difference is the universal as such – universal not as a neutral frame elevated above its two species, but as their constitutive antagonism; and the third element (chimney sweeper, Jew, *objet a*) stands for the difference as such, for the 'pure' difference/antagonism that precedes the differentiated terms. If the division of the social body into two classes had been completed, without the excessive element (Jew, rabble . . .[27]), there would have been no class struggle, just two clearly divided classes. This third element is not the mark of an empirical remainder that escapes the classification of classes (the pure division of society into two classes), but *the materialization of their antagonistic difference itself*, insofar as this difference precedes the differentiated terms. In the space of anti-Semitism, the 'Jew' stands for the social antagonism as such: without the Jewish intruder, the two classes would live in harmony . . . We can see now how the third intruding element is evental: it is not just another positive entity, it stands for what is forever unsettling the harmony of the two, opening it up to an incessant process of re-accommodation. A supreme example of this third element, *objet a*, which supplements the couple, comes, again, from Turkey – it is provided by a weird incident that occurred in the Kemalist Turkey of 1926. Part of the Kemalist modernization was to enforce new 'European' models for women, for how they should dress, talk and act, in order to get rid of the oppressive Oriental traditions. As is well known, there was a Hat Law prescribing how men and women, at least in big cities, should cover their heads. Then,

> in Erzurum in 1926 there was a woman among the people who were executed under the pretext of 'opposing the Hat Law'. She was a very tall (almost 2 m.) and very masculine-looking woman who peddled shawls for a living (hence her name '*Şalcı Bacı*' [Shawl Sister]). Reporter Nimet Arzık described her as, 'two meters tall, with a sooty face and snakelike thin dreadlocks [. . .] and with manlike steps'. Of course as a woman she was not supposed to wear the fedora, so she could not have been 'guilty' of anything, but probably in their haste the gendarmes mistook her for a man and hurried her to the scaffold. Şalcı Bacı was the first woman to be executed by hanging in Turkish history. She was definitely not 'normal' since the description by Arzık does not fit in any framework of feminine normalcy at that particular time, and she probably belonged to the old tradition of tolerated and culturally included 'special people' with some kind of genetic 'disorder'. The coerced and hasty transition to 'modernity', however, did not allow for such an inclusion to exist, and therefore she had to be eliminated, crossed out of the equation. 'Would a woman wear a hat that she be hanged?' were the last words she was reported to have muttered on the way to the scaffold. Apart from making no sense at all, these words represented a semantic void and only indicated that this was definitely a scene from the Real, subverting the rules of semiotics: she was first emasculated (in its primary etymological sense of 'making masculine'), so that she could be 'emasculated'.[28]

How are we to interpret this weird and ridiculously excessive act of killing? The obvious reading would be a Butlerian one: through her provocative trans-sexual appearance and acting, Şalcı Bacı rendered visible the contingent character of sexual difference, of how it is symbolically constructed – as such, she was a threat to normatively established sexual identities ... My reading is slightly (or not so slightly) different: rather than undermining sexual difference, Şalcı Bacı stood for this difference as such, in its traumatic Real, irreducible to any clear symbolic opposition. Her disturbing appearance transforms clear symbolic difference into the impossible-real of an antagonism. So, again, in the same way as class struggle is not just 'complicated' when other classes that do not enter the clear division of the ruling class and the oppressed class appear (this excess is, on the contrary, the very element which makes the class antagonism real and not just a symbolic opposition), the formula of sexual antagonism is not M/F (the clear opposition between masculine and feminine) but MF+, where + stands for the excessive element that transforms the symbolic opposition into the Real of an antagonism.

This brings us back to our topic, the big opposition that is emerging today: on the one hand, the violent imposition of a fixed symbolic form of sexual difference as the basic gesture of counteracting social disintegration; on the other hand, the total transgender 'fluidification' of gender, the dispersal of sexual difference into multiple configurations. This opposition is false. Both poles share a key feature: they both miss sexual difference as the real/impossible of an antagonism.

What goes on is also the neglect of the class and race dimension by the PC proponents of women's and gay rights.

In '10 Hours of Walking in NYC as a Woman' created by a video marketing company in 2014, an actress dressed in jeans, black t-shirt, and tennis shoes walked through various Manhattan neighborhoods recording the actions and comments of men she encountered with a hidden camera and microphone. Throughout the walk the camera recorded over 100 instances coded as verbal harassment, ranging from friendly greetings to sexualized remarks about her body including threats of rape. While the video was hailed as a document of street harassment and the fear of violence that are a daily part of women's lives, it ignored race and class: the largest proportion of the men presented in the video are minorities: in a number of instances the men commenting at the actress were standing against buildings, resting on fire hydrants, or sitting on folding chairs on the sidewalk, postures used to characterize lower class and unemployed men – or, as a reader commented on it: 'The video was meant to generate outrage . . . and it used cryptoracism to do it.'[29]

The great mistake in dealing with this opposition is to search for a proper measure between the two extremes.[30] What one should do instead is bring out what both extremes share: a peaceful world where the antagonistic tension of sexual difference disappears, either in a clear and stable hierarchic distinction of sexes or in the happy fluidity of a desexualized universe. And it is not difficult to discern in this fantasy of a peaceful world the fantasy of a society without social antagonisms; in short, without class struggle.

UNIVERSAL ANTAGONISM

To conclude, transgender people are not simply marginals who disturb the hegemonic heterosexual gender norm; their message is universal, it concerns us all, they bring out the anxiety that underlies every sexual identification, its constructed/unstable character. This, of course, does not entail a cheap generalization that would blunt the edge of the suffering of transgender people ('we all have anxieties and suffer in some way') – it is in transgender people that anxiety and antagonism, which otherwise remain mostly latent, break open. So, in the same way in which for Marx, if one wants to understand the 'normal' functioning of capitalism one should take as a starting point economic crises, if one wants to analyse 'normal' heterosexuality, one should begin with the anxieties that are rife in transgender people.

So what are transgender individuals, from the clinical standpoint? They are not a clinical category – certainly no more 'pathological' than the majority of 'normal' people. Catherine Millot[31] was right in emphasizing that each case should be approached in its uniqueness, focusing on the specific subjective economy which brought the subject to formulate a demand for gender change, an uneasiness with the socially allotted gender identity, etc. Transgender subjects can perform the fetishist disavowal of castration (when their identity functions as a fetish), they can be caught in hysterical questioning, etc., so one should avoid quick generalizations and bear in mind that real castration (like the one performed by the ancient Bulgarian sect of *skopci*) is the ultimate form of the disavowal of castration. Those who follow Butler in emphasizing the infinite plasticity of the discursive construction of gender ('choose your sex') ignore the real, not the biological real supposed to pose a limit to discursive transformations but the real of sexual antagonism.

This is why antagonism is not between heterosexuality and LGBT; the antagonism (or again, as Lacan put it, the fact that 'there is no sexual relationship') is at work in the very core of normative heterosexuality. It is what the violent imposition of gender norms endeavours to contain and obfuscate. It is here that my parallel with the anti-Semitic figure of the Jew enters: the (anti-Semitic figure of the) 'Jew' as the threat to the organic order of a society, as the element which brings into it from the outside corruption and decay, is a fetish whose function is to mask the fact that antagonism does not come from the outside but is immanent to every class society.

One – traditional – way to avoid this anxiety is to impose a heterosexual norm that specifies the role of each gender, and the other is, as we have seen, to advocate the overcoming of sexuality as such (the postgender position). Today, with the rise of the 'internet of things' and biogenetics, this perspective has received a new boost. And, as part of this new perspective, new demands for overcoming old limitations will emerge; among them will be demands for legalizing multiple marriages (which already exist, not only as polygamy but also as polyandry, especially in the Himalaya region), as well as demands for some kind of legalization of intense emotional ties with animals (legally described 'emotional support animals' are already a huge thing in the US). I am not talking about sex with animals (although I remember from my youth, in the late 1960s, the widespread tendency all around Europe to practise sex with animals), even less about 'bestiality,' but about a tendency to recognize some animals (say, a faithful dog) as legitimate partners.

And this brings us back to the topic of normativity: the predominant stance of today's consumerist-capitalist ethics is effectively beyond normativity, 'beyond good and evil', but there is nothing even vaguely 'progressive' about it; this 'beyond' should rather be read as 'beneath'. Normativity cannot and should not be reduced to the scarecrow of 'normative impositions of hegemonic ideology'. Is the fact that, at least in our public space, homophobia and tolerance for rape are inadmissible not a case of normativity that should be endorsed without qualification? The normativity we should fight for should be different from the hegemonic heterosexual/conservative one as well as from the politically correct fake.

Nancy Fraser[32] has shown how the predominant form of US feminism was basically co-opted by neoliberal politics, while the animosity of the Third World countries towards gay struggles is widely known, the saddest thing about them being that they present their rejection of homosexuality and so on as part of their anti-imperialist struggle. So in the same way that homophobia and anti-feminism in many Third World movements should make us suspicious about the level of their anti-imperialism, we should also at least take note of the fact that individuals who personify the cutting edge of global capitalism, like Tim Cook, emphatically support LGBT+ rights. There is nothing *a priori* bad in this fact, of course – there is a long history of big corporations acting against apartheid. In the old South Africa, foreign companies with factories there (like Mercedes) began paying black workers the same as white and thus definitely contributed to the end of apartheid. It is nonetheless symptomatic to listen to stories of how LGBT individuals are oppressed, victimized, etc. – true, but one should nonetheless also note that they enjoy the full support of the hegemonic political space and big business. This, of course, should not in any way problematize our support for LGBT+, but it should make us aware of the politico-ideological background of the affair.

Whenever one mentions class struggle, multicultural theorists tend to fire off warnings against 'class essentialism', against the reduction of anti-racist and anti-sexist struggles to a secondary phenomenon;

however, a quick look at their work shows that (with some rare exceptions) they simply ignore class struggle. Although they officially promote the mantra of 'sex–race–class', the class dimension is never actually dealt with. Class struggle is *de facto* prohibited in multiculturalist discourse, but this prohibition is itself prohibited, one cannot enounce it openly – the penalty is the instant accusation of 'class essentialism'. This is why those critics of my texts on LGBT+ who accused me of old-style class essentialism that ignores new forms of cultural struggles totally miss the point: my problem is precisely how to effectively bring together the anti-capitalist struggle with anti-sexist etc. struggles. The problem is not one of communication, of a deeper understanding of the other, but of radical self-transformation: each side will have to undergo such a radical change that the problem is not resolved but simply disappears.

Maybe, the problem is much more serious than it appears – maybe, the desperate calls for the unification of struggles bear witness to the fact that today's predominant form of anti-sexist struggle in developed Western countries is to such an extent constrained by the ideological coordinates of highly developed late capitalist society that direct unification is simply impossible. Maybe, the phrase 'class struggle and anti-sexist struggle' conceals a hidden 'castrative' dimension, a dimension of a 'vel', of a hard choice: one *or* the other, never both of them. In spite of all the rhetoric of solidarity, today's actual 'nomadic proletariat' (immigrants from non-Western countries – this new form of what Frantz Fanon called 'the wretched of the earth') and today's actual anti-sexist movements cannot find the same language. Once again, to construct a shared space for both of them is a difficult task that requires long and hard work of self-transformation from both sides. To put it in brutal terms, without this shared space, one cannot get rid of the suspicion that the politically correct cultural Left is getting so fanatical in advocating 'progress', in fighting battles against newly discovered cultural and sexual 'apartheids', only in order to cover up its own full immersion in global capitalism. Their shared space is the space in which LGBT+ meets Tim Cook.

No wonder that this process of the progressive radicalization of the liberal demands for the overcoming of the different forms of 'segregation' recently found its peak in the demand for the desegregation of toilets – there is a long history behind this demand. In 2012, Viggo Hansen, a Leftist MP, proposed in the Swedish parliament a law prohibiting masculine individuals from urinating in a standing position, in order to end toilet segregation and enforce the same model of urination for all.[33] But we can reach even further back: in 1934, Gabriel Chevalier published *Clochemerle*, a novel set in a fictional French village in the Beaujolais region. The book satirizes the conflicts between Catholics and Republicans in the French Third Republic by telling the story of the installation of a urinal in Clochemerle's village square. The 'Leftist radical' mayor and the principal teacher concoct the idea of a public urinal as a big symbol of Republican egalitarianism that will bring secular Enlightenment into the village and thereby deal a heavy blow to the Catholic reactionaries. It is difficult to miss the ironic reference to Duchamp's urinal (*Fountain*, first exhibited in 1917), the ultimate example of radical artistic egalitarianism (any object can be art if it is displayed as such). Furthermore, we should bear in mind the arbitrariness with which an activity is chosen to be considered worthy of liberation or desegregation. Why, for example, is smoking more and more prohibited while the use of drugs is increasingly considered an unalienable right? Another example: decades ago, the French 'progressive' press published a whole series of petitions demanding the decriminalization of paedophilia, claiming that in this way the artificial and oppressive culturally constricted frontier that separates children from adults would be abolished and the right to freely dispose with one's body would be extended also to children; only the dark forces of 'reaction' and oppression could oppose such a measure – among the signatories were Sartre, de Beauvoir, Derrida, Barthes, Foucault, Aragon, Guattari, Deleuze, Dolto, Lyotard . . .[34] Today, however, paedophilia is perceived as one of the worst crimes and, instead of fighting for it in the name of anti-Catholic progress, it is rather associated with the dark side of the Catholic church, so that fighting against paedophilia is today a progressive task directed at the forces of reaction . . . The comic victim of this shift is Daniel Cohn-Bendit, who, still living in the old spirit of the '60s, recently described in an interview how, while working in his younger years in a kindegarten, he regularly played masturbatory games with young girls. To his surprise he faced a brutal backlash, and his removal from the European parliament and prosecution were demanded.

At a more general methodological level, one cannot distinguish in a direct way the universal dimension of the emancipatory project and the identity of a particular way of life, so that while we are all together engaged in a universal struggle, we simultaneously fully respect the right of each group to its particular way of life. One should never forget that, for a subject who lives a particular way of life, *all universals appear to him 'coloured' by this way of life*. Each identity (way of life) comprises also a specific way to relate to *other* ways of life. So when we posit as a guideline that each group should be left to enact its particular identity, to practise its own way of life, the problem immediately arises: where do customs that form my identity stop and where does injustice begin? Are women's rights just our custom, or is the struggle for women's rights also universal (and part of the emancipatory struggle, as it was in the entire socialist tradition from Engels to Mao)? Is homophobia just a thing of a particular culture, to be tolerated as a component of its identity? Should arranged marriages (which form the very core of kinship structures in some societies) also be accepted as part of a particular identity? And so on.

This 'mediation' of the universal with the particular (way of life) holds for all cultures, ours (Western) included, of course. The 'universal' principles advocated by the West are also coloured by the Western way of life, so the task is thus to bring the struggle *into* every particular way of life: each particular way of life is antagonistic, full of inner tensions and inconsistencies, and the only way to proceed is to work for an alliance of struggles in different cultures. From here I would like to return to the project of the alliance between progressive middle classes and nomad proletarians: in terms of concrete problematic, this means that the politico-economic struggle against global capitalism and the struggle for women's rights etc. have to be conceived as two moments of the same emancipatory struggle for equality.

The transgender theorists who endeavour to assert the link between their struggle and the struggle against racism get caught in the line of argumentation that reaches its peak in Che Gossett's claim that 'trans and gender nonconforming people are situated (like the violence of the gender binary which we oppose) within the theoretical and political coordinates of history and history's present tense – the afterlife of slavery and colonialism. Žižek ignores the fact that we can't think the gender binary outside of the context of racial slavery and colonialism within which it was forged.'[35] So it's not just that racism and colonialism mobilize and manipulate – the gender binary emerged in the context of racial slavery . . . So what about the obvious fact that all premodern cosmologies are based precisely on the 'gender binary', on the interaction of masculine and feminine 'cosmic principles'? (Not to mention the usual confusion between sexual difference/antagonism and 'gender binary'.)

These two aspects – the imposition of Western values as universal human rights, and the respect for different cultures independently of the horrors that can be part of these cultures – are the two sides of the same ideological mystification. The multiculturalist anti-colonialist defence of the multiplicity of ways of life is also false: it covers up the antagonisms within each of these particular ways of life, justifying acts of brutality, sexism and racism as expressions of a particular culture that we have no right to judge by foreign Western values.

This aspect should in no way be dismissed as marginal: from Boko Haram and Mugabe to Putin, anti-colonialist critiques of the West more and more appear as a rejection of Western 'sexual' confusion, and as a demand for a return to the traditional sexual hierarchy. It is, of course, true that the immediate export of Western feminism and individual human rights can serve as a tool of ideological and economic neo-colonialism (we all remember how some American feminists supported the US intervention in Iraq as a way to liberate women there, while the result is exactly the opposite). But one should nonetheless absolutely reject drawing from this the conclusion that Western Leftists should make here a 'strategic compromise', silently tolerating 'customs' that humiliate women and gays, on behalf of the 'greater' anti-imperialist struggle.

However, the opposition between the sexual politics of religious fundamentalism (whose extreme cases are ISIS and Boko Haram) and the radicalism of LGBT+ forms an axis of excesses from which one should distinguish another axis, the opposition between the two 'normal' (and much more predominant) stances, the 'normal' conservative family ideology, which is ready to deplore the extremist excesses, and the 'normal' stance of liberal permissiveness, which supports feminism and gay rights but prefers to mockingly dismiss the excesses of LGBT+. The basic axis is this one, and each of its two opposed poles tends to dismiss its radicalized version (Muslim-style extreme subordination of women is rejected by moderate-conservative Muslims; the excessive measures advocated by LGBT+ are also rejected by the mainstream advocates of women's rights and of gay rights). Each side rejects such extremes as its own pathological outgrowth, as something belonging to those who have lost the proper human measure.

The communist struggle for universal emancipation means *a struggle that cuts into each particular identity, dividing it from within.* When there is racism, when there is domination over women, it is always an integral part of a particular 'way of life', a barbarian integral underside of a particular culture. In the 'developed' Western world, communist struggle means a brutal and principled struggle against all ideological formations that, even if they present themselves as 'progressive', serve as an obstacle to universal emancipation (liberal feminism, etc.); it means not only attacking our own racist and religious fundamentalisms, but also demonstrating how they arise out of the inconsistencies of the predominant liberalism. And in Muslim countries, communist strategy should in no way endorse the traditional 'way of life', which includes honour killings, etc.; it should not only collaborate with the forces in these countries that fight traditional patriarchy, it should make a crucial step forward and demonstrate how, far from serving as a point of resistance against global capitalism, such traditional ideology is a direct tool of imperialist neo-colonialism.

6

The Populist Temptation

THE SIMPLE ART OF
DEFECATING IN PUBLIC

On 18 February 2017, discussing terror, Donald Trump mentioned the incident 'last night in Sweden' – but, as commentators from Sweden were quick to point out, there had been no 'incident' in Sweden the previous night . . . One can't help but remember here the famous dialogue between the Scotland Yard detective Gregory and Sherlock Holmes in the story 'Silver Blaze':

> 'Is there any other point to which you would wish to draw my attention?'
> 'To the curious incident of the dog in the night-time.'
> 'The dog did nothing in the night-time.'
> 'That was the curious incident.'

Or, in Trump's version, a journalist asks him: 'Is there any other point to which you would wish to draw the attention of the press, Mister President?' Trump replies: 'To the curious incident last night in Sweden.' The surprised journalist reacts: 'But no incident occurred last night in Sweden.' Trump snaps back: 'That was the curious incident.' This brief dialogue spills out the truth of Trump's scandal-mongering propaganda of 'alternative facts': the 'curiosity' does not reside in facts mentioned by Trump but in how he presents non-events as facts.

However, Trump's sloppiness with facts is just an effect of a much deeper disturbance. When it was announced that, from July to

September 2015, 'Jade Helm 15' – a series of large military exercises – would take place in southwestern USA, the news immediately gave rise to a suspicion that they were part of a Federal plot to place Texas under martial law, in direct violation of the Constitution. We find all the usual suspects participating in this conspiracy paranoia, up to Chuck Norris; the craziest among them is the website All News Pipe-Line, which linked the exercises to the closure of several Walmart megastores in Texas: 'Will these massive stores soon be used as "food distribution centers" and to house the headquarters of invading troops from China, here to disarm Americans one by one as promised by Michelle Obama to the Chinese prior to Obama leaving the White House?'[1] What makes the affair ominous is the ambiguous reaction of the leading Texas Republicans: Governor Greg Abbott ordered the State Guard to monitor the exercise, while Ted Cruz demanded details from the Pentagon … Texas conservatives were so much driven by their hatred of Obama that they were ready to believe that Obama wanted to actually facilitate a Chinese takeover of the US southwest, and while the leading Texas Republicans were of course not ready to publicly embrace such crazy conspiracy theories, they nonetheless wanted to signal their solidarity with the anti-Obama fanatics among their voters.

Such weird incidents can only be understood against the background of the conflict between the Republican Party establishment and its religious-populist element active in phenomena like the Tea Party. Trump as a media phenomenon is an answer to this predicament: it is simply an attempt to keep together the two heterogeneous components of the Republican Party – big business and populism. Although he has supported the Tea Party, he is definitely not one of the lunatic Rightists. If one looks closely at his programme, it is the standard Republican list: deregulation and low taxes in the economy, dismissal of Global Warming as a hoax, pro-Israel foreign policy, anti-abortion Christianity, etc. If anything, his programme is even relatively moderate (he acknowledges many Democratic achievements, and his stance towards gay marriages is ambiguous). The function of his 'refreshing' provocations and vulgar outbursts is precisely to mask this ordinariness of his programme.

That's why the moderate 'rational' Republican Right is in a panic:

after the decline of the fortunes of Jeb Bush, it is desperately looking for a new face, toying with the idea of mobilizing Bloomberg, etc. What has to be done here is to address a more basic question: the true problem resides in the moderate 'rational' position itself. The fact that the majority cannot be convinced by the 'rational' capitalist discourse and is much more prone to endorse a populist anti-elitist stance is not to be discounted as a case of lower-class primitivism: populists correctly detect the irrationality of this rational approach, their rage directed at faceless institutions that regulate their lives in a non-transparent way is fully justified.

Trump is the purest expression of this tendency towards the debasement of our public life. What does he do in order to 'steal the show' at public debates and in interviews? He offers a mixture of 'politically incorrect' vulgarities: racist stabs (against Mexican immigrants), suspicions on Obama's birthplace and university diploma, bad taste attacks on women, offending war heroes like John McCain . . . In mid December 2015 Trump mocked Hillary Clinton for returning late to a debate following a commercial break because she'd been using the bathroom: 'What happened to her? I'm watching the debate, and she disappeared. Where did she go?!' he said at a rally in Michigan, and went on: 'I know where she went. It's disgusting, I don't want to talk about it.'[2] There is a mystery in his words: in what precise sense is going to the bathroom disgusting? Are we not all (with the exception of Kim Yong-Il, according to some North Korean official media) doing it? What makes it really disgusting is talking publicly about it – so it is Trump himself who is disgusting in his remarks. Such tasteless quips are meant to indicate that Trump doesn't care about false manners and 'says openly what he (and many ordinary people) thinks'. In short, he makes it clear that, in spite of his billions, he is an ordinary vulgar guy like all of us common people.

However, these vulgarities should not deceive us: whatever Trump is, he is not a dangerous outsider. His true secret is that, now that he has won, nothing will really change – in contrast to Bernie Sanders, the Leftist Democrat whose key advantage over the academic politically correct liberal Left was that he understood and respected the problems and fears of ordinary workers and farmers. The really interesting electoral duel would have been between

Trump as the Republican candidate and Sanders as the Democratic candidate.

A while ago, Donald Trump was unflatteringly compared to a man who noisily defecates in the corner of a room in which a high-class drinking party is going on[3] – OK, but were the other Republican candidates for the US presidency substantially any better? We probably all remember the scene from Buñuel's *Phantom of Freedom* in which relations between eating and excreting are inverted: people sit at their toilets around the table, pleasantly talking, and when they want to eat, they silently ask the housekeeper 'Where is that place, you know?' and sneak away to a small room in the back. Are the Republican candidates – to prolong the metaphor – not like this reunion in Buñuel's film? And does the same not hold for many leading politicians around the globe? Was Erdogan not defecating in public when, in a paranoiac outburst, he dismissed critics of his policy towards the Kurds as traitors and foreign agents? Was Putin not defecating in public when (in a well-calculated public vulgarity aimed at boosting his popularity at home) he threatened a critic of his Chechen politics with medical castration? Was Sarkozy not defecating in public when, back in 2008, he snapped at a farmer who refused to shake his hand *'Casse-toi alors, pauvre con!'* (a very soft translation would be 'Get lost then you bloody idiot!', but its actual meaning is much closer to something like 'Fuck you, prick!')? And the list goes on – even the Left is not exempt from this debasement. Here is an example of the racism of the alleged Leftist 'radicals' at its most brutal, combined with breathtaking ignorance of facts[4] – the author is the late John Pilger:

> Yugoslavia was a uniquely independent and multi-ethnic, if imperfect, federation that stood as a political and economic bridge in the Cold War. This was not acceptable to the expanding European Community, especially newly united Germany, which had begun a drive east to dominate its 'natural market' in the Yugoslav provinces of Croatia and Slovenia. By the time the Europeans met at Maastricht in 1991, a secret deal had been struck; Germany recognized Croatia, and Yugoslavia was doomed. In Washington, the US ensured that the struggling Yugoslav economy was denied World Bank loans and the defunct NATO was reinvented as an enforcer.[5]

Incidentally, Slovenia and Croatia were not 'provinces', but autonomous sovereign republics whose right to secession was explicitly recognized by the federal constitution. Reducing other republics to 'provinces' was part of the Serb nationalist policy – Yugoslavia was doomed years before 1991. Pilger then surpasses even his own standards of slander with the openly racist characterization of Kosovo as a land 'which has no formal economy and is run, in effect, by criminal gangs that traffic in drugs, contraband and women' – even the standard Serb nationalist propaganda wouldn't have put it so openly (although, of course, they would have agreed with it). But Pilger is in no way alone in resorting to racism apropos Yugoslavia: in order to justify the shift towards more 'balanced' (i.e., basically pro-Serb) position in the last years of the post-Yugoslav war and its aftermath, some senior peers of the *New Left Review* were fond of evoking Slovene 'egotism' as the main cause of the disintegration of Yugoslavia and the ensuing war. One of them told me in private that, before the outbreak of the war, the Yugoslav Army (the same army which, a little bit later, put itself fully in the service of Milošević's politics!) should have been bribed not to take side with Milošević, i.e., that it should have been given a couple of billion dollars more for its budget – the logic of this statement is simply that, basically, Slovenes should have bribed the bandit who planned to attack them. And, incidentally, the same senior peer told me privately in 1994, when a bomb exploded in a crowded Sarajevo market, killing dozens of civilians, that he learned from confidential sources in the Foreign Office that Bosnians had bombed themselves in order to gain Western sympathy . . .

This strange 'old boys' pact between the UK's radical Left senior peers and the shadowy figures of the UK conservative establishment is not without irony – and one can see how Pilger, the great critic of Western neo-colonialism, joined in, buying the French-British establishment story of the dark German-Vatican plan to extend their influence in Balkans by ruining Yugoslavia – another case of the 'radical' Left relying on data provided by the conservative diplomatic establishment.[6]

The problem here is the one that Hegel called *Sittlichkeit*: mores, the thick background of (unwritten) rules of social life, the thick and impenetrable ethical substance which tells us what we can and what we cannot do. These rules are disintegrating today: what was a couple of decades ago simply unsayable in a public debate can now be pronounced with impunity. It may appear that this disintegration is counteracted by the growth of political correctness, which prescribes exactly what cannot be said; however, a closer look immediately makes it clear how politically correct regulation participates in the same disintegration of the ethical substance.

This specific dimension of politeness is located between the two extremes of pure inner morality and external legality: while both of these two extremes are constructed in a very precise conceptual way (the subject acts morally only if the motive for his act is pure duty that is not contaminated by any pathological considerations; the subject acts legally if his external acts do not violate any legal prohibitions and regulations), politeness (manners, gallantry, etc.) is more than just obeying external legality and less than pure moral activity – it is the ambiguously imprecise domain of what one is not strictly obliged to do (if one doesn't do it, one doesn't break any laws), but what one is nonetheless expected to do. We are dealing here with implicit unspoken regulations, with questions of tact, with something towards which the subject has as a rule a non-reflected relationship: something that is part of our spontaneous sensitivity, a thick texture of customs and expectations which is part of our inherited substance of mores. As such, this domain is the domain of ideology par excellence, at its purest: the air that we breathe spontaneously in our daily interactions, attitudes that we accept as self-evident givens. To put it in Althusserian terms, this domain is the domain of ideological apparatuses and practices, the domain which, to use the terms of Kant himself, allows individuals to 'schematize' their abstract moral and legal norms, to make them part of their living experience.

But why talk about politeness and public manners today, when we are facing what appears to be much more pressing 'real' problems? In doing so, do we not regress to the level of de Quincey's famous quip about the simple art of murder – 'How many people began with unleashing terror and economic catastrophes, and ended up with behaving badly at a party?' But manners *do* matter – in tense situations, they are a matter of life and death, a thin line that separates barbarism from civilization. There is one surprising fact about the latest outbursts of public vulgarity that deserves to be noted. Back in the 1960s, occasional vulgarities were associated with the political Left: student revolutionaries often used common language to emphasize their contrast to official politics with its polished jargon. Today, vulgar language is almost exclusively the prerogative of the radical Right, so that the Left finds itself in a surprising position of the defender of decency and public manners. (*Almost* exclusively – there are also signs of the new vulgarities among the PC Left. On the website of *The New Republic*, Alex Shephard begins his commentary on me: 'The last time we checked in on collection of bodily fluids Slavoj Žižek ...'[7] – and this comes from a journal that otherwise deplores Trump's vulgarity and degradation of public speech ...)

This defence is, of course, always in danger of degenerating into political correctness: the need for PC rules arises when unwritten mores are no longer able to regulate effectively everyday interactions – instead of spontaneous customs followed in a nonreflexive way, we get explicit rules ('blacks' become 'African-Americans', 'fat' becomes 'weight-challenged', etc.). The great victim of such operations is precisely the level of 'sincere lies', of pretending. Under the PC discursive regime, it is not enough to follow external rules of politeness: one is expected to be 'sincerely' respectful of others, and one is questioned endlessly about the sincerity of one's innermost convictions. In short, the PC attitude, brought to its extreme, resembles a proto-psychotic who is suspicious about the sincerity of our politeness in an almost paranoiac way: after we greet him – 'Hello, glad to meet you!' – his reaction is: 'Are you really glad to see me, or are you just a hypocrite?'

As to the replacement of the word 'torture' by 'enhanced interrogation technique', one should note that we are dealing here with an extension of the politically correct logic: in exactly the same way that 'disabled' becomes 'physically challenged', 'torture' becomes 'enhanced interrogation technique' (and again, 'rape' could become 'enhanced seduction technique'). The crucial point is that torture – brutal violence practised by the state – was made publicly acceptable at the very moment when public language was rendered politically correct in order to protect victims from symbolic violence. These two phenomena are two sides of the same coin.

A parallel with rape imposes itself here: what if a film were to show a brutal rape in the same neutral way, claiming that one should avoid cheap moralism and start to think about rape in all its complexity? Our guts tell us that there is something terribly wrong here: I would like to live in a society where rape is simply considered unacceptable, so that anyone who argues for it appears an eccentric idiot, not in a society where one has to argue against it – and the same goes for torture: a sign of ethical progress is the fact that torture is 'dogmatically' rejected as repulsive, without any need for argumentation.

Furthermore, the Leftist public space is increasingly dominated by the rules of tweet culture: short snaps, retorts, sarcastic or outraged remarks, with no space for considered discussion and argument. One passage (or a sentence, or even just a part of it) is cut out and reacted to. For example, many critics reacted to my analysis of the anti-Semitic figure of the Jew as a foreign intruder that disturbs social harmony by accusing me of anti-Semitism, totally ignoring the fact that the claim about 'Jews as the foreign intruder' is for me the very claim I reject as the exemplary ideological operation of obfuscating social antagonisms – they simply cut out the words they wanted and used them to attack me ... The stance that sustains these tweet rejoinders is a mixture of self-righteousness, political correctness and brutal sarcasm: the moment anything that sounds problematic is perceived, a reply is automatically triggered, usually a PC commonplace. Although critics like to emphasize how they reject normativity ('the imposed heterosexual norm', etc.), their stance is one of ruthless normativity, denouncing every minimal deviation from the PC dogma as 'transphobia' or 'fascism' or whatever. Such a tweet culture, which combines official tolerance and openness with extreme intolerance towards actually different views, simply renders critical thinking impossible. It is a true mirror-image of the blind populist rage à la Donald Trump, and it is simultaneously one of the reasons why the Left is so often inefficient in confronting Rightist populism, especially in today's Europe. If one just mentions that this populism draws a good part of its energy from the popular discontent of the exploited, one is immediately accused of 'class essentialism' ...

THE BEGINNING OF A BEAUTIFUL FRIENDSHIP? WHEN THE LEFT DISCOVERS BELONGING

Apart from the temptation to join the liberal centre against the Big Bad Wolf, another no less deplorable Leftist reaction to the rise of populist rage is a variation on the old theme 'if you can't beat them, join them!' From Greece to France, a new trend is arising in what remains of the radical Left: the rediscovery of nationalism. All of a sudden, universalism is out, dismissed as a lifeless political and cultural counterpart of the 'rootless' global capital and its technocratic financial experts, at best the ideology of Habermasian social democrats who advocate global capitalism with a human face. The reason for this rediscovery of nationalism is obvious: the rise of the Rightist nationalist populism in Western Europe is now the strongest political force advocating the protection of working-class interests, and simultaneously the strongest political force able to give rise to proper political passions. So the idea is: why should the Left leave this field of nationalist passions to the radical Right, why should it not 'reclaim *la patrie* from the Front National'? Could the radical Left not mobilize these same nationalist passions as a mighty tool against the central fact of today's global society, which is the increasingly unfettered reign of rootless financial capital? Anti-immigrant populism brings passion back into politics, it speaks in terms of antagonisms, of Us against Them, and one of the signs of the confusion among what remains of the Left is the idea that one should take this passionate approach from the Right: 'If Marine le Pen can do it, why should we also not do it?' So one should return to the ideal of a strong nation-state and mobilize national passions? A ridiculous struggle, lost in advance.

Once we accept this horizon, the very fact that the critique of the Brussels technocracy from the standpoint of national sovereignty is the main feature of today's radical Right, it's clear why it has become a reason for Leftist patriotism. In Greece, it's the opposition between Varoufakis and Lapavitsas, who mocks Varoufakis's DIEM initiative for its lifeless pan-Europeanism that in advance accepts the terrain of the enemy.

Of special interest in this controversy is, once again, Frédéric Lordon, a relentless critic of financialized global capitalism (especially its EU Brussels version). Lordon endeavours to provide a philosophical grounding for the Leftist rehabilitation of 'belonging' (to a particular community, way of life, etc.) in Spinoza's thought. He attacks the Cartesian individualist tradition of the abstract subject possessing free will, with no substantial roots, which survives in existentialism and today's postmodern celebration of hybridity, from the position of Spinoza as 'the thinker who can emancipate us from the delusions of free will or untrammeled individual choice, allowing us to grasp human struggles for existence in a disabused materialist fashion'.[8] Against post-national individualism and direct universalism, Lordon advocates

> a Spinozian conception of the community constituted by convergence around a shared emotion – a common view of good and evil, for example – which the vertical of sovereignty then establishes as a condition of membership. The community's feeling for itself exceeds the individual emotions of its members, creating something that is part of them yet goes beyond them. For Spinoza, this excess is the potential of the multitude, which will duly bring forth a potestas.[9]

The mechanism which accounts for the constitution and closure of social totalities, the mechanism that regulates how individuals are 'captured' in a social space, is that of 'imitation of affects' (*imitatio afecti*), and its status is universal, it is an 'anthropological necessity of closure and exclusion',[10] the elementary mechanism of how groups as self-enclosed bodies that exclude others emerge. Imitation of affects works at a more basic level than the liberal-individualist notion of singular subjects who establish links that fit their interests. Spinoza's starting point is not the individual but the multitude, a pluriverse field of chaotic interconnections that resists centralization (subordination to a One). The concept of multitude *qua* crowd is fundamentally ambiguous: multitude is resistance to the imposing One, but, at the same time, it designates what we call the 'mob', a wild, 'irrational' explosion of violence which, through *imitatio afecti*, feeds on and propels itself. This profound insight of Spinoza gets lost in today's ideology of the multitude: the thorough 'undecid-ability' of the crowd designates a certain mechanism that engenders social links, and *this very same* mechanism that supports, say, the enthusiastic formation of social solidarity also supports the explosive spread of racist violence. As Deleuze later developed in a Spinozan vein, affects are not something that belong to a subject and are then passed over to another subject; affects function at the pre-individual level, as free-floating intensities that belong to no one and circulate at a level 'beneath' intersubjectivity.

The next philosophical consequence is the thorough rejection of negativity: each entity strives towards its full actualization – every obstacle comes from outside. In short, since every entity endeavours to persist in its own being, nothing can be destroyed from within, for all change must come from without. (And the same holds for Lordon: the conflict of passions is irreducible, but it remains external, between groups totalized by a shared *conatus* (striving).)

It is this assertion of the positivity of being that grounds Spinoza's radical equation of power and right: justice means that every entity is allowed to freely deploy its inherent power-potentials, that is, the amount of justice owed to me equals my power. Spinoza's ultimate thrust is here anti-legalistic: the model of political impotence is for him the reference to an abstract law that ignores the concrete differ-ential network and the relationship of forces. A 'right' is, for Spinoza, always a right to 'do', to act upon things according to one's nature, not the (judicial) right to 'have', to possess things. It is precisely this equation of power and right that, on the very last page of his *Trac-tatus Politicus*, Spinoza evokes as the key argument for the 'natural' inferiority of women:

> if by nature women were equal to men, and were equally distinguished
> by force of character and ability, in which human power and therefore
> human right chiefly consist; surely among nations so many and differ-
> ent some would be found, where both sexes rule alike, and others,
> where men are ruled by women, and so brought up, that they can
> make less use of their abilities. And since this is nowhere the case, one
> may assert with perfect propriety, that women have not by nature
> equal right with men.[11]

One should here oppose Spinoza to the standard bourgeois liberal ideology, which would publicly guarantee women the same legal status as men, relegating their inferiority to a legally irrelevant 'pathological' fact (and, in fact, all great bourgeois anti-feminists, from Fichte up to Otto Weininger, were always careful to emphasize that, 'of course', the inequality of the sexes should not be translated into inequality in the eyes of the law). Furthermore, one should read this Spinozan equation of power and right against the background of Pascal's famous *pensée*: 'Equality of possessions is no doubt right, but, as men could not make might obey right, they have made right obey might. As they could not fortify justice they have justified force, so that right and might live together and peace reigns, the sovereign good.'[12] Crucial in this passage is the underlying *formalist* logic. The *form* of justice matters more than its content – the form of justice should be maintained even if it is, as to its content, the form of its opposite, of injustice. And, one might add, this discrepancy between form and content is not just the result of particular unfortunate circumstances, but constitutive of the very notion of justice: justice is 'in itself', in its very notion, the form of injustice, namely, a 'justified force'. Usually, when we are dealing with a fake trial in which the outcome is fixed in advance by political and power interests, we speak of a 'travesty of justice' – it pretends to be justice, while it is merely a display of raw power or corruption posing as justice. What, however, if justice is 'as such', in its very notion, a travesty? Is this not what Pascal implies when he concludes, in a resigned way, that if power cannot come to justice, then justice should come to power (i.e., subordinate itself to power)?

In contrast to Spinoza, Lordon does not see the sub-individual play of passions as a dangerous mechanism to be controlled and regulated by the conscious rational subject, but as a mechanism that can (also) ground 'radical democratic progress, understood as the "enrichment of life by joyous affects" '[13] – the affects shared can also be those of a joyful affirmative life. (Even consumerism has a good side: what motivates consumers is not hunger and other painful needs but the joys of sensual satisfactions and entrepreneurialism.) Referring to – among others – Marx, Durkheim, Mauss and Bourdieu, Lordon thus proposes a kind of 'structuralism of passions'. Social and economic structures determine individuals directly, at a sub-individual level of collectivized passions: 'human beings are in the first instance moved by their passions, which in turn, in the final analysis, are determined by social structures.'[14] Unless we get rid of political and social philosophies of the subject, we cannot supplement objective structures with a regime of desires and affects grounded in these structures. Even communism as the most radical idea of universal emancipation should not be deprived of 'belonging' as the fundamental feature of every social link:

> Governed by divergent passions, humans will never be combined and pacified in spontaneous harmony [. . .] To simply assert a communism of reason is to wish away the weight of common affect. To avert implosion, all numerous collectives require a vertical right or power – which, having the multitude as its only basis [. . .] nevertheless rises up over it.[15]

Consequently, any post-nationalism is 'the denial of this fragmentary condition of human social life, its separation in different groupings of belonging'[16] – vertical forms of emancipation can only emerge at this base of a shared affective belonging. Lordon thus attacks the anti-nationalist Left, dismissing their demands as '"the grotesque claims of the well-off" for a "liberation from belonging", without acknowledging how much they benefit from their own belonging'. Once again, Lordon contrasts this hidden belonging of self-proclaimed rootless universalists with

> the reality of statelessness, the nightmare of absolute non-inclusion, surviving like the sans-papiers without rights – and indeed fighting for citizenship, for belonging [. . .] To disavow national affects in the metropole while allowing them, romantically or condescendingly, for the subaltern, is mere hypocrisy. One is never totally free of national belonging: we are seized by a nation from our very first day.[17]

Lordon attacks here Badiou, who, in his very radical universalism, remains 'profoundly French', but above all Habermas and Ulrich Beck, for their lifeless universalism: in Europe today, the nationalist popular call for sovereignty against its financial confiscation 'signals the urgency of rethinking the national state in its relation to collective emancipation'.[18] We should get rid of the dangerous idea that every 'territorialization' – delimitation, drawing a line of separation – is in itself almost proto-fascist, a possessive act of separating 'ours' from 'theirs', and that only the limitless open flow is truly 'progressive', as if there is not also a properly Leftist way of drawing a border. The irony of such a passion for 'de-territorialization' is that it occurs at a time when, from Palestine to many other places, desperate actions to protect a territory against capitalist global free-flow are abounding.

Closely linked to this reassertion of national belonging as a component of the Left identity is the idea of Leftist populism, whose main theoretical proponent is Chantal Mouffe.[19] According to her diagnosis of our predicament, the main reason for the defeat of the Left is the non-combative stance of rational argument and lifeless universalism, of the end of old passionate ideological struggles, epitomized by the names of Giddens, Beck and Habermas. This post-political Third Way cannot combat in an efficient way the antagonistic logic of Us against Them successfully mobilized by anti-immigrant Rightist populists like Marine le Pen in France. Consequently, the way to combat this Rightist populism is to have recourse to a Leftist populism that, while retaining the basic populist coordinates (the logic of Us against Them, of the 'people' against a corrupted elite), fills them in with a Leftist content: 'They' are not poor refugees or immigrants but financial capital, technocratic state bureaucracy, etc. This populism moves beyond the old working-class anti-capitalism: it tries to bring together a multiplicity of struggles, from ecology to feminism, from the right to employment to free education and healthcare, etc., as Podemos is doing in Spain. Is, however, such a formula of antagonistic politicization, of passionate confrontation, against lifeless universalism, not precisely all too formal? Does it not ignore the big question that lurks in the background: why did the Left abandon the antagonistic logic of Us against Them decades ago? Was it not because of deep structural changes in capitalism, changes that cannot be undone with simple populist mobilization?

Podemos stands for populism at its best. Against the arrogant politically correct intellectual elites who despise the 'narrowness' of the ordinary people who are considered 'stupid' for 'voting against their interests', its organizing principle is to listen to and organize those 'from below' against those 'from above', beyond all traditional Left and Right models. The idea is that the starting point of emancipatory politics should be the suffering and injustices concretely experienced by ordinary people in their local life-world (home, workplace, etc.), not abstract visions of a future communist or whatever society. (Incidentally, although the new digital media seem to open up the space for new communities, the difference between these new communities and the old life-world communities is crucial: these old communities are not chosen, I am born into them, they form the very space of my socialization, while the new (digital) communities induct me into a specific domain defined by my interests and thus dependent on my choice. Far from rendering the old 'spontaneous' communities defunct, the fact that the old communities do *not* rely on my free choice makes them superior to the new digital communities, since they compel me to find my way through a pre-existing, not-chosen life-world in which I encounter (and have to learn to deal with) real differences, while the new digital communities, dependent on my choosing them, sustain the ideological myth of the individual who somehow pre-exists a communal life and is free to choose it.) While this approach undoubtedly contains a (very big) grain of truth, its problem is that, to put it bluntly, *'people' doesn't exist*. This idea is not to be taken as an abstract theoretical statement about the inconsistency of multiplicities, etc., but as a thesis referring to a quite concrete, even experiential, fact. 'People' is a false name for the social totality out of which we draw all aspects of our lives. In our global capitalism, the totality is 'abstract', invisible – there is no way to ground it in concrete life-worlds. In other words, in the global capitalist universe, a 'concrete experience' of being a member of a particular life-world, with its customs, living links, forms of solidarity, etc., is *already something 'abstract'* in the strict sense of a particular experience that obliterates the thick network of financial, social, etc., processes that rule and regulate this concrete particular world. We are not dealing here only with the 'alienated', non-transparent activities of state and capital but also with the thick network of social services (water, electricity, education, health) that are necessary for particular communities to operate. Here, Podemos will encounter problems if it at some point takes power: what specific economic measures (beyond the standard Keynesian bag of tricks) will it enact to limit the power of the capital?

Formally, the problem is how to combine the two axes: hybridity/universality versus patriotic belonging, and capitalism versus Leftist anti-capitalism. All four possible combinations are occupied: we have global multicultural capitalism, we have a universalist Left, we have an anti-globalist patriotic Left, and we have capitalism with local ethnic/cultural 'characteristics' (China, India . . .). This last combination is getting stronger and stronger, proving that global capitalism can coexist with particular cultural identities.

To sum up, one can clearly discern two opposed readings of the ongoing disintegration of the predominant mode of 'manufacturing consent' that opens up the space for public vulgarity: liberal and populist. And we should reject both of them – again, our stance should be the one of 'against the double blackmail'. First, there is the liberal complaint: popular rage exploited by figures like Donald Trump and anti-immigrant populists in Europe entails a 'regression of political culture' – demagogic vulgarities that, even a couple of years ago, would not be tolerated in the public space now become a commonplace, providing a 'clear and present danger' to our democracy. Then, there is the Leftist advocacy of populism: in the popular rage that abounds all around us, people have awoken, they have made their discontent clear, and what the dominant big media denounce as a dangerous turn is basically a forceful return of class struggle to the scene. From this standpoint, the movements identified by the names 'Trump' and 'Sanders' are two forms of populism, of returning antagonistic anti-establishment passion to politics. (It is of course absurd to consider Trump, a billionaire exploiting all the legal loops, 'anti-establishment' in any meaningful sense – but this has been the paradox of populism from the very beginning.)

Each of the two positions has a point. On the one hand, good manners should never be underestimated in politics – a vulgar public speech by definition indicates a deeper political disorientation; on the other hand, it is true that the Rightist populist rage is a distorted form of class struggle – as was the case with fascism (it is clear that 'the Jew' in Nazism is a coded figure of the class enemy). However, each of the two positions is also fundamentally flawed. Liberal critics of the new populism don't see that the popular rage is not a sign of the primitivism of ordinary people but a sign of the weakness of the hegemonic liberal ideology itself, which can no longer manufacture consent, so that a recourse to a more 'primitive' functioning of ideology is needed. The Leftist advocates don't see that 'populism' is not a neutral form that can be given a Rightist-fascist or a Leftist spin: already at the level of its form, populism denies immanent social antagonisms, displacing the struggle to one with a constructed external intruder. Although it is, of course, clear that populism does not necessarily overlap with the disintegration of the public discourse into vulgarity, there is nonetheless clearly something like a natural propensity of populism to slide into vulgar simplification and personalized aggressiveness.

A CRISIS IN MANUFACTURING CONSENT

Back to the US, the reactions of both party establishments, Republican and Democrat, to Trump's and Sanders' unexpected success in the US primaries was basically the same: their success demonstrates the crisis of our democracy, it is an abnormality that we should somehow control and contain . . . (The same holds also for the political establishments all around Europe.) This reaction tells us a lot about how our democracy effectively functions: it is tolerated if it is properly controlled by the political establishment, or, as Noam Chomsky noted years ago, 'it is only when the threat of popular participation is overcome that democratic forms can be safely contemplated.'[20]

Walter Lippmann, the icon of American journalism in the twentieth century, played a key role in the self-understanding of US democracy. Although politically progressive (advocating a fair policy towards the Soviet Union, etc.), he proposed a theory of the public media that has a chilling truth. He coined the term 'manufacturing consent', later made famous by Herman and Chomsky – but Lippmann intended it in a positive way. In *Public Opinion* (1922), he wrote that a 'governing class' must rise to face the challenge – he saw the public as Plato did, a great beast or a bewildered herd, floundering in the 'chaos of local opinions'. So the herd of citizens must be governed by 'a specialized class whose interests reach beyond the locality' – this elite class is to act as a machinery of knowledge that circumvents the primary defect of democracy, the impossible ideal of the 'omni-competent citizen'. This is how our democracies function – with our consent. There is no mystery in what Lippmann was saying, it is an obvious fact; the mystery is that, knowing it, we play the game. We act as if we are free and freely deciding, silently not only accepting but even demanding that an invisible injunction (inscribed into the very form of our free speech) tells us what to do and think. As Marx knew long ago, the secret is in the form itself. In this sense, in a democracy, every ordinary citizen effectively is a king – but a king in a constitutional democracy, a king who only formally decides, whose function is to sign measures proposed by executive administration. This is why the problem of democratic rituals is homologous to the big problem of constitutional democracy: how to protect the dignity of the king? How to maintain the appearance that the king effec-tively decides, when we all know this is not true? This, then, is our sad predicament: those rare moments when our democracy really functions and voters get a real choice – recall recent events in Greece – are perceived as a crisis of democracy. The disturbing fact is that this distrust of popular opinion is double-edged: it can be directed also against anti-immigrant populism judged unacceptable by the liberal establishment. We got the first big taste of the mixture of Rightist and Leftist populism in the Brexit vote in UK.

BREXIT, OR, DISORDER UNDER HEAVEN

Late in his life, Freud asked the famous question '*Was will das Weib?*', 'What does a woman want?', admitting his perplexity when faced with the enigma of female sexuality. A similar perplexity arises today, apropos the Brexit referendum: what does Europe want?

The true stakes of this referendum become clear if we locate it in its larger historical context. In Western and Eastern Europe, there are signs of a long-term rearrangement of the political space. Until recently, the political space was dominated by two main types of party, which addressed the entire electoral body: a Right-of-centre party (Christian-Democrat, liberal-conservative, people's . . .) and a Left-of-centre party (socialist, social-democratic . . .), with smaller parties addressing narrower sections of the electorate (ecologists, neo-fascists, etc.). Now, there is progressively emerging a single party that stands for global capitalism as such, usually with relative tolerance towards abortion, gay rights, religious and ethnic minorities, etc.; opposing this party is a stronger and stronger anti-immigrant populist party which, on its fringes, is accompanied by directly racist neo-fascist groups. Once again, the exemplary case here is Poland: after the disappearance of the ex-communists, the main parties are the 'anti-ideological' centrist liberal party of the ex-prime-minister Donald Tusk and the conservative Christian party of the Kaczynski brothers. The stakes of the struggle are: which of the two main parties, conservatives or liberals, will succeed in presenting itself as embodying the post-ideological non-politics while dismissing the other party as 'still caught in old ideological spectres'? In the early 1990s, the conservatives were better at it; later, it was liberal Leftists who seemed to be gaining the upper hand, and now, it's again the conservatives.

So what does Europe want? Basically, Europe is caught in a vicious cycle, oscillating between the Brussels technocracy, unable to drag it out of its inertia, and the popular rage against this inertia, a rage appropriated by new more-radical Leftist movements but primarily by Rightist populism. The Brexit referendum moved along the lines of this new opposition, which is why there was something terribly wrong with it. To see this, one should only look at the strange bedfellows that found themselves together in the Brexit camp: right-wing 'patriots', populist nationalists fuelled by the fear of immigrants, mixed with desperate working-class rage . . . is such a mixture of patriotic racism with the rage of 'ordinary people' not the ideal ground for a new form of fascism?

The intensity of the emotional investment in the referendum

should not deceive us. The choice offered obfuscated the true questions: how to fight 'agreements' like TTIP, which present a real threat to popular sovereignty, how to confront ecological catastrophes and economic imbalances, which breed new poverty and migrations, etc. The choice of Brexit means a serious setback for these true struggles – suffice it to bear in mind what an important argument for Brexit was the 'refugee threat'. The Brexit referendum is the ultimate proof that ideology (in the good old Marxist sense of 'false consciousness') is well and alive in our societies. For example, the case of Brexit exemplifies perfectly the falsity of the calls to restore national sovereignty (the 'British people themselves, not some anonymous and non-elected Brussels bureaucrats, should decide the fate of the UK' motif):

> At the heart of the Brexit is a paradox worth articulating. England wants to withdraw from the bureaucratic, administrative control of Brussels, control seen as compromising its sovereignty, in order to be better able to organize the dismantling of its sovereignty (by way of more radical submission to the logic of global capital) on its own. Does this not have the markings of the death drive? The organism wants to die in its own way, on its own terms. This is the paradox at the heart of American Republican thinking: we want to 'take back our country' in order to be better able to submit it and pretty much all of life to the logic of the market.[21]

Is this paradox not confirmed by a quick look at the conflicts between the UK and the EU in the past decades? When they concerned workers' rights, it was the EU that demanded a limiting of weekly work hours, etc., and the UK government complained that such a measure would affect the competitiveness of British industry ... In short, the much-vilified 'Brussels bureaucracy' was also a protector of minimal workers' rights – in exactly the same way as it is today the protector of the rights of refugees against many 'sovereign' nation-states that are not ready to receive them.

Recall again Stalin's exclamation that both choices are worse. Was it not the same with the choice British voters were confronting? Remain was 'worse' since it meant persisting in the inertia that keeps Europe mired down. Exit was 'worse' since it made changing nothing look desirable. In the days before the referendum, there was a pseudo-deep thought circulating in our media: 'Whatever the result, the EU will never be the same, it will be irreparably damaged.' However, it's the opposite that is true: nothing really changed, just the inertia of Europe became impossible to ignore. Europe will again lose time in long negotiations among the EU members, which will continue to make any large-scale political project unfeasible. This is what those who oppose Brexit didn't see: shocked, they now complain about the 'irrationality' of the Brexit voters, ignoring the desperate need for change that the vote made palpable.

For this reason, one should fully support the EU stance that the UK withdrawal should be enacted as fast as possible, without any long preliminary consultations. Understandably, the Brexit partisans in the UK now want to have their cake and eat it (or, as a commentator wittily remarked, they want a divorce that would still allow them to share the marital bed). They desperately want to strike a middle road (Boris Johnson's proposal that the UK should maintain free access to the common market was quite appropriately dismissed as a pipe dream).

The confusion that underlies the Brexit referendum is not limited to Europe: it is part of a much larger process of the crisis of manufacturing democratic consent in our societies, of the growing gap between political institutions and popular rage, the rage that gave birth to Trump as well as to Sanders in the US. Signs of chaos are everywhere – recently, a debate over gun control in the US congress turned into banana-republic mayhem, with congressmen involved in the sort of rough-and-tumble that we usually associate with Third World countries . . .

Is this a reason to despair? Although crises are painful and dangerous, they are the terrain on which battles have to be waged and won. Is there not a struggle also in heaven, is heaven also not divided – and does the ongoing confusion not offer a unique chance to react to the need for a radical change in a more appropriate way, with a project that will break the vicious cycle of EU technocracy and nationalist populism? The true division of our heaven is not between anemic technocracy and nationalist passions, but between their vicious cycle and a new pan-European project that addresses the true challenges that humanity confronts today. Now that, in an echo of the Brexit victory, calls for other exits from the EU are multiplying all around Europe, the situation calls for such a heretical project – but who will grab the chance? Unfortunately, not the existing Left, which is well-known for its breathtaking ability to never miss a chance to miss a chance . . .

A FORCE OF LAW THAT CANCELS ITSELF

Far from being just a phenomenon of 'bad manners', the disintegration of *Sittlichkeit* materializes itself in the decline of trust in the rule of law. Recall how, after the two cases in which a white policeman shot a black man in cold blood, a black sniper (who had previously served as a sniper in the US army in Afghanistan) set an ambush in Dallas during a protest march and shot to death five white policemen. Conservative media declared this act of revenge an act of war, for which the organization Black Lives Matter should be held responsible, and promised retaliation – the killing of policemen was perceived as a much stronger crime than the killing by a white policeman of a black suspect. The underlying reasoning is easy to reconstruct: in the case of the white policeman killing a black man, the policeman went too far in pursuing his duty of cleansing the streets of violent crime, since the black victims were all suspected of some crime, while the shooting of policemen who were just maintaining order during a peaceful protest is a much more heinous attack on the very force that maintains social peace. However, this classification remains blind to the crucial dimension that opposes the two crimes. While the killing of the five white policemen was simply a private citizen's revenge against the representatives of the force of law, the policemen who were responsible for the killing of unarmed black men did something much more radical: they threatened in a much stronger way the status of the law since they performed their criminal acts in their capacity as agents of the law, so that a crime was performed as part of the enforcement of the law itself, blurring the distinction between crime and law. When representatives of law commit crimes in their very enforcement of the rule of law, the rule of law is not just weakened but undermined from within – it directly appears as its own self-negation.

And is something quite similar not going on in Israel? The cruel irony of the history of relations between capitalist-colonialist nations (whose basic principle was equivalent exchange regulated by law) and the colonized (who were not yet fully within the market economy of exchange) is that it is a long history of broken laws/treaties, from the US treatment of native Americans to the Israeli treatment of Palestinians, which is why the role of Shylock (who just demands what the law gives him) is played by Palestinians. Recently, a Palestinian lawyer in the West Bank made a quite logical Shylockian demand on the State of Israel:

> A lawyer for the family of a Palestinian teen whose 2014 murder was part of a chain of events that sparked the Gaza war says he wants Israel to punish the teenager's killers in the same way it does Palestinian militants. Lawyer Mohannad Jubara is petitioning Israel's Supreme Court to demolish the family homes of the three Israeli men who abducted 16-year-old Mohammed Abu Khdeir and burned him to death in 2014.[22]

Since Israel carries out demolitions of militants' homes to deter future attacks, is this demand not quite logical? (Recall also the outcry after the adolescents responsible for this attack were arrested. Rumours started to spread that they had been tortured by the Israeli police, and the public protested . . . against what? Against the fact that they appeared to be treated in the same way as Palestinian adolescents suspected of terrorism!) A long time ago Golda Meir allegedly said that, after the Holocaust (or, according to another version, after the Eichmann trial), Israel could do whatever it wants. Although Jews are supposedly defined by the strict rule of law, the State of Israel exploits the Holocaust as the ground for a superego exception from the law.

FACES OF DEMOCRATIC DEFICIT

Apart from joining the centrist consensus and trying to appropriate populist rage, the main liberal Left's third reaction to populism is to see it as an effect of a 'democratic deficit' – so what we need is a more authentic democracy. Here, however, we finally face the true deadlock.

After Dijsselbloem and Malmström, a new anonymous EU face has emerged: Frans Timmermans, the First Vice-President of the European Commission, who on 23 December 2015 scolded the Polish government for adopting a new law that poses a threat to the democratic constitutional order since it subordinates the constitutional court to the authority of government. Furthermore, Timmermans condemned a new media law that was rushed through Poland's parliament: the law will enable the parliament to immediately sack all executives at the country's public television and radio companies and to appoint their replacements. The ruling party justifies this law as necessary to stifle unfair criticism of its actions, while the opposition decries it as a severe limitation of the freedom of the press. In an immediate and sharp reply, the Polish side warned Brussels 'to exercise more restraint in instructing and cautioning the parliament and the government of a sovereign and democratic state in the future'.

From the standard Left-liberal view, it is of course inappropriate to put these three names into the same series: Dijsselbloem and Malmström personify the pressure of the Brussels bureaucrats (without democratic legitimization) on states and their democratically elected governments, while Timmermans intervened to protect basic democratic institutions (the independence of courts, a free press) from a government that overstepped its legitimate powers. However, although it may appear obscene to equate the brutal neo-liberal pressure on Greece with the justified criticism of Poland, did the Polish government's reaction also not hit the mark? Timmermans, an EU administrator without any clear democratic legitimization, exerted pressure on the democratically elected government of a sovereign state.

This is what makes problematic the calls for transparency in EU decision-making: since in many countries the majority of the public was against the Greek debt reduction, rendering EU negotiations public would make representatives of these countries advocate even tougher measures against Greece ... We encounter here the old problem: what happens to democracy when the majority is inclined to vote for racist and sexist laws? I am not afraid to draw the conclusion that emancipatory politics should not be bound *a priori* by formal-democratic procedures of legitimization. People quite often do *not* know what they want, or do not want what they know, or they simply want the wrong thing. There is no short-cut here, and, as we have already seen, we can well imagine a democratized Europe with much more engaged citizens in which the majority of governments are formed by anti-immigrant populist parties.

The context of these impasses is the Big Bad Wolf of the European liberal Left: the threat of a new fascism embodied in anti-immigrant Rightist populism. This scarecrow is perceived as the principal enemy against which we should all unite, from (whatever remains of) the radical Left to mainstream liberal democrats (including EU administrators like Timmermans). Europe is portrayed as a continent regressing towards a new fascism that feeds on the paranoiac hatred and fear of the external ethnic-religious enemy (mostly Muslims). While this fascism is directly predominant in some post-communist East European countries (Hungary, Poland, etc.), it is also getting stronger in many other countries, where the view is that the invasion of Muslim refugees poses a threat to the European legacy.

It is here that one should not lose nerve but persist in the basic Marxist insight: this 'fascism' is strictly a secondary phenomenon engendered by its apparent opposite, the 'open' liberal-democratic universe, so the only way to truly defeat it is to overcome the imma-nent limitations of the latter.

The situation is here exactly the same as with the so-called 'authoritarian personality' from the legendary study in which Adorno participated.[23] The features of the 'authoritarian personal-ity' are clearly opposed to the standard figure of the 'open' democratic personality, and the underlying dilemma is whether these two types of personality are opposed in a struggle, so that we should fight for one against the other, or whether the 'authoritarian' personality is in fact the symptomal 'truth' of the 'democratic' personality. The shift from Adorno to Habermas apropos modernity can itself be formulated in these terms: at the heart of Adorno's and Horkheimer's 'dialectic of enlightenment' is the idea that phenomena such as fascism are 'symptoms' of modernity, its necessary consequence. For Habermas, by contrast, they are 'symptoms' or indicators of the fact that modernity remains an 'unfinished project', that it has not yet deployed all its potential.

The source of unease is, of course, the unpleasant fact that this new 'fascism' is democratically legitimized. Leftist critics of the EU now find themselves in a strange predicament: on the one hand, they deplore the 'democratic deficit' of the EU and propose plans to make more transparent the decision-making in Brussels; on the other hand, they support the 'non-democratic' Brussels administrators when they exert pressure on (democratically legitimized) new 'fascist' tendencies.

But is this fascism really fascism? There are currently two wrong generalizations about contemporary society circulating. The first one is that we live in an era of universalized anti-Semitism. With the military defeat of fascism, the role once played by (the anti-Semitic figure of) the 'Jew' is now played by any foreign group experienced as a threat to our identity – Latinos, Africans and, especially, Muslims, who are today in Western society more and more treated as the new 'Jew'. The other wrong generalization is that the fall of the Berlin Wall led to the proliferation of new walls intended to separate us from the dangerous Other (the wall separating Israel from the West Bank, the planned wall between the US and Mexico, etc.) – true, but there is a key distinction between the two types of wall. The Berlin Wall stood for the Cold War division of the world, and although it was perceived as the barrier that kept isolated the populations of the 'totalitarian' communist states, it also signalled that capitalism was not the only option, that an alternative to it, although a failed one, existed. The walls that we see rising today are, on the contrary, walls whose construction was triggered by the very fall of the Berlin Wall (i.e., the disintegration of the communist order): they don't stand for the division between capitalism and communism but for the division that is strictly immanent to the global capitalist order. In a nice

Hegelian move, when capitalism triumphed over its external enemy and united the world, the division returned in its own space.

As for the first generalization, there is a rather obvious distinction between fascism proper and today's anti-immigrant populism.[24] Let's recall the basic premise of the Marxist analysis of capitalism: capitalism is a reign of abstraction; in it, social relations are permeated, regulated and dominated by abstractions that are not just subjective abstractions, abstractions performed by our minds, but 'objective' abstractions, abstractions that rule social reality itself, what Marx called *Realabstraktion*, 'real abstraction'. These abstractions are part of our social experience of capitalism: we directly experience our social life as regulated by impenetrable mechanisms that are beyond representation, which cannot be embodied in any individuals – even the capitalists who replaced the old Masters are enslaved by powers beyond their control. The (anti-Semitic figure of the) 'Jew' embodies this abstraction: it is the invisible Master who secretly pulls the strings. Jews are fully integrated into our society, they deceivingly appear as one of us, so the problem and task is to clearly identify them (recall all the ridiculous Nazi attempts to exactly measure racial identities). Muslim immigrants are *not* today's Jews: they are all too visible, not invisible, they are clearly not integrated into our societies, and nobody claims they secretly pull the strings. If one sees in their 'invasion of Europe' a secret plot, then Jews have to be behind it, a view expressed in an article that recently appeared in one of the main Slovene Rightist weekly journals, where we could read that 'George Soros is one of the most depraved and dangerous people of our time,' responsible for 'the invasion of the negroid and Semitic hordes and thereby for the twilight of the EU [. . .] as a typical Talmudo-Zionist, he is a deadly enemy of the Western civilization, nation-state and white, European man.' His goal is to build a 'rainbow coalition composed of social marginals like faggots, feminists, Muslims and work-hating cultural Marxists', which would then perform 'a deconstruction of the nation-state, and transform the EU into a multicultural dystopia of the United States of Europe'. So which forces are opposing Soros? 'Victor Orban and Vladimir Putin are the perspicuous politicians who wholly grasped Soros's machinations and, logically, prohibited the activity of his organizations.' Furthermore, Soros is inconsistent in his promotion of multiculturalism: 'He promotes it exclusively in Europe and the USA, while in the case of Israel, he, in a way which is for me totally justified, agrees with its monoculturalism, latent racism and building a wall. In contrast to EU and USA, he also does not demand from Israel to open its borders and accept "refugees". A hypocrisy proper to Talmudo-Zionism.'[25]

Apart from the stunning racist directness of this text, one should note two features. First, it brings together anti-Semitism and Islamophobia: the threat to Europe is hordes of Muslim refugees, but behind this chaotic phenomenon are the Jews. Second, it clearly takes sides in the conflict within the European Right with regard to Putin: on the one hand, Putin is bad, a threat to Europe, especially to neighbouring post-communist countries, trying to undermine the EU with his machinations; on the other hand, he saw the danger of Western multiculturalism and permissiveness and wisely prevented his country from being overrun by it.

The term 'fascism' is all too often used as a means of avoiding a detailed analysis of what is actually going on. The Dutch Rightist populist politician Pim Fortuyn, killed in early May 2002, two weeks before elections in which he was expected to gain one fifth of the votes, was a paradoxical symptomal figure: a Rightist populist whose personal features and even (most of his) opinions were almost perfectly 'politically correct'. He was gay, had good personal relations with many immigrants, had an innate sense of irony, and so on – in short, he was a good tolerant liberal with regard to everything except his basic political stance: he opposed fundamentalist immigrants because of their hatred towards homosexuality, women's rights, etc. What he embodied was thus the intersection between Rightist populism and liberal political correctness – before his death he was the living proof that the opposition between Rightist populism and liberal tolerance is a false one, that we are dealing with two sides of the same coin.

Furthermore, many Leftist liberals (like Habermas) who bemoan the ongoing decline of the EU seem to idealize its past: but the 'democratic' EU, the loss of which they bemoan, never existed. Recent EU policy is just a desperate attempt to make Europe fit for new global capitalism. The usual Left-liberal critique of the EU – it's basically OK, just with a 'democratic deficit' – betrays the same naivety as the critics of ex-communist countries who basically supported them, just complaining about the lack of democracy: in both cases, the 'democratic deficit' was a necessary part of the overall structure.

But I am here even more of a sceptical pessimist. When I was recently answering questions from the readers of *Süddeutsche Zeitung* about the refugee crisis, the question that attracted by far the most attention concerned precisely democracy, but with a Rightist-populist twist: when Angela Merkel made her famous public appeal inviting hundreds of thousands of immigrants into Germany, what was her democratic legitimization? What gave her the right to bring such a radical change to German life without democratic consultation? My point here, of course, is not to support anti-immigrant populists, but to clearly show the limits of democratic legitimization. The same goes for those who advocate a radical opening of the borders: are they aware that, since our democracies are nation-state democracies, their demand equals suspension of democracy – should a gigantic change be allowed to affect a country without democratic consultation of its population? (Their answer would have been, of course, that refugees should also be given the right to vote – but this is clearly not enough, since this is a measure that can only happen after refugees are already integrated into the political system of a country.)

Yuval Harari points out how the ongoing troubles with immigrants in Germany confronts us with the limits of democracy: how are we to counter anti-immigrant populists who demand a referendum on immigrants, assured that the majority of Germans will vote against them? Is then the solution to give voting rights also to immigrants? To whom among them? To those who are already in Germany, to those who want to go there . . . ? At the end of this line of thought, we get the idea of worldwide elections, which is self-defeating for a simple and precise reason:

> People feel bound by democratic elections only when they share a basic bond with most other voters. If the experience of other voters is alien to me, and if I believe they don't understand my feelings and

don't care about my vital interests, then even if I am outvoted by a hundred to one, I have absolutely no reason to accept the verdict. Democratic elections usually work only within populations that have some prior common bind, such as shared religious beliefs and national myths. They are a method to settle disagreements between people who already agree on the basics.[26]

In larger contexts, the only procedure at our disposal (outside outright war, of course) are negotiations. That's why the Middle East conflict cannot be solved by elections but only by war or negotiations. Let's take an (artificially) clear-cut case: imagine a democracy in which a large majority of voters succumb to the anti-immigrant populist propaganda and decide in a referendum to close the borders to the refugees and make life more difficult for those already in the country; imagine then a country in which, despite such propaganda, voters assert in a referendum their commitment to solidarity and their will to help the refugees. The difference is not just objective, i.e., it is not just that, in one case, voters made a reactionary racist decision and, in the other case, they made the right choice of solidarity; the difference is also 'subjective', in the precise sense that a different type of political passion is at work in each of the two cases. However, one should not be afraid to posit that, in the first case, no matter how sincerely convinced they appear to be, the voters somehow 'deep in themselves' know that what they have done is a shameful act – all their agitated reasoning just covers up their bad feeling. And, in the second act, people always are somehow aware of the liberating effect of their act: even if what they have done is risky and crazy, they have achieved a true breakthrough. Both acts, in a sense, achieve the impossible, but in an entirely different way. In the first case, the public space is spoiled, the ethical standards are lowered. What was, up to that moment, a matter of private dirty prejudices, unacceptable in the public space, becomes something one can talk about publicly – one can be openly racist and sexist, preach hatred and spread paranoia. Today's model of such 'liberation' is, of course, Donald Trump, who, as we are told, 'says publicly what others are only thinking about'. In the second case, most of us are ashamed that we don't trust people more: before the referendum, we were silently expecting a defeat, and the ethical composure of the voters surprises us. Such 'miracles' are worth living for.

Obviously, the only way to counteract the 'democratic deficit' of global capitalism would be through some trans-national entity – was it not Kant who, more than two hundred years ago, saw the need for a trans-nation-state legal order grounded in the rise of the global society? 'Since the narrower or wider community of the peoples of the earth has developed so far that a violation of rights in one place is felt throughout the world, the idea of a law of world citizenship is no high-flown or exaggerated notion.'[27] This, however, brings us to what is arguably the 'principal contradiction' of the New World Order: the structural impossibility of finding a global political order that could correspond to the global capitalist economy. What if, for structural reasons and not only because of empirical limitations, there cannot be a worldwide democracy or a representative world government? That the structure of global capitalism means the global market economy cannot be directly organized as a global liberal democracy with worldwide elections? In politics, the 'repressed' of the global economy returns: archaic fixations, particular substantial (ethnic, religious, cultural) identities. This tension defines our predicament today: while commodities circulate increasingly freely, people are kept apart by new walls.

A TRIUMPH OF IDEOLOGY

The lesson to be learned from the Trump phenomenon is thus that the greatest danger for the true Left is to accept a strategic pact with Clinton liberals against the Big Danger embodied in Trump. Alfred Hitchcock once said that a film is as good as its villain – does this mean that the US elections were good, since the 'bad guy' (Trump) is an almost ideal villain? Do the revelations about his comments on the sexual availability of women not make it clear that we have already moved beyond politics proper? There is something ridiculous in the ongoing wave of these revelations: why do people act 'surprised' by how Trump behaves towards women? Was something like this not to be fully expected? Was such acting not part of his public image? To put it in a tasteless way, it is almost like inviting Hitler to dinner and then being surprised when he starts throwing out anti-Semitic remarks. What did Republicans who supported him expect him to be? Any consternation now is thoroughly hypocritical and is, in itself, much more than Trump's vulgarities, a sad symptom of where we are.

For the liberal majority, the 2016 US elections represented a clear-cut choice: the figure of Trump is a ridiculous excess, vulgar and exploiting our worst racist and sexist prejudices, a male chauvinist without a minimum of decency, so that even Republican big names abandoned him in droves . . . However, this democratic consensus should worry us. We should take a step back and turn the gaze on ourselves: which is the exact 'colour' of this all-embracing democratic unity? Everybody is there, from Wall Street to Sanders supporters in what remains of the Occupy movement, from big business to trade unions, from army veterans to LGBT+, from ecologists (horrified by Trump's denial of global warming) and feminists (delighted by the prospect of the first female president) to the 'decent' Republican establishment figures (terrified by Trump's inconsistencies and irresponsible 'demagogic' proposals). However, these very inconsistencies make his position unique. For example, recall the ambiguity of his stance towards LGBT or abortion:

> After Orlando, he came out all warm and fuzzy about LGBT victims/ people – in a manner that no other Republican would have dared. Also, it is common knowledge that he is not a 'faithful' Christian and that he only says that he is for show – and by 'common knowledge' I mean that this is known by the Methodists and the Mormons and the other Christian sects that make up the US Fundamentalist Front. Lastly, his position on abortion has for decades been a liberal one and it is, again, common knowledge that he does not favour a repeal of the Roe vs Wade Supreme Court decision. In short, Trump has managed to change the cultural politics of the Republican Party for the first time since Nixon. By adopting a crass, misogynist, racist language he has managed to release the Republican Party from its traditional reliance on the Fundamentalist, the homophobic and the anti-abortion ideological straitjacket. It is a remarkable contradiction that only a Hegelian can grasp![28]

The reference to Hegel is here fully justified: Trump's vulgar racist and misogynist style is what enabled him to undermine the Republican conservative-fundamentalist dogma (whose pure representative is a freak like Ted Cruz, which is why Cruz's hatred of Trump is understandable) – Trump is *not* simply the candidate of conservative fundamentalists, he is perhaps an even greater threat to them than to 'rational' moderate Republicans. This complexity, of course, disappears in the standard Left-liberal demonization of Trump – why? To see this, we should again turn our gaze towards the Clinton consensus and ask: what disappears in this apparently all-embracing conglomerate?

The popular rage which gave birth to Trump also gave birth to Sanders, and while they both express widespread social and political discontent, they do it in opposite senses, the one engaging in Rightist populism and the other opting for the Leftist call for justice. And here comes the trick: the Leftist call for justice tends to be combined with struggles for women's and gay rights, for multiculturalism and against racism, etc., while the strategic aim of the Clinton consensus was clearly to dissociate all these struggles from the Leftist call for economic justice.

This same stance was brought to the extreme with Madeleine Albright, a big 'feminist' Clinton supporter. Imagine that, after the Orlando shooting in June 2016 that killed forty-nine people and wounded fifty-three in a gay bar, a representative of some Muslim fundamentalist organization had said that, deplorable as this act is, it is justified as an act in the war against Western decadence and military aggression against Muslims – imagine the public outcry and rage at the barbarian madness of such claims totally alien to our Judeo-Christian culture. But wait, on CBS's *60 Minutes* (12 May 1996), Albright, at that time the US ambassador to the UN, was asked a question about the Iraq war: 'We have heard that half a million children have died. I mean, that's more children than died in Hiroshima. And, you know, is the price worth it?' Albright replied: 'I think this is a very hard choice, but the price – we think the price is worth it.' Let's ignore all the questions that this reply raises (up to the interesting shift from 'I' to 'we': 'I think it's a hard choice' but 'we think the price is worth it'), and focus on just one aspect: can we imagine all the hell that would break out if the same answer was given by somebody like Putin or the Chinese president or Iranian president? Would they not be immediately denounced in all our headlines as cold and ruthless barbarian monsters? Campaigning for Hillary Clinton, Albright said: 'There's a special place in hell for women who don't help each other!' (Meaning: women who voted for Sanders instead of Clinton.) Maybe we should amend this statement: there is a special place in hell for women (and men) who think half a million dead children is an affordable price for a military intervention that ruins a country while wholeheartedly supporting women's and gay rights at home ... Are Albright's words not infinitely more obscene and lewd than all Trump's sexist banalities?

Trump is not the dirty water one should throw out to keep safe the healthy baby of US democracy; he is himself the dirty baby who should be thrown out in order to reveal the true dirty water of social relations that sustain the Clinton consensus. The message of this consensus to the Leftists is: you can get everything, we just want to keep the essentials, the unencumbered functioning of global capital. President Obama's 'Yes, we can!' acquires now a new meaning: yes, we can concede all your cultural demands ... without endangering the global market economy – so there is no need for radical economic measures. Or, as Todd McGowan puts it: 'The consensus of "right-thinking people" opposed to Trump is frightening. It is as if his excess licenses the real global capitalist consensus to emerge and to congratulate themselves on their openness.'[29]

This is why Julian Assange was right in his crusade against Clinton, and the liberals who criticized him for attacking the only person who they thought could save us from Trump were wrong: the thing to attack and undermine now is precisely this democratic consensus against the Villain.[30]

CLINTON DUTERTE TRUMP

José Saramago's *Seeing*[31] tells the story of strange events in the unnamed capital city of an unidentified democratic country. When the election-day morning is marred by torrential rain, voter turnout is disturbingly low, but the weather breaks by mid-afternoon and the population heads en masse to their voting stations. The government's relief is short-lived, however, when vote counting reveals that over 70 per cent of the ballots cast in the capital have been left blank. Baffled by this apparent civic lapse, the government gives the citizenry a chance to make amends just one week later with another election day. The results are worse: now 83 per cent of the ballots are blank . . . Is this an organized conspiracy to overthrow not just the ruling government but the entire democratic system? If so, who is behind it, and how did they manage to organize hundreds of thousands of people into such subversion without being noticed? The city continues to function near-normally throughout, the people parrying each of the government's thrusts in inexplicable unison and with a truly Gandhian level of non-violent resistance. The lesson of this thought-experiment is clear. The voters' abstention is a true political act: it forcefully confronts us with the vacuity of today's democracies.

This, exactly, is how the US citizens should have acted when faced with the choice between Clinton and Trump – to refer again to Stalin's answer, they are both worse. Trump is obviously 'worse' since he promises a Rightist turn and enacts a decay of public morality; however, he at least promises a change, while Clinton is 'worse' since she makes changing nothing look desirable. In such a choice, one should not lose nerve; one should choose the 'worse' that means change. Even if it is a dangerous change, it opens up the space for a different, more authentic change. The point is thus not to vote for Trump – not only should one not vote for such scum, one should not even participate in such elections. The point is to approach coldly the question: whose victory is better for the fate of the radical emancipatory project, Clinton's or Trump's?

Trump wants to make America great again, to which Obama responded that America already is great – but is it? Can a country in which a person like Trump is president be really considered great? The dangers of a Trump presidency are obvious: he not only promised to nominate conservative judges to the Supreme Court, he not only mobilized the darkest white-supremacy circles and openly flirts with anti-immigrant racism; he not only flouts basic rules of decency and symbolizes the disintegration of basic ethical standards; while advocating concern for the misery of ordinary people, he effectively promotes a brutal neo-liberal agenda, including tax breaks for the rich, further deregulation, etc. Trump is a vulgar opportunist, and he is also a vulgar specimen of humanity (in contrast to entities like Ted Cruz or Rick Santoro, whom I suspect of being aliens). What Trump is definitely not is a successful, productive and innovative capitalist – he excels in getting into bankruptcy and then making the taxpayers cover up his debts. One of the stories circulating about Trump is that, a couple of years ago, he was approaching the parking lot of an exclusive restaurant with his daughter Ivanka. They saw a homeless person lying in a corner and Ivanka made a dismissive gesture, but Donald interrupted her: 'Show some respect to this guy! He is worth two billion more than me!' The implication being, of course, that he was so much in debt that his net worth was minus $2 billion. (Although we could also argue that Trump is precisely capitalism as such: in his figure, the innermost core of capitalism becomes visible on the surface.) When a man wears a wig, he usually tries to make it look like it's real hair. Trump achieved the opposite: he made his real hair look like a wig; and maybe this reversal provides a succinct formulation of the Trump phenomenon. At the most elementary level, he is not trying to sell us his crazy ideological fictions as reality – what he is really trying to sell us is his own vulgar reality as a beautiful dream.

Liberals panicked by Trump dismiss the idea that Trump's victory can start a process out of which an authentic Left can emerge – their counter-argument is a reference to Hitler. Many German communists welcomed the Nazi takeover as a new chance for the radical Left as the only force that could defeat them, but, as we know, their appreciation was a catastrophic mistake. The question is: are things the same with Trump? Is Trump a danger that should bring together a broad front in the same way that Hitler did, a front where 'decent' conservatives and libertarians fight together with mainstream liberal progressives and (whatever remains of) the radical Left? Fredric Jameson was right to warn against the hasty designation of the Trump movement as a new fascism: 'People are saying "this is a new fascism" and my answer is – not yet!'[32] (Incidentally, the term 'fascism' is today often used as an empty word when something obviously dangerous appears on the political scene but of which we lack a proper understanding – no, today's populists are *not* simply fascists!) Why not yet?

First, the fear that a Trump victory could turn the US into a fascist state is a ridiculous exaggeration. The US has such a rich texture of divergent civic and political institutions that their direct *Gleichshaltung* (Nazification) cannot be enacted. Where, then, does this fear come from? Its function is clearly to unify us all against Trump and thus to obfuscate the true political divisions that run between the Left, resuscitated by Sanders, and Clinton, who is *the* establishment candidate supported by a wide rainbow coalition that includes old Bush cold warriors like Paul Wolfowitz and Saudi Arabia. Second, the fact remains that Trump draws support from the same rage out of which Bernie Sanders mobilized his partisans – he is perceived by the majority of his supporters as the anti-establishment candidate, and what one should never forget is that popular rage is by definition free-floating and can be redirected. Liberals who fear the Trump victory are not really afraid of a radical Rightist turn. What they are really afraid of is simply an actual radical social change. To paraphrase Robespierre once again, they admit (and are sincerely worried about) the injustices of our social life, but they want to cure them through a 'revolution without revolution' (in exact parallel to today's consumerism which offers coffee without caffeine, chocolate without sugar, beer without alcohol, multiculturalism without violent clashes, etc.): a vision of social change with no actual change, a change where no one gets really hurt, where well-meaning liberals remain cocooned in their safe enclaves. If Clinton had won, we can imagine the sounds of relief among the liberal elite: 'Thank God, the nightmare is over, we just avoided the catastrophe . . .' But such a relief would have been the sign of a true catastrophe, since it would really amount to: 'Thank God, the cold warrior figure of the political establishment who represents the interest of big banks got elected, the danger is over!' Or, even more pointedly: 'The danger over, now we can breathe easily and continue walking calmly towards catastrophe. . .'

*

Who really rules in the US? Before the elections, we could have heard the murmur of secret meetings in which members of the financial and other elites negotiated the distribution of key posts in the upcoming Clinton administration. To get an idea how these negotiations in the shadows work, it suffices to read the John Podesta emails, or *Hillary Clinton: The Goldman Sachs Speeches* (to be published in early 2017 by OR Books, New York, with an introduction by Julian Assange). Clinton's victory would have been the victory of a status quo overshadowed by the prospect of a new world war (and Clinton definitely is a typical Democrat cold warrior), a status quo in which we gradually but inevitably slide towards ecological, economic, humanitarian and other catastrophes. That's why I consider extremely cynical the 'Leftist' critique of my position which claims that

> to intervene in a crisis the left must be organized, prepared and with support among the working class and oppressed. We cannot in any way endorse the vile racism and sexism which divides us and weakens our struggle. We must always stand on the side of the oppressed, and we must be independent, fighting for a real left exit to the crisis. Even if Trump causes a catastrophe for the ruling class, it will also be a catastrophe for us if we have not laid the foundations for our own intervention.[33]

True, the Left 'must be organized, prepared and with support among the working class and oppressed' – but in this case, the question should be: which candidate's victory would have contributed more to the organization of the Left and its expansion? Isn't it clear that Trump's victory will 'lay the foundations for our own intervention' much more than Clinton's would have? Yes, there is a great danger in Trump's victory, but the Left will be mobilized *only* through such a threat of catastrophe – if we maintain the inertia of the status quo, there will for sure be *no* Leftist mobilization. I am tempted to quote Hoelderlin here: 'Only where there is danger the saving force is also rising.' In the choice between Clinton and Trump, neither of them 'stands on the side of the oppressed', so the real choice is: abstain from voting or choose the

one who, worthless as s/he is, opens up a greater chance of unleashing a new political dynamic that might lead to massive Leftist
radicalization. In contrast to this true cynicism, *my* cynicism is
simply along the lines of Lenin's 'collaboration' (the 'sealed train')
with the German Empire in the spring of 1917, which brought the
Bolsheviks to power half a year later (although my cynicism is
much less radical than Lenin's).

Many of the poorer voters claim that Trump speaks for them –
how can they recognize themselves in the voice of a billionaire whose
speculations and failures are one of the causes of their misery? Like
the ways of god, the paths of ideology are mysterious . . . (although,
incidentally, some data suggest that the majority of Trump supporters are not of low income). When Trump supporters are denounced
as 'white trash', it is easy to discern in this designation the fear of the
lower classes that characterizes the liberal elite. Here is the title and
strapline of a Guardian report from a recent Trump electoral meeting: 'Inside a Donald Trump Tally: Good People in a Feedback Loop
of Paranoia and Hate. Trump's crowd is full of honest and decent
people – but the Republican's invective has a chilling effect on fans
of his one-man show'.[34] But how did Trump become the voice of so
many 'honest and decent' people? Trump single-handedly ruined the
Republican Party, antagonizing both the old party establishment
and the Christian fundamentalists. What remains as the core of his
support are the bearers of populist rage against the establishment,
and this core is dismissed by liberals as 'white trash' – but are they
not precisely those who should be won over to the radical Leftist
cause (this is what Bernie Sanders achieved)?

Clinton's defeat was the price she had to pay for neutralizing
Bernie Sanders. She did not lose because she moved too much to
the Left but precisely because she was too centrist and in this way
failed to capture the anti-establishment revolt that sustained both
Trump and Sanders. Trump reminded them of the half-forgotten
reality of class struggle, although, of course, he did it in a distorted
populist way, and he masks this distortion through the obvious
self-enjoyment contained in his outbursts – no wonder his rage is
often characterized as 'ragegasm'. Trump's anti-establishment rage
was a kind of return of what was repressed in the moderate liberal

Left's politics focusing on cultural and PC issues. This Left got from Trump its own message in its inverted true form. That's why the only way to reply to Trump would have been to fully appropriate the anti-establishment rage, not to dismiss it as white-trash primitivism.

Remember how many times the liberal media announced that Trump was caught with his pants down and committing public suicide (mocking the parents of a dead war hero, boasting about pussy grabbing, etc.). Arrogant liberal commentators were shocked at how their continuous acerbic attacks on Trump's vulgar racist and sexist outbursts, factual inaccuracies, economic nonsense, etc., did not hurt him at all but maybe even enhanced his popular appeal. They missed how identification works: we as a rule identify with another's weaknesses, not only or even not principally with their strengths, so the more Trump's limitations were mocked the more ordinary people identified with him and perceived attacks on him as condescending attacks on themselves. The subliminal message to ordinary people of Trump's vulgarities was: 'I am one of you!', while ordinary Trump supporters felt constantly humiliated by the liberal elite's patronizing attitude towards them. As Alenka Zupančič put it succinctly, 'the extremely poor do the fighting for the extremely rich, as was clear in the election of Trump. And the Left does little else than scold and insult them.'[35] Or, we should add, the Left does what is even worse: it patronizingly 'understands' the confusion and blindness of the poor . . . This Left-liberal arrogance emerges at its purest in the new genre of political-comment-comedy talk shows (Jon Stewart, John Oliver), which mostly enact the pure arrogance of the liberal intellectual elite:

> Parodying Trump is at best a distraction from his real politics; at worst it converts the whole of politics into a gag. The process has nothing to do with the performers or the writers or their choices. Trump built his candidacy on performing as a comic heel – that has been his pop culture persona for decades. It is simply not possible to parody effectively a man who is a conscious self-parody, and who has become president of the United States on the basis of that performance.[36]

In my past work, I used a joke popular among dissidents from the good old days of 'really-existing socialism'. In fifteenth-century Russia, when it was occupied by Mongols, a farmer and his wife walk along a dusty country road. A Mongol warrior on horseback stops at their side and tells the farmer that he will now rape his wife. He then adds: 'But, since there is a lot of dust on the ground, you should hold my testicles while I'm raping your wife, so that they will not get dirty!' After the Mongol finishes his job and rides away, the farmer starts to laugh and jump with joy. The surprised wife asks him: 'How can you be jumping with joy when I was just brutally raped in your presence?' The farmer answers: 'But I got him! His balls are full of dust!' This sad joke tells of the predicament of dissidents: they think they are dealing serious blows to the party *nomenklatura*, but all they are doing is getting a little bit of dust on the *nomenklatura*'s testicles, while the *nomenklatura* continue raping the people. And can we not say exactly the same about Jon Stewart and co. making fun of Trump – do they not just dust his balls, or perhaps in the best of cases scratch them?

So when we are bombarded by sarcastic remarks about Trump, could we not imagine Trump answering them with Loge's words from Wagner's *Rhinegold*. 'To cover their disgrace, the fools revile me'? (In German, the phrase sounds much better, because of its middle rhyme: '*Ihre Schmach zu decken schmähen mich Dumme.*') But there is another, deeper, problem with parodying Trump. Imagine that, a couple of years ago, a comedian enacted on stage Trump's statements, tweets and decisions – it would have been experienced as an unrealistic, exaggerated joke. So Trump already is his own parody, with the uncanny effect that the reality of his acts is more outrageously funny than most parodies.

In one of the tell-tale ironies of the 2016 US presidential elections, Trump won by getting more electoral college delegate votes than Clinton, while Clinton got more individual votes (the 'popular vote') – in short, the populist candidate won by a legalistic technicality. Before the elections, Trump himself criticized the delegate system as non-democratic and demanded that the winner should be elected by a simple majority of votes – so, to be consistent, he should now step down and concede victory to Clinton. But we should not expect consistency from any of the two big candidates: a feature shared by Clinton and Trump in the election campaign was that they were both saying (almost) everything, appealing to all sides. And the predictable result was that the main reason to vote was in both cases a desperate negative one: 'Trump/Clinton is not as bad as the other!' In both cases, but especially in the case of Trump, it would be wrong to speculate about 'what he really stands for'. It's not only that we, the observers, don't know: probably even Trump himself, the ultimate opportunist, doesn't really know. As for Clinton, the enigma is: how could it have gone so wrong when *all* were included in her rainbow coalition, from Wall Street to Occupy Wall Street, from Saudi Arabian money to LGBTQ+? The catch is that 'all' is never truly 'all' but always based on an exclusion – Clinton's vision excluded division itself, the true division (between the status quo and the Leftist alternative voiced by Sanders), replacing it with the wrong one (between the liberal status quo and the populist threat to it).

The title of Sarah Churchwell's comment in the *Guardian* – 'Hillary Clinton Didn't Fail Us. We Failed Her'[37]– should thus be turned around: we should totally reject the gesture of putting the burden of guilt on us, ordinary voters. This is why the title of Jill Abramson's comment (also in the *Guardian*) on the result of the US elections – 'Hillary Clinton Once Believed Anything Possible. Now Her Tragedy is Ours'[38] – should be given a different spin than intended. Clinton believed that 'anything is possible' in the sense that she could bring together all of us, from Wall Street to OWS, and now we are paying the price for it – not for her tragedy, but for her short-sighted opportunism. Although it is inappropriate to characterize Trump as a fascist, what phenomena like Trump demonstrate is that Walter Benjamin's old thesis – 'every rise of fascism bears witness to a failed revolution' – not only still holds today, but is perhaps more pertinent than ever.

When a protester in Portland declared 'I have a leader I fear for the first time in my life,'[39] he professed his unawareness of what he should really fear: the mainstream liberal consensus that gave birth to Trump, even if it now reacts in a panicky way to his victory. There is a moment of truth in the claim that Clinton lost because of political correctness – not in the simplistic sense that political correctness clashes with the spontaneous stance of many ordinary people but in a more precise sense of what is fundamentally wrong with political correctness. Although proponents of PC are denounced by the conservative media as Marxists, PC is ultimately not Leftist at all but rather the neutralization of social antagonisms through the regulation of how we speak and act. The Leftist reaction to Trump's victory should thus leave behind the self-satisfied moral outrage and engage in tough self-criticism: Trump's victory provides a unique chance for the renewal of the Left. Populism and PC are thus two complementary forms of lying which follow the classic distinction between hysteria and obsessional neurosis: a hysteric tells the truth in the guise of a lie (what is said is literally not true, but the lie expresses in a false form an authentic complaint), while what an obsessional neurotic claims is literally true, but it is a truth that serves a lie. In a homologous way, PC is 'like lying with truth. It says the right things, but it somehow comes across as wrong nevertheless. Populism, on the other hand, is somewhat like telling the truth in the form of a lie. It says all the wrong things, yet we feel that something about it is nevertheless right.'[40] The populist protest displaces onto the external enemy the authentic frustration and sense of loss, while the PC Left uses its true points (detecting sexism and racism in language, etc.) to re-assert its moral superiority and thus prevent true social-economic change.

But are we not playing with fire here? Can good ever come out of evil? Should we not resist such a nihilistic-manipulative stance? My reply is that, precisely, good can come out of evil and (more often, sadly) evil can come out of good. Recent history is full of such dialectical reversals, where actions have created results opposite to what was intended – was the ultimate result of Mao's Cultural Revolution not the explosion of capitalism triggered by Deng Xiaoping's 'reforms'?

But, one might retort, even if a newly awakened Left might arise out of Trump's victory, is the price simply too high? For a vague chance of that awakening, we will have to endure gigantic setbacks in the ecological struggle, further demolition of the welfare state, the rude awakening of open racism, the reduction of Muslims to second-rate human beings, and so on. My reply is that the risk is worth taking because (1) one shouldn't lose nerve too quickly and over-estimate the danger – Trump will definitely not be able to realize the dark scenario feared by panicky liberals, and (2) one should not underestimate the danger of where the continuation of the status quo would lead (a possible new world war, ecological catastrophes, etc.).

Prior to the presidential elections, Noam Chomsky said that the Republican Party is 'literally a serious danger to human survival' (principally because of its denial of global warming and other ecological threats) and supported 'strategic voting' for Clinton (in spite of his well-known critical stance towards her).[41] While I fully agree with his dark outlook, I think it should be broadened to the claim that our entire global capitalist system is the true danger to our survival, and that, because of this, we should coldly explore how to mobilize the people against this threat. The danger of the strategic voting for Clinton was that it would bring a wrong complacency: 'We avoided the worst, Clinton admits the reality of ecological crisis and advocates measures against it, so now we can relax. . .' A much stronger sense of urgency is needed.

In a speech at UCLA on the eve of the presidential elections,[42] Alain Badiou defined Trump as a symptom of global capitalism – to which I would just add that Trump's rise is not merely the symptom of what is wrong in global capitalism as such but above all the symptom of Hillary Clinton, of what was wrong with her project. Jacques Lacan said that woman is a symptom of man – here we have the opposite, a man as the symptom of a woman. We speak of medicines which do not cure the disease itself but only alleviate the symptoms, thereby making it easier for us to endure the disease (they diminish the temperature, lower the pain, etc.). Criticizing Trump without criticizing Clinton is a pure case of such symptomal healing. It is not enough to look just for small tactical mistakes in the Clinton campaign: its fault was more basic. The only way to really get rid of Trump-the-symptom is to cure the Clinton-disease. The liberal panic is false because it remains focused on the *urbi* of Trump, forgetting how the *orbi* of global capitalism is implicated in it, i.e., how Trump emerged out of the Fukuyamaist happy global liberal capitalism. Recall again how Horkheimer retorted to liberal critics of fascism:

those who do not want to talk (critically) about capitalism should also keep silent about fascism. Today, we should say: those who do not want to talk (critically) about the global capitalist world (dis)order should also keep silent about Trump. One is tempted to paraphrase Brecht's old motto, 'What is the robbing of a bank compared to the founding of a new bank?': what is the brutality of Trump's racist and sexist outburst compared to the brutality and violence of today's global capitalism?

Am I arguing here in the vein of Badiou's motto *mieux vaut un désastre qu'un désêtre* (better a disaster – the catastrophic outcome of an event – than a non-eventful survival in a hedonist-utilitarian universe)? The origin of Badiou's motto is Julien Gracq's *The Opposing Shore* (original title *Le rivage des Syrtes*), a novel about Orsenna, a fictional stand in for Italy, a country ruled by the ancient and decadent city of the same name which, for the last 300 years, has been in a state of suspended war with Farghestan, the barbarian desert country across the sea to the south. The leadership of Orsenna decides to provoke an open war with Farghestan in order to break the spell of decadent inertia and bring authentic life back to Orsenna, although they are aware that the war may well result in Orsenna's destruction. The underlying existential dilemma is: what is more desirable, a still, inert life of small satisfactions, not a true life at all, or taking a risk that may well end in a catastrophe? But is Gracq's example not misleading? The hedonist-decadent non-being of the Orsenna society is a false state that obfuscates the underlying social antagonisms – and the pseudo-event of the war with Farghestan continues this obfuscation. So there are three terms and not two: the event (which may end up in disaster), the pseudo-event (fascism or, in this case, war), and the hedonist-utilitarian bio-politics of non-being, of regulating animal-human life. (It is worth noting that, back in the early 1990s, in Gracq-like mode, Badiou wrote that a victory of Milošević in the post-Yugoslav war would be more interesting politically than the victory of the forces opposed to him – a clear preference for the nationalist pseudo-event over the non-evental life ... At a deeper level, the problem is Badiou's dismissal of the mere order of being, of economy, as 'non-evental'.) The difficulty today is how to distinguish the first from the second, since they often share many features. In short, even if we agree with the formula *mieux vaut un désastre qu'un désêtre*, what about *mieux vaut un pseudo-événement qu'un désêtre*? Is a fascist 'event' also better than a non-eventful capitalist survival? So am I saying: better the Trump-as-president disaster, which may even end in total catastrophe, than liberal vegetating? This is definitely *not* my position, for two reasons: first, the Trump presidency is not the full catastrophe painted by the scared Democrats, and, above all, the true catastrophe is the continuing rule of the liberal consensus which, as is becoming more and more obvious, brings us closer and closer to a true catastrophe.

Hopefully, the first steps in the renewal of a more authentic Left are already being taken. With all the uncertainties about what Bernie Sanders' initiative 'Our Revolution' actually amounts to, it is at this moment the only movement that harbours a potential to evolve into a larger political movement, reaching beyond small sectarian Leftist groups. When radical Leftists cast doubts as to whether Sanders is really radical, the answer should be that the situation is genuinely open, things are not yet decided, we have to engage in the struggle of what 'Our Revolution' will become.

So what about the fact that Hillary Clinton would have been the first woman president of the US? In his new book *The True Life*,[43] Alain Badiou warns about the dangers of the growing post-patriarchal nihilist order that presents itself as the domain of new freedoms. We live in an extraordinary era, when there is no tradition on which we can base our identity, no frame of meaningful life that might enable us to live a life beyond hedonist reproduction. This New World Disorder, this gradually emerging world-less civilization, exemplarily affects the young, who oscillate between the intensity of fully burning out (sexual enjoyment, drugs, alcohol, up to violence), and the endeavour to succeed (study, make a career, earn money . . . within the existing capitalist order), the only alternative being a violent retreat into some artificially resuscitated tradition.

Badiou notes here that we are getting a reactive decadent version of the withering-away of the state announced by Marx: today's state is increasingly an administrative regulator of market egotism with no symbolic authority, lacking what Hegel perceived as the essence of a state (the all-encompassing community for which we are ready to sacrifice ourselves). This disintegration of the ethical substance is clearly signalled by the abolition of universal military conscription in many developed countries: the very notion of being ready to risk one's life for a common-cause army appears more and more pointless, if not directly ridiculous, so that an armed force as the body in which all citizens equally participate is gradually turning into a mercenary force.

This disintegration of a shared ethical substance affects the two sexes differently. Men are gradually turning into perpetual adolescents, with no clear passage of initiation enacting their entry into maturity (military service, acquiring a profession, even education no longer play this role). No wonder, then, that, in order to supplant this lack, post-paternal youth gangs proliferate, providing ersatz-initiation and social identity. In contrast to men, women are today more and more precociously mature, treated as small adults, expected to control their lives, to plan their career . . . In this new version of sexual difference, men are ludic adolescents, out-laws, while women appear as hard, mature, serious, legal and punitive. Women are today not called upon by the ruling ideology to subordinate themselves; they are called – solicited, expected – to be judges, administrators, ministers, CEOs, teachers, policewomen and soldiers. A paradigmatic scene occurring daily in our security institutions is that of a female teacher/judge/psychologist taking care of an immature and asocial young male delinquent . . . A new figure of the feminine One is thus arising: a cold competitive agent of power, seductive and manipulative, attesting to the paradox that 'in the conditions of capitalism, women can do better than men' (Badiou).[44] This, of course, in no way makes women suspicious as agents of capitalism; it merely signals that contemporary capitalism has invented its own ideal image of woman.

There is a political triad that renders perfectly the predicament described by Badiou: Clinton – Duterte – Trump. Hillary Clinton and Donald Trump are today's ultimate political couple: Trump is the eternal adolescent, a reckless hedonist prone to irrational brutal outbursts that hurt his chances, while Clinton exemplifies the new feminine One, a self-controlled ruthless manipulator who recklessly exploits her femininity and presents herself as caring for the marginal and for victims. So one should not be seduced by her image as the victim of Bill merrily philandering around and allowing women to suck him off in his office – *he* was the true clown, while *she* is the master in the relationship, allowing her servant small irrelevant pleasures. What, then, about Rodrigo Duterte, the Philippine president openly soliciting extra-judicial murders of drug-addicts and dealers, and comparing himself with Hitler? He stands for the decay of the rule of law, for the transformation of state power into an extra-legal mob rule administering its wild justice; as such, he does what it is not yet permissible to do openly in our 'civilized' Western countries. If we condense the three into one, we get an ideal image of *the* politician today: *Clinton Duterte Trump* – 'Clinton Trump', the main opposition, plus 'Duterte', the embarrassing intruder who signals the violence that sustains both.

WHAT IS TO BE DONE, WITH TRUMP AND WITH US?

A couple of months ago, the front-page story of our big media was LGBTQ+, as if the key problem in our societies is how to overcome toilet segregation or how to enforce a third-person-singular pronoun that would provide an option for those who do not recognize themselves either in 'he' or in 'she' (they, ze . . .). Now, we have the brutal return of the repressed: the electoral victory of a man who consciously breaks all PC rules in a direct and vulgar way. Trump is a perfect case of the 'two-spirit capitalist', whose formula was provided by *Citizen Kane*: when Kane is attacked by Thatcher, a representative of big banking capital, for using his money to finance a newspaper that speaks for the underprivileged, Kane replies:

> The trouble is, Mr Thatcher, you don't realize you're talking to two people. As Charles Foster Kane, who has eighty-two thousand, six hundred and thirty-one shares of Metropolitan Transfer – you see, I do have a rough idea of my holdings – I sympathize with you. Charles Foster Kane is a dangerous scoundrel, his paper should be run

out of town and a committee should be formed to boycott him. You may, if you can form such a committee, put me down for a contribution of one thousand dollars. On the other hand, I am the publisher of the *Enquirer*. As such, it is my duty – I'll let you in on a little secret, it is also my pleasure – to see to it that decent, hard-working people of this city are not robbed blind by a group of money-mad pirates because, God help them, they have no one to look after their interests! I'll let you in on another little secret, Mr Thatcher. I think I'm the man to do it. You see, I have money and property. If I don't defend the interests of the underprivileged, somebody else will – maybe somebody without any money or any property, and that would be too bad.[45]

The last sentence gives the succinct formula of what is wrong with the billionaire Trump posing as the voice of the dispossessed: his strategic function is to prevent the dispossessed from defending themselves . . . Trump is thus far from being simply inconsistent: what appears as inconsistency is the very core of his project. Trump's first presidential acts already indicate inconsistencies: he reiterated his intention to roll back Dodd-Frank financial regulations – clearly a favour to big banks, etc. – and his flurry of executive orders mocks the notion of government for and by the people. However, one should not conclude too quickly that such inconsistencies will hurt him: for some time, they may work. In principle, it is easy to see how we should deal with the inconsistencies that sustain Trump's project. Lately, passages from Richard Rorty's *Achieving Our Country* have mushroomed on the internet[46] – for good reasons, since, almost two decades ago, Rorty clearly foresaw not only the conflict between identity politics and the struggle of the dispossessed but also how this conflict may give rise to a populist anti-identity-politics leader. When the poor white electorate realizes how, in spite of all the talk about social justice, the predominant Left-liberal establishment basically ignores their plight,

something will crack. The nonsuburban electorate will decide that the system has failed and start looking around for a strongman to vote for – someone willing to assure them that, once he is elected, the smug bureaucrats, tricky lawyers, overpaid bond salesmen, and post-modernist professors will no longer be calling the shots [. . .] One thing that is very likely to happen is that the gains made in the past 40 years by black and brown Americans, and by homosexuals, will be wiped out. Jocular contempt for women will come back into fashion [. . .] All the resentment which badly educated Americans feel about having their manners dictated to them by college graduates will find an outlet.[47]

Rorty was not alone in this insight – many saw it coming but, as is usually the case in politics, being aware of the dangerous turn things may take not only doesn't prevent it from happening but, in a case of political life imitating the Oedipus plot, even helps it to happen. No wonder that liberal attacks on Sanders for his alleged rejection of identity politics are appearing, unfairly accusing him of ditching such politics, while Sanders is doing the exact opposite, insisting on a link between class, race and gender. One has to support him unconditionally when he rejects identity in itself as a reason to vote for someone:

It is not good enough for somebody to say, I'm a woman, vote for me. What we need is a woman who has the guts to stand up to Wall Street, to the insurance companies, to the drug companies, to the fossil fuel industry [. . .] It's a step forward in America if you have an African-American CEO of some major corporation. But if that guy is going to be shipping jobs out of this country, and exploiting his workers, it doesn't mean a whole hell of a lot whether he's black or white or Latino.[48]

Sanders is thereby touching a sore point of racism (also) within the LGBT community:

'How can I be a bigot when I am myself a member of an oppressed minority?' is a prevailing attitude among some white LGBT people. But another far more pernicious reason is that the LGBT world revolves around white gay men to the exclusion of others. The rainbow flag is whiter than it appears.[49]

No wonder that far-right movements 'are consciously trying to co-opt the LGBT rights campaign for their own agenda. There are those who only talk about LGBT rights if it is to bash Muslims or migrants as a whole. American white nationalists websites now sell LGBT pride flags along with the Confederate flag.'[50] Empty calls for all-round solidarity and coalitions are not enough here; we need to confront the limitations of identity politics, depriving it of its privileged status. It is absolutely crucial to take note of a feature shared by politically correct respect for particular identities and the anti-immigrant hatred of others: the fear that a particular identity will be swallowed by the nameless universality of a global New World Order. When conservative nationalists point out that they just want for their own nation (for Germans, French, British . . .) the same right to identity that sexual and ethnic minorities want for themselves, this utterly hypocritical demand nonetheless makes a valid point, namely the need to move beyond *all* forms of identity politics, Rightist and Leftist. What one should reject is, at a more basic level, the perspective of multiple local struggles for emancipation (ethnic, sexual, religious, legal . . .) which should then gradually be united by way of building an always-fragile 'chain of equivalences' among them (to use Laclau's expression). Universality is not something that should emerge through a long and patient process: it is something that is 'always-already' here as the starting point of every authentic emancipatory process, as its very motivation.

There are two reactions to the Trump victory that should be rejected as unacceptable and ultimately self-destructive. The first is the arrogant fascination with the stupidity of ordinary voters who didn't get that they were voting against their own interests and fell for Trump's superficial demagoguery; the second is the call for an immediate counter-offensive ('No time to philosophize, we have to act'), which strangely echoes Trump's own anti-intellectual stance. Judith Butler has noted that, as is the case with every populist ideology, Trump is giving to the people 'an occasion not to think, an occasion not to have to think. To think is to think of a very complex global world, and he's making everything very, very simple.'[51] (Of course, as Butler is fully aware, while Clinton presented herself as someone well-versed in the complexities of real politics, her reference to 'complexity' was no less false, since it was used also to diffuse Leftist demands.)

The urgency of the present situation should in no way serve as an excuse – an urgent situation *is* the time to think. We should not be afraid here to turn around Marx's famous Thesis XI: 'till now we have tried to change our world too quickly; the time has come to re-interpret it self-critically, examining our own (Leftist) responsibility'. There is a classic Soviet joke about Lenin that refers to the fact that, in socialist countries, Lenin's advice to young people, his answer to what they should do – 'Learn, learn and learn!' – was displayed on the walls of thousands of classrooms. The joke goes: Marx, Engels and Lenin are asked whether they would prefer to have a wife or a mistress. As expected, Marx, rather conservative in private matters, answers, 'A wife!', while Engels, more of a *bon vivant*, opts for a mistress. But, to everyone's surprise, Lenin says: 'I'd like to have both!' Why? Is there a hidden stripe of decadent *jouisseur* behind his austere revolutionary image? No, he explains: 'So that I can tell my wife that I am going to my mistress, and my mistress that I have to be with my wife.' 'And then, what do you do?' 'I go to a solitary place to learn, learn and learn!' Is this not exactly what Lenin did after the catastrophe of 1914? He withdrew to a lonely place in Switzerland, where he 'learned, learned and learned', reading Hegel's logic. And this is what we should do today when we are under the spell of Trump's victory (which is, we should not forget, just one in a series of similar bad surprises): we need to reject both defeatism and blind activism and 'learn, learn and learn' what caused this fiasco of liberal-democratic politics.

The point is not to withdraw from activity into inner reflection – in tense situations like today's, not to act is in itself a mode of (re)acting, i.e., it amounts to accepting what goes on. But we should not forget that the opposite also holds: acting can also be a mode of non-acting, of not effectively intervening in a situation. This brings us to the notion of *false activity*: people not only act in order to change something, they can also act in order to prevent something from happening, i.e., so that *nothing will change*. Therein resides the typical strategy of the obsessional neurotic: he is frantically active in order to prevent the real thing from happening. For example, in a group situation in which some tension threatens to erupt, the obsessional talks all the time, tells jokes, etc., in order to prevent the awkward moment of silence that would compel the participants to openly confront the underlying tension. This is why, in psychoanalytic treatment, obsessional neurotics talk all the time, flooding the analyst with anecdotes, dreams, insights: their incessant activity is sustained by the underlying fear that, if they stop talking for a moment, the analyst will ask them the question that truly matters. In other words, they talk in order to keep the analyst immobile.

Even in much of today's progressive politics, the danger is not passivity but pseudo-activity, the urge to 'be active', to 'participate': people intervene all the time, 'do something', academics participate in meaningless debates, etc., and the truly difficult thing is to step back, to withdraw from it. Those in power often prefer even a 'critical' participation to silence – just to engage us in a dialogue, to make sure that our ominous passivity is broken. Against such an 'interpassive' mode of our participation in socio-ideological life in which we are active all the time in order to make sure that nothing happens, that nothing really changes, the first truly critical step is to *withdraw into passivity*, to refuse to participate – this is the necessary first step that as it were clears the ground for true activity, for an act that will effectively change the coordinates of the constellation. And does something similar not hold for the reaction of the Left to Trump's victory? All the protests against Trump court the danger of being a way to avoid a self-critical look into how Trump could have happened, and we need to step back and think in order to be able to effectively intervene in our predicament.

The most depressing aspect of the post-electoral period in the US is not the measures announced by the President-elect but the way the bulk of the Democratic Party is reacting to its historic defeat: the oscillation between the two extremes, the horror at the Big Bad Wolf called Trump and the obverse of this panic and fascination, the renormalization of the situation, the idea that nothing extraordinary happened, that it is just another reversal in the normal exchange of Republican and Democratic presidents: Reagan, Bush, Trump . . . Along these lines, Nancy Pelosi 'repeatedly brings up the events of a decade ago. For her, the lesson is clear – past is prologue. What worked before will work again. Trump and the Republicans will overreach, and Democrats have to be ready to jump at the opportunity when they do.'[52] Such a stance totally ignores the real meaning of Trump's victory, the weaknesses of the Democratic Party that rendered possible this victory, and the radical restructuring of the entire political space this victory announces.

This restructuring is made clear by yet another version of Trump's inconsistency, which concerns his stance towards Russia: while hardline Republicans were continually attacking Obama for his all too soft stance towards Putin, tolerating Russian military aggressions (Georgia, Crimea . . .) and thereby endangering Western allies in Eastern Europe, the Trump supporters now advocate a much more lenient approach to Russia. The underlying problem is here: how are we to unite the two ideological oppositions, the opposition of traditionalism versus secular relativism and the other big ideological opposition on which the entire legitimacy of the West and its 'war on terror' relies, the opposition between liberal-democratic individual rights and religious fundamentalism embodied primarily in 'Islamofascism'? Therein resides the symptomatic inconsistency of the US neo-conservatives: while, in their inner politics, they privilege the fight against liberal secularism (abortion, gay marriages, etc.), i.e. their struggle is one of so-called 'culture of life' against 'culture of death', in foreign politics, they privilege the very opposite values of the liberal 'culture of death'.

At some deep and often obfuscated level, the US neo-cons perceive the European Union as *the* enemy. This perception, kept under control in the public political discourse, explodes in its underground obscene double, the extreme Right Christian fundamentalist political vision with its obsessive fear of the New World Order (Obama is in secret collusion with the United Nations, international forces will intervene in the US and erect concentration camps for all true American patriots). One way to resolve this dilemma is the hardline Christian fundamentalist one, articulated in the works of Tim LaHaye and his followers: to unambiguously subordinate the second opposition to the first one. The title of one of LaHaye's novels points in this direction: *The Europa Conspiracy*. The true enemies of the US are not Muslim terrorists – they are merely puppets secretly manipulated by the European secularists, who are the true forces of the anti-Christ, wanting to weaken the US and establish the New World Order under the domination of the United Nations. In a way, they are right in this perception: Europe is not just another geo-political power block, but a global vision that is ultimately incompatible with nation-states. This dimension of the EU provides the key to the so-called European 'weakness': there is a surprising correlation between European unification and its loss of global military-political power. If, however, the European Union is a less and less important and more and more disunited confederacy of states, why is then the US – among other things – so ill at ease with it and so keen to undermine it? Recall the indications of financial support for those forces in Ireland that organized the campaign for 'no' to the new European treaty. Opposed to this minority view is the predominant liberal-democratic view which sees the principal enemy in all kinds of fundamentalisms, and perceives the US Christian fundamentalism as a deplorable homegrown version of 'Islamo-fascism'. However, this predominance is now threatened: what was till now a marginal opinion limited to conspiracy theories that thrived in the underground of the public space is becoming the hegemonic stance of our public space.

This brings us back to Trump and Putin: they both supported Brexit, they both belong to the extreme conservative-nationalist line of 'America/Russia first', which perceives united Europe as its biggest enemy – and they are both right. The problem of Europe is to remain faithful to this legacy, threatened by the conservative-populist onslaught – how? In his *Notes Towards a Definition of Culture*, the great conservative T. S. Eliot remarked that there are moments when the only choice is the one between heresy and non-belief, when the only way to keep a religion alive is to perform a sectarian split from its main body. This is what has to be done today: the 2016 elections were the final blow to the Fukuyama dream, the final defeat of liberal democracy, and the only way to really defeat Trump and to redeem what is worth saving in liberal democracy is to perform a sectarian split from liberal democracy's main body – in short, to shift the weight from Clinton to Sanders. The next election should be between Trump and Sanders.

Elements of the programme for this new Left are relatively easy to imagine. Trump promises the cancellation of the big free trade agreements supported by Clinton, and the Left alternative to both should be a project of new different international agreements, agreements that would establish control of the banks, agreements about ecological standards, about workers' rights, healthcare, protection of sexual and ethnic minorities, etc. The big lesson of global capitalism is that nation-states alone cannot do the job – only a new political international could posibly reign in global capital. An old anti-communist Leftist once told me the only good thing about Stalin was that he really scared the big Western powers, and one could say the same about Trump: the good thing about him is that he really scares liberals. Western powers learned a lesson and self-critically focused on their own shortcomings, which led them to develop the welfare state – will our Left liberals be able to do something similar?

And the story of Trump and Clinton goes on: in the second instalment, the couple's names are changed to Marine le Pen and François Fillon. Now that Fillon has been chosen as the Right's candidate in the forthcoming French presidential elections, and with the (almost full) certainty that, in the second round of the elections, the choice will be between Fillon and Marine le Pen, our democracy has reached its (till now) lowest point. In her *Guardian* column headlined 'François Fillon is as Big a Threat to Liberal Values as Marine le Pen', Natalie Nougayrède wrote:

> It is no coincidence that Fillon was publicly lauded by Putin. This wasn't just because the Kremlin hopes to find a French presidential ally on foreign policy. It's also because Putin detects in Fillon streaks of his own ultra-conservative ideology. Witness how Russian propaganda has dubbed Europe 'Gayropa'.[53]

If the difference between Clinton and Trump was the difference between the liberal establishment and Rightist populist rage, this difference shrinks to a minimum in the case of le Pen versus Fillon. While both are cultural conservatives, in matters of economy Fillon is pure neo-liberal, while le Pen is much more oriented towards protecting workers' interests. In short, since Fillon stands for the worst combination around today – economic neo-liberalism and social conservativism – one is seriously tempted to prefer le Pen. The only argument for Fillon is a purely formal one: he *formally* stands for a united Europe and a minimal distance from the populis. But with regard to content he seems to be worse than le Pen. He stands for the immanent decadence of the establishment itself – here is where we end up after a long process of defeats and withdrawals. First, the radical Left had to be sacrificed as out of touch with our new postmodern times and its new 'paradigms'. Then the moderate social-democratic Left was sacrificed as also out of touch with the necessities of the new global capitalism. Now, in the last epoch of this sad tale, the moderate liberal Right itself (Juppé) is sacrificed as out of touch with conservative values, which have to be enlisted if we, the civilized world, want to beat le Pen. Any resemblance with the old anti-Nazi story of how we first passively observed when the Nazis in power took away the communists, then the Jews, then the moderate Left, then the liberal centre, then even honest conservatives . . . is purely accidental. The Saramago reaction – to abstain from voting – is here obviously the *only* appropriate thing to do. Even if the scandal with his wife disqualifies Fillon, the very fact that, for some time, he appeared as the main opponent of le Pen is telltale enough.

One should get rid of the false panic, fearing the Trump victory as the ultimate horror which made us support Clinton in spite of all her obvious shortcomings. Trump's victory created a totally new political situation, with chances for a more radical Left. Today's liberal Left and populist Right are both caught in the politics of fear: fear of the immigrants, of feminists, etc., or the fear of fundamentalist populists. The first thing to do here is to accomplish the move from fear to *Angst*: fear is the fear of an external object that is perceived as posing a threat to our identity, while anxiety emerges when we become aware that there is something wrong with our identity itself, with what we want to protect from the feared external threat. Fear pushes us to annihilate the external object, while the way to confront anxiety is to transform ourselves.

One is tempted to turn around Benjamin's famous statement about monsters which thrive when the old is dying and the new is not yet born: when an order rules, horrors and monstrosities are normalized, but in the process of passage, when the old order is dying and the new order is not yet here, horrors become visible as such, they are de-normalized, and, in such moments of hope, great acts become possible. So if you love America (as I do), now is the time for the hard work of love, for becoming engaged in the long process of the formation of a radical political Left in the US – or, to quote Mao again: 'Everything under heaven is in utter chaos; the situation is excellent.'

Finale: The Loneliness of the Global Policeman in a Multi-centric World

Towards the end of September 2014, after declaring war on ISIS, President Obama gave an interview to *60 Minutes* in which he tried to explain the rules of US engagement: 'When trouble comes up anywhere in the world, they don't call Beijing, they don't call Moscow. They call us. That's always the case. America leads. We are the indispensable nation.' This holds also for environmental and humanitarian disasters: 'When there's a typhoon in the Philippines, take a look at who's helping the Philippines deal with that situation. When there's an earthquake in Haiti, take a look at who's leading the charge helping Haiti rebuild. That's how we roll. That's what makes us Americans.'

In mid-October 2014, however, Obama himself made a call to Tehran, sending a secret letter to Ayatollah Ali Khamenei in which he suggested a broader rapprochement between the US and Iran based on the shared interest in combatting Islamic State militants. Not only did Iran reject the offer, but when the news of the letter reached the broad public, the US Republicans denounced it as a ridiculous gesture of self-humiliation that could only strengthen Iran's arrogant view of the US as a superpower in decline. That's how the US rolls effectively: acting alone in a multi-centric world, they more and more gain wars and lose the peace, doing the dirty job for others: for China and Russia, who have their own problems with Islamists, and even for Iran – the final result of the invasion of Iraq was to deliver Iraq to the political control of Iran.

The ultimate source of these problems is the changed role of the US in the global economy. An economic cycle is coming to an end, the 'American century' is over and we are witnessing the gradual formation of multiple centres of global capitalism – the US, Europe, China, maybe Latin America – each of them standing for capitalism with a specific twist: the US for neo-liberal capitalism; Europe for what remains of the welfare state; China for the 'Asian values' (authoritarian) capitalism; Latin America for populist capitalism ... In this world, the old and new superpowers are testing each other, trying to impose their own version of global rules, experimenting with them through proxies, which, of course, are other small nations and states.

The present situation thus bears an uncanny resemblance to the situation around 1900, when the hegemony of the British empire was questioned by new rising powers, especially Germany, which wanted their piece of the colonial cake, and the Balkans was one of the places of confrontation. Today, the role of the British empire is played by the US, the new rising superpowers are Russia and China, and our Balkans is the Middle East. It is the same old battle for geo-political influence: not only the US, but also Moscow hears calls from Georgia, from Ukraine; maybe it will start hearing voices from the Baltic states ... (Furthermore, one should note that, at the beginning of the twentiethth century, Russia was perceived by many in England and Germany as the next world superpower, which would surpass others in twenty to twenty-five years; but although the Russian economy was exploding, so were social antagonisms. The same holds for today's China, where social tensions are the dark obverse of fast economic development.)

There is another unexpected parallel with the situation before the outbreak of the First World War: recently the media have continuously warned us about the threat of a Third World War. Headlines like 'The Russian Air Force's Super Weapon: Beware the PAK-FA Stealth Fighter' or 'Russia is Ready for Shooting War, Will Likely Win Looming Nuclear Showdown with US' abound; at least once a week Putin makes a statement seen as a provocation to the West, and a notable Western statesman or NATO figure warns against Russian imperialist ambitions; Russia expresses concerns about being contained by NATO, while Russia's neighbours fear Russian invasion; and so on. The very worried tone of these warnings seems to heighten the tension – exactly as in the decades before 1914. And, in both cases, the same superstitious mechanism is at work: as if talking about it will prevent it happening. We know about the danger, but we don't believe it can really happen – and that's why it can happen. That is to say, even if we don't really believe it can happen, we are all getting ready for it – and these actual preparations, largely ignored by the big media, are mostly reported in marginal media:

> America is on a war footing. While a World War Three scenario has been on the drawing board of the Pentagon for more than ten years, military action against Russia is now contemplated at an 'operational level.' We are not dealing with a 'Cold War'. None of the safeguards of the Cold War era prevail. The adoption of a major piece of legislation by the US House of Representatives on December 4 2014 (H.Res.758) would provide (pending a vote in the Senate) a *de facto* green light to the US president and commander in chief to initiate – without congressional approval – a process of military confrontation with Russia. Global security is at stake. This historic vote – which potentially could affect the lives of hundreds of millions of people worldwide – has received virtually no media coverage. A total media blackout prevails [. . .] On December 3, the Ministry of Defence of the Russian Federation announced the inauguration of a new military-political entity which would take over in the case of war. Russia is launching a new national defense facility, which is meant to monitor threats to national security in peacetime, but would take control of the entire country in case of war. (RT, December 3, 2014)[1]

What further complicates matters is that the competing new and old superpowers are joined by a third factor, the radicalized fundamentalist movements in the Third World that oppose all of them but are prone to making strategic pacts with some of them. No wonder our predicament is getting more and more obscure: who is who in the ongoing conflicts? How to choose between Assad and ISIS in Syria? Between ISIS and Iran? Such obscurity – not to mention the rise of drones and other arms that promise a clean high-tech war without casualties (on our side) – gives a boost to military spending and makes the prospect of war more appealing.

In August 2016, when the monstrous battle for the city of Aleppo began, with two million human lives threatened, the so-called civilized world should have put all its efforts into stopping the carnage. Now we see a future gigantic flow of refugees in gestation. Now we are just watching how the struggle is escalating into a potential direct conflict between Russia and the US. In view of the high stakes, the lack of serious international anti-war mobilization is just stunning.

What to do with the flow of immigrants? What if the only consequent answer is that there is no clear solution and that some kind of war is the only visible outcome? While we appear to be in the midst of the clash of civilizations (the Christian West versus radicalized Islam), in fact there are clashes within each civilization: in the Christian space, it is the US and Western Europe against Russia; in the Muslim space it is Sunnis against Shias. The monstrosity of ISIS serves as a fetish covering all these struggles, in which every side pretends to fight ISIS in order to hit its true enemy.

There is, of course, a complex multiplicity of causes that triggered the Syrian war and the ensuing flow of refugees, even including environmental changes: 'the disastrous 2007–2010 drought in Syria, the most severe in the instrumental record and a principal catalyst to social unrest, was likely part of a "long-term drying trend" associated with rising greenhouse emissions.'[2] However, it seems clear that there are two factors the status of which is exceptional: while the *dominant* factor is political (where Arab tensions play the main role), the *determination in the last instance* is exerted by the global capitalist economy.

If the basic underlying axiom of the Cold War was MAD (Mutually Assured Destruction), the axiom of today's War on Terror seems to be the opposite one, that of NUTS (Nuclear Utilization Target Selection), i.e., the idea that, by means of a surgical strike, one can destroy the enemy's nuclear capacities while the anti-missile shield is protecting us from a counter-strike. More precisely, the US adopts a differential strategy: it acts as if it continues to trust the MAD logic in its relations with Russia and China, while it is tempted to practise NUTS with Iran and North Korea. The paradoxical mechanism of MAD inverts the logic of the 'self-realizing prophecy' into a 'self-stultifying intention': the very fact that each side can be sure that, should it decide to launch a nuclear attack, the other side will respond with full destructive force, guarantees that no side will start a war. The logic of NUTS is, on the contrary, that the enemy can be forced to disarm if it is assured that we can strike at them without risking a counter-attack. The very fact that two directly contradictory strategies are mobilized simultaneously by the same superpower bears witness to the fantasmatic character of this entire reasoning. In December 2016, this inconsistency reached an almost unimaginably ridiculous peak: both Trump and Putin emphasized the chance for new, more friendly relations between Russia and the US, and simultaneously asserted their full commitment to the arms race – as if peace among the superpowers can only be provided by a new Cold War . . .

The same combination of incompatible strategies is at work in the way we relate to the threat of ecological catastrophes. In December 2016, smog in big Chinese cities became so thick that thousands fled to the countryside, trying to reach places where one could still see blue sky – this 'airpocalypse' affected half a billion people. For those who remained, moving around began to resemble life in a post-apocalyptic movie: people walking around with large gas masks in a smog where even nearby trees were invisible.[3] The class dimension played a crucial role: before the authorities had to close airports because of the bad air, cities were abandoned by those who could afford an expensive flight . . . And, to add insult to injury, Beijing's lawmakers considered listing smog as a meteorological disaster, an act of nature, not an effect of industrial pollution, to prevent blaming the authorities for the catastrophe.[4] A new category was thus added to the long list of refugees from wars, droughts, tsunamis, earthquakes, economic crises, etc. – smog refugees.

Perhaps the most surprising thing about this airpocalypse is its quick renormalization: after the authorities could no longer deny the problem, they tried to establish a new procedure that would somehow enable people to continue their daily life by following new routines, as if the catastrophic smog was just a new fact of life. On designated days, you try to stay at home as much as possible and, if necessary, walk around with masks. Children rejoice in the news that, on many days, schools are closed – an opportunity to stay at home and play. Making a trip to the countryside where the blue sky is still visible becomes a special occasion one looks forward to (there are already agencies in Beijing specializing in such one-day trips). The important thing is not to panic but to maintain the appearance that, in spite of everything, life goes on.

One thing is sure: an extraordinary social and psychological change is taking place right in front of our eyes – the impossible is becoming possible. An event first experienced as impossible but not real (the prospect of a forthcoming catastrophe which, however probable we know it is, we do not believe will effectively occur and thus dismiss as impossible) becomes real but no longer impossible (once the catastrophe occurs, it is renormalized, perceived as part of the normal run of things, as 'always-already' having been possible). The gap that makes these paradoxes possible is the one between knowledge and belief: we *know* the (ecological) catastrophe is possible, probable even, yet we do not *believe* it will really happen.

Recall the siege of Sarajevo in the early 1990s: the fact that a 'normal' European city of half a million inhabitants could be encircled, starved, regularly bombed, its citizens terrorized by sniper fire, and that this could go on for three years, would have been considered unimaginable before 1992. It would have been extremely easy for the Western powers to break the siege and open a small safe corridor to the city. When the siege began, even the citizens of Sarajevo thought, this is a short-term event, trying to send their children to safety 'for a week or two, till this mess is over'. And then, very quickly, the siege was 'normalized'. As we have already seen, this same passage from impossibility to normalization (with a brief intermediary stage of panicky numbness) is clearly discernible in how the US liberal establishment reacted to Trump's victory. It is also clearly at work in how state powers and big capital relate to ecological threats like the ice meltdown at the poles. The very same politicians and managers who, until recently, dismissed the fears of global warming as the apocalyptic scare-mongering of ex-communists, or at least as premature conclusions based on insufficient evidence, assuring us that there is no reason for panic, that, basically, things will go on as usual, are now all of a sudden treating global warming as a simple fact, as part of the way things are 'going on as usual' . . .

In July 2008, CNN repeatedly showed a report, 'The Greening of Greenland', celebrating the new opportunities that the melting of ice offers to Greenlanders – they could grow vegetables in the open land, etc. The obscenity of this report is not only that it focuses on the minor benefit of a global catastrophe; to add insult to injury, it plays on the double meaning of 'green' in our public speech ('green' for vegetation; 'green' for ecological concerns), so that the fact that more vegetation can grow on the Greenland soil because of global warming is associated with the rising of ecological awareness. Are such phenomena not yet another example of how right Naomi Klein was when, in her *Shock Doctrine*, she described the way global capitalism exploits catastrophes (wars, political crises, natural disasters) to get rid of the 'old' social constraints and impose its agenda on the slate cleared by the catastrophe? Perhaps, the forthcoming ecological disasters, far from undermining capitalism, will serve as its greatest boost . . .

A similarly perverted strategy of profiting from the very threat to one's survival (and from the worst outcome of one's own reign) is at work in a new type of state socialism that is emerging in North Korea (and up to a point also in Cuba and Venezuela): it combines ruthless Party rule with the wildest capitalism. While state power is firmly entrenched in the ruling Party, the state is no longer able to provide life's daily necessities, especially food, to the general population, so it has to tolerate wild local capitalism. In North Korea, there are hundreds of 'free' markets where individuals sell home-grown food, commodities smuggled from China, etc. The North Korean state is thus relieved of the burden of taking care of ordinary people and can concentrate on new arms and the life of the elite – in an unheard-of cruel irony, the North Korean basic ideological notion of *juche* (self-reliance) arrives at its truth: not the nation but individuals themselves have to rely on their own forces. But is something similar not going on in China itself, where the Party functions as the most efficient manager of capitalism? Maybe, airpocalypses are the price we have to pay for such socio-political perversions.

We have to finish with such games. The airpocalypse in China is a clear indication of the limits of our predominant environmentalism, this strange combination of catastrophism and routine, of guilt-feeling and indifference. Let's take the case of genetically modified crops: instead of getting involved in the endless debates about its pluses and minuses, one should take a step back and focus on the socio-economic changes imposed by a large corporation like Monsanto. When farmers begin to buy their seeds, the self-sufficient cycle of agricultural reproduction is broken, farmers are obliged to get their seeds again and again from Monsanto, so that the simple cycle of growing wheat etc. is irreducibly 'mediated' by a large corporation with a quasi-monopolistic position. Is this not yet another example of the privatization of commons?

How to stop our slide into this vortex? In both cases, the threat of ecological catastrophe as well as the threat of global war, the first step is to leave behind all the pseudo-rational talk about 'strategic risks' that we have to assume, as well as the notion of historical time as the linear process of evolution where, at each moment, we have to choose between different courses of action. We have to accept the threat as our fate: it is not just a question of avoiding risks and making the right choices within the global situation, the true threat resides in the situation in its entirety, in our 'fate' – if we continue to 'roll on' the way we do now, we are doomed, no matter how carefully we proceed. So the solution is not to be very careful and avoid risky acts – in acting like this, we fully participate in the logic that leads to catastrophe. The solution is to become fully aware of the explosive set of interconnections that makes the entire situation dangerous. Once we do this, once we embrace the courage that comes with hopelessness, we should embark on the long and difficult work of changing the coordinates of the entire situation. Nothing less will do.

In a weird coincidence with President Obama's 'that's how we roll', when the passengers of the United flight 93 attacked the hijackers on 9/11, the last audible words of Todd Beamer, one of the passengers, were: 'Are you guys ready? Let's roll.' That's how we all roll, so let's roll, we may say – and bring down not only a plane but our entire planet. With the election of Donald Trump, this rolling down entered a new mode. A couple of days before Trump's inauguration, Marine le Pen was seen sitting at the Trump Tower café on Fifth Avenue, as if waiting to be called up by the president-to-be. Although no meeting took place, what happened just days after the inauguration seems an after-effect of that failed meeting: on 21 January, in Koblenz, representatives of the European right-wing populist parties met under the slogan of 'Freedom for Europe'. The meeting was dominate by le Pen, who called on voters across Europe to 'wake up' and follow the example of US and British voters. She predicted that Brexit and Trump's victory would unleash an unstoppable wave of 'all the dominoes of Europe'. Trump made it clear that he 'does not support a system of the oppression of peoples': '2016 was the year the Anglo-Saxon world woke up. I am certain 2017 will be the year when the people of continental Europe wake up.'[5]

What does awakening mean here? In his *Interpretation of Dreams*, Freud reports on a rather terrifying dream: a tired father who has spent the night watching at the coffin of his young son, falls asleep and dreams that his son is approaching him all in flames, addressing to him the horrifying reproach: 'Father, can't you see I am burning?' Soon afterwards, the father awakens and discovers that, owing to a fallen candle, the cloth of his dead son's shroud had caught fire – the smoke that he smelled while asleep was incorporated into the dream of the burning son to prolong his sleep. So was it that the father awoke when the external stimulus (smoke) became too strong to be contained within the dream-scenario? Was it not rather the obverse: the father first constructed the dream in order to prolong his sleep, i.e. to avoid the unpleasant awakening; however, what he encountered in the dream – literally the burning question, the creepy spectre of his son making the reproach – was much more unbearable than the external reality, so the father woke, escaping into external reality – why? *To continue to dream*, to avoid the unbearable trauma of his own guilt for the son's painful death. And is it not the same with the populist awakening? In the 1930s, Adorno remarked that the Nazi call, *Deutschland, erwache!* ('Germany, awaken!') effectively meant its exact opposite: follow our Nazi dream (of the Jews as the external enemy ruining the harmony of our societies) so that you can continue to sleep! To sleep and to avoid the rude awakening, the awakening to the social antagonisms that cut across our social reality! Today, the populist Right is doing the same: it calls upon us to 'awaken' to the immigrant threat in order to enable us to continue to dream, i.e. to ignore the antagonisms that traverse our global capitalism.

Trump's inaugural address was, of course, ideology at its purest, its simple, straight message relying on a whole series of rather obvious inconsistencies. As they say, the devil dwells in the details. If we take Trump's address at its most elementary, it may sound like something that Bernie Sanders could have said: I speak for all those forgotten, neglected and exploited hard-working people, I am your voice, you are now in power . . . However, notwithstanding the obvious contrast between these proclamations and Trump's first nominations (how can Trump's secretary of state Rex Tillerson, the chief executive of Exxon Mobil, be the direct voice of exploited hard-working people?), there is a series of clues which give a specific spin to his message. Trump talks about 'Washington elites', not about capitalists and big bankers. He talks about the disengagement from the role of the global policeman, but he promises the destruction of Muslim terrorism, the prevention of the North Korean ballistic tests and the containment of the Chinese occupation of South China sea islands . . . So what we are getting is global military interventionism exerted directly on behalf of American interests, with no human-rights-and-democracy mask. Back in the 1960s, the motto of the early ecological movement was 'Think globally, act locally!' Trump promises to do the exact opposite: 'Think locally, act globally.'

There is something hypocritical about the liberals who criticize the slogan 'America first' – as if this is not what more or less *every* country is doing, as if America did not play a global role precisely because it fitted its own interests. The underlying message of 'America first!' is nonetheless a sad one: the American century is over, America has resigned itself to being just one among the (powerful) countries. The supreme irony is that the Leftists who for a long time criticized the US pretension to be the global policeman may begin to long for the old times when, with all hypocrisy included, the US imposed democratic standards onto the world.

What makes Trump's inaugural address interesting (and efficient) is that its inconsistencies mirror the inconsistencies of the liberal Left. Now, at the beginning of Trump's reign, the situation remains ambiguous. A broad anti-Trump front is gradually building in the US and around the world, and one should especially emphasize here the rise of women as perhaps even the main power of political protest (not only in the US but also in Poland).[6] The big question is: will this protest be contained by the liberal Left or will it reach further? Remember the wonderful title of that Werner Herzog movie: *Auch Zwerge haben klein angefangen*, 'Dwarfs also Started Small'; I am always reminded of this title when I hear about wonderful marginal political protest acts, like veiled Palestinian women and Israeli lesbians protesting together. But will such events that begin small in all probability not also remain small and marginal?

Indicative of this tension is a recent incident with the Democrat Nancy Pelosi. At a town-hall meeting in January 2017 covered by CNN, NYU student Trevor Hill asked her: 'My experience is that the younger generation is moving left on economic issues and I've been so excited to see how Democrats have moved left on social issues. As a gay man, I've been very proud to see you fighting for our rights and for – many Democratic leaders fighting for our rights. But I wonder if there's anywhere you feel that the Democrats could move farther left to a more populist message, the way the alt-right has sort of captured this populist strain on the right wing, if you think we could make a more stark contrast to right-wing economics?' He got a prompt answer: 'Well, I thank you for your question. But I have to say, we're capitalist. That's just the way it is.'[7] It is here that the break (with the automatic 'that's the way it is' acceptance of capitalism) should happen if we are truly to defeat Trump. In a great piece for *In These Times* with the title 'The End of History?: The Short, Strange Era of Human Civilization Would Appear to be Drawing to a Close', Noam Chomsky reports on a set of phenomena which augur 'the likely end of the era of civilization'.[8] One should note that Chomsky, who criticized me ferociously for my idea that a Trump victory may lead to a renewed more radical Left, enumerates here phenomena (global warming, deforestation, warzone devastations, etc.) which have been going on for decades – the most one can say is that Trump's blatant denial of the ecological threat pushes the danger a step further. What is needed is thus not only strong opposition to Trump but also a clear break with the entire liberal-capitalist tradition out of which Trump grew.

The 2016 elections were the final defeat of liberal democracy or, more precisely, of what we could call the Left-Fukuyamaist dream.

No wonder, then, that the predominant liberal reaction to Trump's inauguration address was full of doomsday visions – suffice it to mention MSNBC host Chris Matthews who detected in it a 'Hitlerian background'. Trump's taking power was the end of their world, and, at one point, Marine le Pen definitely hit the mark: 2017 will be the moment of truth for Europe. Alone, pinched between the US and Russia, it will have to reinvent itself or die. In the years to come, the big battlefield will be in Europe, and at stake will be the very core of European emancipatory legacy.

Notes

INTRODUCTION: *V for Vendetta*, PART 2

1. Alenka Zupančič, 'The End' (unpublished manuscript).
2. George Orwell, *The Road to Wigan Pier* (1937), available online at http://gutenberg.net.au/ebooks02/0200391.txt.
3. V. I. Lenin, *Collected Works*, Vol. 33, Moscow: Progress Publishers, 1966, p. 479.
4. Göran Therborn, 'An Age of Progress?', *New Left Review*, 99 (May–June 2016), p. 37.
5. Axel Honneth, *Die Idee des Sozialismus*, Frankfurt: Suhrkamp, 2015.
6. Quoted from https://www.project-syndicate.org/commentary/lesson-of-populist-rule-in-poland-by-slawomir-sierakowski-2017-01.
7. See http://french.about.com/od/grammar/a/negation_form_2.htm.
8. Jean-Claude Milner, *Relire la Révolution*, Paris: Verdier, 2016, pp. 232–3.
9. Quoted from http://www.cnbc.com/2016/11/04/elon-musk-robots-will-take-your-jobs-government-will-have-to-pay-your-wage.html.
10. Quoted from https://www.marxists.org/reference/archive/hegel/works/pr/preface.htm.
11. Ibid.

I. GLOBAL CAPITALISM AND ITS DISCONTENTS

1. Incidentally, the way Western media report on the refugee crisis subtly resuscitates the old racist cliché about the Balkans being the wild frontier between the civilized West and the barbarian Orient, the place of confusion and broken border fences, with hordes of refugees wandering around – as if civilization proper begins in Austria. If the same number of refugees were to enter UK or France, one can be sure that a quick solution would be found.

2. Peter Sloterdijk, *In the World Interior of Capital*, Cambridge: Polity Press, 2013, pp. 8–9.

3. At http://www.other-news.info/2016/06/song-do-the-global-city-with out-soul/.

4. https://www.adbusters.org/article/the-twilight-of-the-west/

5. Saroj Giri, 'Parasitic Anticolonialism' (unpublished manuscript).

6. ibid.

7. Boris Buden noted that the post-communist *Ostalgie* in some Eastern European countries is not the longing for the lost emancipatory potential that survived in socialist regimes, but is structured like nostalgia for a lost culture, a lost way of life – we are, of course, dealing with the retroactively constructed memory of mythic times when life was modest but stable and safe. This is why getting rid of *Ostalgie* is a *sine qua non* of a renewed emancipatory movement in these countries. The large public that has no sympathy with or longing for communism perceive it (from the standpoint of the neo-liberal universe) as some weird foreign culture, incomprehensible and irrational in its premises and rituals. What the two opposed stances share is the same ignorance of the radical emancipatory dimension of the communist project: in both cases, communism is treated as a particular culture. (See Boris Buden, *Zone des Uebergangs*, Frankfurt: Suhrkamp, 2009.) What makes the situation in post-communist countries politically interesting is that the new capitalist class is not yet fully constituted as a class: it remains – as Céline put it almost a century ago – 'an embryonic bourgeoisie that hasn't yet negotiated its contract'.

8. Tana French's outstanding murder mystery *Likeness* also refers to a social background of an impossible choice: students of humanities who co-own a house in which they live, establishing it as a kind of utopian community that provides a safe haven from the brutal competitive world outside, collectively kill one of them, a girl who wanted to sell her part, since that would mean the end of their communal life – in short, the girl is killed for using her right to choose. The novel can effectively be read as a new version of Agatha Christie's *Murder on the Orient Express*: since the murder is committed by the entire group of suspects, it is the victim who should be seen as the real criminal.

9. Aaron Schuster, *The Trouble with Pleasure: Deleuze and Psycho-analysis*, Cambridge, Mass.: MIT Press, 2016, p. 89.

10. Lee Williams, http://www.independent.co.uk/voices/comment/what-is-ttip-and-six-reasons-why-the-answer-should-scare-you-9779688.html.

11. George Monbiot, at https://www.theguardian.com/commentisfree/2016/sep/06/transatlantic-trade-partnership-ttip-canada-eu.
12. I rely here on the work of Jela Krečič.
13. Personal communication. Incidentally, some Leftists in Europe and the US refer to Badiou, to his notion of subtraction, to justify their struggle for 'autonomous zones' to be defended.
14. Ibid.
15. Quoted from http://www.project-syndicate.org/commentary/joseph-e--stiglitz-blames-rising-inequality-on-an-ersatz-form-of-capitalism-that-benefits-only-the-rich.
16. Alain Badiou, 'Prefazione all'edizione italiana', in his *Metapolitica*, Napoli: Cronopio, 2002, p. 14.
17. See Axel Honneth, *Die Idee des Sozialismus*, Frankfurt: Suhrkamp, 2015.
18. Peter Sloterdijk, *Was geschah im 20. Jahrhundert?*, Frankfurt: Suhrkamp, 2016.
19. See Kojin Karatani, *The Structure of World History*, Durham: Duke University Press, 2014.
20. The exemplary cases of such a 'return of the repressed' are radical millenarian religious communities, which we find in Christianity (Canudos in Brazil, etc.) but also in Islam (Alamut in Iran, etc.) – no wonder that, as soon as a religion establishes itself as an ideological institution legitimizing the existing power relations, it has to fight against its own innermost excess. The Christian church faced a common problem from the fourth century onwards, when it became the state church: how do you reconcile the feudal class society, where rich lords rule over impoverished peasants, with the egalitarian poverty of the collective of believers as described in the Gospels? The solution of Thomas Aquinas is that while, in principle, shared property is better, this holds only for perfect humans; for the majority of us, who dwell in sin, private property and difference in wealth are natural, and it is even sinful to demand the abolition of private property or egalitarianism in our fallen societies, i.e. to demand for the imperfect people what befits only the perfect. This is the immanent contradiction at the very core of the Church's identity, making it the main anti-Christian force today.
21. Collaborative commons also seem to imply a citizens' basic income: products are the result of collaboration in which we all participate.
22. Jeremy Rifkin, *The Zero Marginal Cost Society: The Internet of Things, the Collaborative Commons, and the Eclipse of Capitalism*, New York: Palgrave Macmillan, 2014, pp. 19, 18.

23. Quoted from C. J. Dew, at https://medium.com/basic-income/post-capitalism-rise-of-the-collaborative-commons-62b0160a7048#.eywtl-gfgx.

24. Ibid.

25. See *Capitalismo cognitivo*, ed. Carlo Vercellone, Roma: manifestolibri, 2006.

26. Karl Marx, *Grundrisse*, at https://www.marxists.org/archive/marx/works/1857/grundrisse/ch14.htm.

27. Quoted from Dew, op. cit.

28. Ibid.

29. Fredric Jameson, *An American Utopia: Dual Power and the Universal Army*, London: Verso, 2016.

30. See Jean-Pierre Dupuy, *Avions-nous oublié le mal? Penser la politique après le 11 septembre*, Paris: Bayard, 2002.

31. See John Rawls, *A Theory of Justice*, Cambridge, Mass.: Harvard University Press, 1971 (revised edition 1999).

32. See Friedrich Hayek, *The Road to Serfdom*, Chicago: University of Chicago Press, 1994.

33. Ayn Rand, *Atlas Shrugged*, London: Penguin Books, 2007, p. 871.

2. SYRIZA, THE SHADOW OF AN EVENT

1. Stathis Kouvelakis, 'Syriza's Rise and Fall', *New Left Review*, 97 (January–February 2016).

2. Costas Douzinas, 'The Left in Power? Notes on Syriza's Rise, Fall, and (Possible) Second Rise', at http://nearfuturesonline.org/the-left-in-power-notes-on-syrizas-rise-fall-and-possible-second-rise/.

3. ibid.

4. Kouvelakis, 'Syriza's Rise and Fall'.

5. Quoted from http://www.project-syndicate.org/commentary/tsipras-greek-crisis-by-joschka-fischer-2015-04#QyEoUcWhxTFmUJYo.99.

6. http://www.theguardian.com/news/2015/feb/18/yanis-varoufakis-how-i-became-an-erratic-marxist

7. Gideon Rachman,'Eurozone's Weakest Link is the Voters', *Financial Times*, 19 December 2014.

8. Alain Badiou, seminar on Plato at the École normale supérieure, 13 February 2008 (unpublished).

9. http://www.newstatesman.com/world-affairs/2015/07/yanis-varoufakis-full-transcript-our-battle-save-greece.

10. Quoted in Richard McGregor, *The Party: The Secret World of China's Communist Rulers*, London: Allen Lane, 2010, p. 22.
11. Ibid., p. 21.
12. http://krugman.blogs.nytimes.com/2015/07/12/disaster-in-europe/.
13. Ibid.
14. Stathis Kouvelakis, 'From the Absurd to the Tragic', at https://www.jacobinmag.com/2015/07/tsipras-syriza-greece-euro-debt/.
15. http://krugman.blogs.nytimes.com/2015/07/12/disaster-in-europe/.
16. https://www.bloomberg.com/news/articles/2015-07-02/defiant-varoufakis-says-he-ll-quit-if-greeks-endorse-austerity.
17. Stathis Gourgouris, https://opendemocracy.net/can-europe-make-it/stathis-gourgouris/syriza-problem-radical-democracy-and-left-govern mentality-in-greece.
18. Ibid.
19. Ibid.
20. Ibid.
21. Julia Buxton, 'Venezuela After Chavez', *New Left Review*, 99 (May–June 2016), p. 25.
22. http://www.lrb.co.uk/v37/n15/tariq-ali/diary.
23. See https://www.jacobinmag.com/2015/07/tsipras-euro-debt-default-grexit/
24. Gourgouris, op. cit.
25. Incidentally, one has to reject both optimist myths, the Left Platform myth that there is a clear rational way to do Grexit and bring new prosperity, as well as the obverse myth (advocated by, among others, Jeffrey Frankel) that, by faithfully enforcing the bailout plan, Tsipras can become a new Lula. See http://www.project-syndicate.org/commentary/kim-dae-jung-lula-da-tsipras-by-jeffrey-frankel-2015-07.
26. Personal communication from Varoufakis.
27. Alberto Toscano, 'A Structuralism of Feeling?', *New Left Review*, 97 (January–February 2016), p. 93.
28. Thomas Metzinger, *Being No One: The Self-Model Theory of Subjectivity*, Cambridge, Mass.: MIT Press, 2004, p. 165.
29. Ibid., p. 169.
30. Ibid.
31. Ibid., p. 331.
32. Ibid., p. 333.
33. Quoted in Ernest Mandel, *Trotsky as Alternative*, London: Verso Books, 1995, p. 81.

34. Quoted from https://www.marxists.org/archive/lenin/works/1918/mar/x03.htm.
35. For a clear articulation of this stance, see Martin Jay, 'No Power to the Soviets', in his *Cultural Semantics: Keywords of Our Time*, Amherst: University of Massachusetts Press, 1998.
36. Isabel Allende, 'The End of All Roads', *Financial Times*, 15 November 2003.
37. Arthur Miller, 'A Visit with Castro', *The Nation*, 12 January 2004, p. 13.

3. RELIGION AND ITS CONTENTS

1. Liu Cixin, *The Three-Body Problem*, New York: Tor Books, 2014 (Chinese original 2008).
2. Zhang Weiwei, *The China Wave: Rise of a Civilizational State*, Hackensack: World Publishing Corporation, 2012.
3. Ibid., pp. 71–2.
4. Ibid., p. 72.
5. Ibid., p. 107.
6. Ibid., p. 164.
7. Ibid., p. 122.
8. Ibid., p. 124.
9. See http://www.bbc.co.uk/news/world-asia-china-28670719.
10. Zhang, *The China Wave*, p. 123.
11. Ibid., p. 120.
12. Ibid., p. 155.
13. Jonathan Clements, *The First Emperor of China*, Chalford: Sutton Publishing, 2006, p. 34.
14. Claude Lefort, *Essai sur le politique*, Paris: Éditions du Seuil, 1986.
15. Ibid.
16. See http://www.theguardian.com/world/2016/apr/08/china-woman-attacked-hotel-video-bystanders-ignore.
17. Zhang, *The China Wave*, p. 156.
18. Richard McGregor, *The Party: The Secret World of China's Communist Rulers*, London: Allen Lane, 2010, p. 14.
19. Another example: in the last days of the German Democratic Republic, the protesting crowds often sang the official national anthem of the GDR – why? Because from late 1950s, its words ('*Deutschland einig Vaterland*' ('Germany, the united Fatherland')) were prohibited from being sung in public. Composed in 1949, they reflected the party line

of that moment (a united socialist Germany), so they no longer fitted the changed emphasis on East Germany as a new socialist nation. So at official ceremonies, only the orchestral version was performed – the GDR was thus a unique country in which singing the national anthem was a criminal act.

20. There was another unwritten regulation in the Yugoslav army: every soldier was expected to mix with soldiers of other nationalities and to communicate with them in Serbocroat (say, if a group of Slovenes was caught talking among themselves in Slovene, they were reproached for nationalist separatism, for ruining brotherhood and the unity of Yugoslav nations) – every soldier except the Albanians, who were considered a lost cause (other soldiers were just told to watch closely if Albanians were involved in some suspicious activity).

21. See 'Even What's Secret is a Secret in China', *Japan Times*, 16 June 2007, p. 17.

22. McGregor, *The Party*, p. 10.

23. Alberto Toscano, 'A Structuralism of Feeling?', *New Left Review*, 97 (January–February 2016), p. 76.

24. See http://chinadigitaltimes.net/2015/06/xinjiang-official-sinicize-religion-to-combat-hostile-forces/.

25. http://www.rfa.org/english/news/china/china-religion-05252015112309.html

26. See Karl Marx and Friedrich Engels, *Collected Works*, Vol. 10, London: Lawrence and Wishart, 1978, p. 95.

27. Zorana Baković, 'Kako bo bog postal Kitajec?', *Delo*, 17 June 2015 (in Slovene).

28. See http://chinadigitaltimes.net/2015/03/unraveling-chinas-campaign-western-values/.

29. Sam Harris, *The End of Faith: Religion, Terror, and the Future of Reason*, New York: Norton, 2005, p. 221.

30. Ibid., p. 253. Incidentally, two similar reproaches are regularly made by the critics of my books, which try to redeem the emancipatory core of the Christian legacy: that I am wrong with regard to Judaism (advocating Christian supercessionism) and especially with regard to Buddhism.

31. See http://gawker.com/orthodox-jews-invent-uber-for-protesting-gay-pride-1714720843.

32. http://www.christianexaminer.com/article/israeli.foreign.minister.bible.says.the.land.is.ours/49013.htm

33. See http://www.theguardian.com/world/2015/oct/21/netanyahu-under-fire-for-palestinian-grand-mufti-holocaust-claim.

34. Quoted from Heinz Hoehne, *The Order of the Death's Head: The Story of Hitler's SS*, London: Penguin, 2000, p. 333.
35. Ibid., pp. 336–7.
36. See Menachem Begin, *The Revolt: Story of the Irgun*, New York: Dell, 1977, pp. 100–101.
37. Quoted from *Time* magazine, 24 July 2006.
38. http://www.nytimes.com/roomfordebate/2014/10/16/should-nations-recognize-a-palestinian-state/there-should-be-no-palestinian-state-23.
39. See http://www.theage.com.au/world/israel-warned-new-zealand-that-un-resolution-was-declaration-of-war-report-20161227-gtiogk.html.
40. http://www.nytimes.com/2014/10/21/arts/music/metropolitan-opera-forges-ahead-on-klinghoffer-in-spite-of-protests.html?_r=0.
41. http://www.israelhayom.com/site/newsletter_article.php?id=19195.
42. http://www.hollywoodreporter.com/news/jon-voight-pens-letter-ignorant-723007.
43. As for the violent dark side of Buddhism, see Brian Victoria, *Zen War Stories*, London: Routledge, 2003, as well as *Buddhist Warfare*, ed. by Michael Jerryson, Oxford: Oxford University Press, 2010.
44. Araeen's quoted texts circulate on the web through his friends and collaborators.
45. See Ernst Bloch, *Avicenna und die Aristotelische Linke*, Frankfurt: Suhrkamp, 1963; first published in Leipzig in 1949.
46. See Joseph M. Bochenski, *Der Sowjet-Russische dialektische Materialismus*, Bern and Munich: Francke Verlag, 1962.
47. Boris Buden, *Zone des Uebergangs*, Frankfurt: Suhrkamp, 2009.
48. Fethi Benslama, *La Psychanalyse à l'épreuve de l'Islam*, Paris: Aubier, 2002, p. 320.
49. Ibid.
50. http://www.goodreads.com/author/quotes/6173212.Ruhollah_Khomeini.
51. Buden, *Zone des Uebergangs*, p. 134.
52. Ibid., p. 111.
53. Ibid., p. 59.

4. THE 'TERRORIST THREAT'

1. Araeen's quoted texts circulate on the web through his friends and collaborators.
2. See Jacques-Alain Miller, 'L'amour de la police', blog written on 13 January 2015 and published on lacan.com.

3. See http://www.corriere.it/cronache/15_settembre_25/attivista-stuprata-un-migrante-mi-chiesero-tacere-non-creare-scandali-496d3388-6370-11e5-9954-7c169e7f3b05.shtml.

4. See http://www.independent.co.uk/news/world/europe/cologne-police-ordered-to-remove-word-rape-from-reports-into-new-year-s-eve-sexual-assaults-a6972471.html.

5. See http://blogs.spectator.co.uk/2016/04/norway-syndrome-a-new-con dition-for-western-victims-of-rape/ and http://www.independent.co. uk/news/world/europe/norwegian-rape-victim-feels-guilty-the-man-who-raped-him-was-deported-a6975041.html.

6. Simon Jenkins, 'Charlie Hebdo: Now is the Time to Uphold Freedoms and Not Give In to Fear', *Guardian*, 7 Janaury 2015.

7. http://ww.theguardian.com/commentisfree/2014/sep/09/isis-jihadi-shaped-by-modern-western-philosophy

8. Sayyid Qutb, *Milestones*, Chapter 7, quoted from http://unisetca. ipower.com/qutb/.

9. Aristotle, *Metaphysics*, Book 12, part 10.

10. And, incidentally, exactly the same logic is at work in Hayek's advocacy of markets: 'Hayek argues that evil arises from the tyranny of personal dependence, the submission of one person to another's arbitrary will. This state of subordination can be escaped only if every member of society willingly subjects himself to an abstract, impersonal, and universal rule that absolutely transcends him' (Jean-Pierre Dupuy, *Economy and the Future: A Crisis of Faith*, East Lansing: Michigan State University Press, 2014, p. 81). Qutb's God thus occupies exactly the same place as Hayek's market, both guaranteeing personal freedom.

11. In an article in their online magazine, ISIS justifies its kidnapping of women as sex slaves by citing Islamic theology (an interpretation that is rejected by the Muslim world at large as a perversion of Islam): 'One should remember that enslaving the families of the kuffar – the infidels – and taking their women as concubines is a firmly established aspect of the Shariah, or Islamic law.' The title of the article sums up the ISIS point of view: 'The Revival (of) Slavery Before the Hour' ('the hour' being Judgment Day). (See http://edition.cnn.com/2014/10/12/world/meast/isis-justification-slavery/index.html?hpt=imi_c2.)

12. http://www.goodreads.com/author/quotes/6173212.Ruhollah_Khomeini.

13. http://www.telegraph.co.uk/news/worldnews/europe/russia/10856197/Putin-attacks-Eurovision-drag-artist-Conchita-for-putting-her-lifestyle-up-for-show.html.

14. http://www.mirror.co.uk/tv/tv-news/russia-slams-eurovision-winner-conchita-3525396.
15. http://www.theage.com.au/news/national/ethnic-leaders-condemn-muslim-cleric/2006/10/26/1161749223822.html.
16. https://www.theguardian.com/world/2016/jul/12/in-russia-and-ukraine-women-are-still-blamed-for-being-raped.
17. See the CNN report http://religion.blogs.cnn.com/2014/05/24/atheists-in-the-bible-belt-a-survival-guide/.
18. See the CNN report 'When Buddhists were Public Enemy No. 1', http://edition.cnn.com/2015/02/04/us/buddhism-us-enemy/index.html.
19. Quoted from http://www.theatlantic.com/magazine/archive/2015/03/what-isis-really-wants/384980/.
20. See http://www.bloomberg.com/view/articles/2016-07-14/israel-s-army-doesn-t-need-a-rabbi-to-settle-debate-on-wartime-rape.
21. I rely here on the paper by Julia Reinhard Lupton and Kenneth Reinhard, 'The Subject of Religion: Lacan and the Ten Commandments', *Diacritics*, 33, 2 (summer 2003), pp. 71–97.
22. Talad Asad, Wendy Brown, Judith Butler and Saba Mahmood, *Is Critique Secular?*, Berkeley: University of California Press, 2009, pp. 37, 40.
23. Ibid., p. 40.
24. Ibid., p. 46.
25. See https://www.washingtonpost.com/world/middle_east/swedish-greens-jolted-by-claims-of-islamist-infiltration/2016/04/26/6e30ee88-0ba6-11e6-bc53-db634ca94a2a_story.html.
26. See Peter Sloterdijk, *Was geschah im 20.Jahrhundert?*, Frankfurt: Suhrkamp, 2016.
27. This and all subsequent quotes on Ali are taken from https://www.theguardian.com/world/2016/jul/23/i-am-german-munich-gunman-took-part-in-shouting-match-during-attack.
28. See Étienne Balibar, 'Violence: idéalité et cruauté', in his *La Crainte des masses*, Paris: Éditions Galilée, 1997.
29. I owe this line of thought to Engin Kurtay, Istanbul.
30. Quoted from http://www.theguardian.com/world/2016/feb/29/we-cant-allow-refugee-crisis-to-plunge-greece-into-chaos-says-merkel.
31. G. K. Chesterton, *The Everlasting Man*, http://www.dur.ac.uk/martin.ward/gkc/books/everlasting_man.html#chap-I-i.
32. Alenka Zupančič, 'Back to the Future of Europe' (unpublished manuscript).

5. THE SEXUAL IS (NOT) POLITICAL

1. Jacques Lacan, *Formations of the Unconscious (Seminar V)*, 25 June 1958, quoted from http://www.valas.fr/IMG/pdf/THE-SEMINAR-OF-JACQUES-LACAN-V_formations_de_l_in.pdf.
2. Quoted from https://newrepublic.com/article/121790/life-triggering-best-literature-should-be-too.
3. Ibid.
4. Quoted from https://www.radicalphilosophy.com/conference-report/benjamin-in-ramallah.
5. http://www.huffingtonpost.com/nikki-johnsonhuston-esq/the-culture-of-the-smug-w_b_11537306.html.
6. Quoted from http://www.independent.co.uk/news/world/asia/north-korea-bans-sarcasm-kim-jong-un-freedom-speech-a7231461.html.
7. I owe this information to Rebecca Carson, London.
8. See http://www.cbc.ca/news/canada/british-columbia/pride-parade-vancouver-protest-1.3694172
9. Graham Harman, *Immaterialism*, Cambridge: Polity Press, 2016, p. 122–3.
10. https://www.theguardian.com/world/2016/aug/30/france-manuel-valls-breasts-headscarf-burkini-ban-row.
11. Quoted from http://gotopless.org/gotopless-day.
12. Mladen Dolar, 'The Art of the Unsaid' (unpublished paper).
13. https://www.facebook.com/dampalestine/posts/10153409978136935.
14. http://www.theguardian.com/world/2016/apr/16/canada-first-nations-suicide-crisis-attawapiskat-history.
15. 'HDPKK' is the author's malevolent condensation of HDP (the legal pro-Kurdish political party, which has over eighty members in the parliament) and PKK (the illegal Kurdish resistance movement decried by the Turkish state as a terrorist organization); the aim is to make it clear that the public and legal HDP is just the public face of the terrorists.
16. The Turkish term *delikanlı* used here means 'dauntless young men', and is a term never used for women; it signifies that the man is strong enough to tell the truth, like *dobra*, which means 'able to say the truth'.
17. The word used, *köleleştirme*, means literally 'making slave'.
18. Quoted from http://www.aktuel.com.tr/yazar/suheyb-ogut/2015/08/17/butch-lezbiyenler-ve-hdpkk. I owe the translation to Engin Kurtay.

19. Jacques Lacan, *Écrits*, trans. Bruce Fink, New York: Norton, 2007, pp. 416–17.
20. Aaron Schuster, 'The Third Kind of Complaint' (unpublished manuscript).
21. Alenka Zupančič, 'Back to the Future of Europe' (unpublished manuscript).
22. And insofar as the other great antagonism is that of classes, could we not also imagine a homologous critical rejection of the class binary? The 'binary' class struggle and exploitation should also supplement it by a 'gay' position (exploitation among the ruling class itself – bankers and lawyers exploiting the 'honest' productive capitalists), a 'lesbian' position (beggars stealing from honest workers, etc.), a 'bisexual' position (as a self-employed worker, I act as both capitalist and worker), 'asexual' (I remain outside capitalist production), etc.
23. Alenka Zupančič, personal communication.
24. Louis Althusser, 'Ideology and Ideological State Apparatuses', in *Essays in Ideology*, London: Verso, 1984, p. 163.
25. I précis here a more detailed critical reading of Althusser's notion of ideology from Chapter 3 of Slavoj Žižek, *The Metastases of Enjoyment*, London: Verso Books, 2005.
26. Here I follow the perspicacious observations of Henry Krips – see his excellent unpublished manuscript 'The Subject of Althusser and Lacan'.
27. There is, of course, a key difference between (the anti-Semitic figure of) the Jew and the (Hegelian) rabble: while 'the Jew as the intruder who disturbs social harmony among classes' is not the real Jew but a figure of anti-Semitic fantasy, the rabble really is a 'class of no class', a group lacking its proper place within the social edifice. While Jews are supposed to act as secret masters pulling the strings behind the scenes, the rabble is just as it appears, a messy conglomerate of disoriented actors – if one suspects a secret agent pulling the strings of the rabble's chaotic activity, the candidate for this role will be again a 'Jew'-like agent. (And, of course, if the rabble were effectively to organize itself, this would be a major radical event.)
28. Bulent Somay, 'L'Orient n'existe pas', doctoral thesis defended at Birkbeck College, University of London, on 29 November 2013.
29. See https://thesocietypages.org/sociologylens/2014/11/18/nice-bag-discussing-race-class-and-sexuality-in-examining-street-harassment/.
30. One should also note that the idea of the 'middle road' between two extremes is regularly used by conservatives, beginning with fascism,

which conceived itself as the organic middle road between the two extremes of bourgeois individualism and communist collectivism. Today, the same goes for Islam and Russian orthodoxy, which both perceive themselves as the middle road between Western active individualism and Oriental passive inertia.

31. See Catherine Millot, *Horsexe: Essays on Transsexuality*, New York: Autonomedia, 1990.
32. See Nancy Fraser, *Fortunes of Feminism*, London: Verso Books, 2013.
33. See Jean-Claude Michea, *Notre ennemi, le capital*, Paris: Climats, 2017, p. 151.
34. Ibid., p. 138.
35. https://lareviewofbooks.org/article/zizeks-transgender-trouble/.

6. THE POPULIST TEMPTATION

1. http://allnewspipeline.com/What_Martial_Law_Will_Look_Like.php.
2. Quoted from http://www.independent.ie/world-news/americas/donald-trump-mocks-hillary-clinton-over-disgusting-toilet-break-34309620.html.
3. See http://www.theguardian.com/commentisfree/2015/dec/13/dont-ban-donald-trump-just-laugh-at-him.
4. Ignorance which is quite usual with quasi-Leftists defending Yugoslavia. I still remember my smile when I read how, in his condemnation of the NATO bombing of Serbia, Michael Parenti gave way to his outrage at the senseless attack on the Crvena Zastava car factory which, he claimed, produced no arms ... Well, while serving in the Yugoslav army for a year in 1975–6, I myself was equipped with a Crvena Zastava automatic gun!
5. John Pilger, 'Don't Forget What Happened in Yugoslavia', *New Statesman*, 14 August 2008.
6. But even conceding the absurd premise of the German-Vatican plot to destroy Yugoslavia, were the US really part of it, i.e., were they really from the outset sympathetic to the disintegration of Yugoslavia? When in June 1991 Slovenia announced that it would soon declare independence, the US Secretary of State James Baker flew to Belgrade and declared in front of the media that if the Slovenes took overt action to secede from Yugoslavia, the US would not object if the Federal army was called in to preserve the unity of Yugoslavia – and, what a sur-

prise, the very next day, Ante Marković, the last Yugoslav Prime Minister, ordered the Federal army into Slovenia. The US thus supported Marković's 'commitment to market-oriented economic reform and building democratic pluralism' as part of his global project, which included 'strong support for Yugoslav independence, unity, and sovereignty'.

7. See https://newrepublic.com/minutes/138412/slavoj-zizek-auditioning-cnn-roundtable.
8. Frédéric Lordon, *Willing Slaves of Capital: Spinoza and Marx on Desire*, London: Verso Books, 2014, p. 78.
9. Ibid., p. 86.
10. Ibid., p. 91.
11. Benedict de Spinoza, *A Theologico-Political Treatise and A Political Treatise*, New York: Dover Publications, 1951, p. 387.
12. Blaise Pascal, *Pensées*, trans. A. J. Kraisheimer, Harmondsworth: Penguin Books, 1966, pp. 21–2.
13. Lordon, *Willing Slaves*, p. 80.
14. Ibid, p. 84.
15. Ibid., pp. 84–5.
16. Ibid., p. 85.
17. Ibid.
18. Ibid., p. 89. A similar line of thought is found in Haim Hazan's *Against Hybridity* (Cambridge: Polity Press, 2015): the 'previously feared, hence marginalized hybrid, the perpetrator of moral panic and disorder, has moved to the legitimate core of social interaction [. . .] Hybridity started with racial theory, and then turned against colonialism, finally becoming a pillar of global popular culture.' Today, 'the infinite tolerance for hybridization is accompanied by zero-tolerance for non-hybridity.' In spite of the problematic nature of many of his lines of argument, Hazan is right in emphasizing the link between global capitalism and politically correct multiculturalism. One should always bear in mind that hybridity is a loose notion covering phenomena as different as globalization, consumerism, cultural theory, multiculturalism, etc.
19. For a short presentation of her position, see Chantal Mouffe, 'Pour un populisme de gauche', *Le Monde*, 20 April 2016, p. 22.
20. Noam Chomsky, *Necessary Illusions: Thought Control in Democratic Societies*, London: Pluto Press, 1989, p. 69.
21. Eric Santner, personal communication.

22. http://bigstory.ap.org/article/b80f7fd3e15e4add9b5ad7a417a73e3b/
lawyer-asks-israel-destroy-homes-palestinians-killers.
23. Theodor W. Adorno, Else Frenkel-Brunswik, Daniel Levinson and
Nevitt Sanford, *The Authoritarian Personality*, New York: Harper &
Brothers, 1950.
24. I rely here on Alenka Zupančič, 'AIMO' (in Slovene), *Mladina*, winter
2016/2017.
25. Quoted from Bernard Brščič, 'George Soros is one of the most depraved
and dangerous people of our time' (in Slovene), *Demokracija*, 25
August 2016, p. 15.
26. Yuval Noah Harari, *Homo Deus: A Brief History of Tomorrow*, London: Harvill Secker, 2016, p. 249.
27. Immanuel Kant, *Perpetual Peace: A Philosophical Sketch*, 1795, available at https://www.mtholyoke.edu/acad/intrel/kant/kant1.htm.
28. Yanis Varoufakis, personal communication.
29. Todd McGowan, personal communication.
30. And poor Bernie Sanders? Unfortunately, Trump hit the mark when he
compared his endorsement of Clinton to an Occupy partisan endorsing
Lehman Brothers. Sanders should have just withdrawn and remained
silent in dignity so that his absence would weigh heavily, reminding us
what was missing in the duel between Clinton and Trump and, in this
way, keeping the space open for future more radical alternatives.
31. José Saramago, *Seeing*, New York: Harcourt, 2006.
32. See http://www.criticatac.ro/lefteast/fredric-jameson-fascism-not-yet-
there/.
33. http://www.leftvoice.org/From-Farce-to-Tragedy-Zizek-Endorses-Trump?
var_mode=calcul.
34. See https://www.theguardian.com/us-news/2016/oct/30/donald-trump-
voters-rally-election-crowd
35. Alenka Zupančič, 'Back to the Future of Europe' (unpublished manuscript).
36. http://www.latimes.com/opinion/op-ed/la-oe-marche-left-fake-news-
problem-comedy-20170106-story.html.
37. https://www.theguardian.com/books/2016/nov/12/hillary-clinton-we-
failed-her-sarah-churchwell.
38. https://www.theguardian.com/commentisfree/2016/nov/11/hillary-clin
ton-progressive-politics-supporters-donald-trump-win.
39. See https://www.yahoo.com/news/outrage-fear-fuel-continuing-anti-
trump-protests-231535430.html.

40. Zupančič, 'Back to the Future of Europe'.
41. See http://www.huffingtonpost.com/entry/noam-chomsky-gop_us_56a
66febe4b0d8cc109aec78.
42. See https://www.youtube.com/watch?v=gRnUpVLc31w.
43. Alain Badiou, *La vraie vie*, Paris: Fayard, 2016.
44. Ibid., p. 67.
45. Quoted from http://www.dailyscript.com/scripts/citizenkane.html.
46. See http://www.nytimes.com/2016/11/21/books/richard-rortys-1998-book-suggested-election-2016-was-coming.html?_r=0.
47. Richard Rorty, *Achieving Our Country*, Cambridge, Mass.: Harvard University Press, 1999, p. 48.
48. Quoted from http://www.salon.com/2016/11/23/reactionary-democrats-trash-bernie-sanders-for-challenging-identity-politics/?utm_source=twitter&utm_medium=socialflow&utm_source=twitter&utm_medium=socialflow.
49. Quoted from https://www.theguardian.com/commentisfree/2016/nov/24/no-asians-no-blacks-gay-people-racism.
50. Ibid.
51. Quoted from https://www.thecairoreview.com/q-a/global-trouble/.
52. Quoted from http://www.politico.com/story/2016/11/nancy-pelosi-donald-trump-house-democrats-231716.
53. https://www.theguardian.com/commentisfree/2016/nov/28/francois-fillon-threat-liberal-values-marine-le-pen-france.

FINALE: THE LONELINESS OF THE GLOBAL POLICEMAN IN A MULTI-CENTRIC WORLD

1. http://www.veteransnewsnow.com/2014/12/06/512430-america-is-on-a-hot-war-footing-house-legislation-paves-the-way-for-war-with-russia.
2. Mike Davis, 'The Coming Desert', *New Left Review*, 97 (January–February 2016), p. 43.
3. See https://www.theguardian.com/world/2016/dec/21/smog-refugees-flee-chinese-cities-as-airpocalypse-blights-half-a-billion.
4. See www.china.org.cn/china/2016-12/14/content_39913139.htm.
5. See https://www.theguardian.com/world/2017/jan/21/koblenz-far-right-european-political-leaders-meeting-brexit-donald-trump.
6. See https://www.project-syndicate.org/commentary/populist-war-on-women-resistance-by-slawomir-sierakowski-2017-02.

7. Quoted from http://www.realclearpolitics.com/video/2017/01/31/student_
   to_pelosi_young_people_do_not_believe_in_capitalism_can_we_fight_
   against_right-wing_economics.html.
8. See http://inthesetimes.com/article/17137/the_end_of_history.